**The Schools, The Courts,
and the Public Interest**

Lexington Books Politics of Education Series
Frederick M. Wirt, Editor

Michael W. Kirst, Ed., *State, School, and Politics: Research Directions*

Joel S. Berke, Michael W. Kirst, *Federal Aid to Education: Who Benefits? Who Governs?*

Al J. Smith, Anthony Downs, M. Leanne Lachman, *Achieving Effective Desegregation*

Kern, Alexander, K. Forbis Jordan, *Constitutional Reform of School Finance*

George R. LaNoue, Bruce L.R. Smith, *The Politics of School Decentralization*

David J. Kirby, T. Robert Harris, Robert L. Crain, Christine H. Rossell, *Political Strategies in Northern School Desegregation*

Philip K. Piele, John Stuart Hall, *Budgets, Bonds, and Ballots: Voting Behavior in School Financial Elections*

John C. Hogan, *The Schools, the Courts, and the Public Interest*

The Schools, the Courts, and the Public Interest

John C. Hogan

Lexington Books
D.C. Heath and Company
Lexington, Massachusetts
Toronto   London

Library of Congress Cataloging in Publication Data

Hogan, John Charles.
    The schools, the courts, and the public interest.

    Bibliography: p.
    1. Right to education—United States. 2. Educational equalization—
United States. I. Title.
KF4155.H6   344'.73'079   73-1005
ISBN-0-669-86892-2

Second printing June 1976

Published simultaneously in Canada.

Printed in the United States of America.

International Standard Book Number: 0-669-86892-2

Library of Congress Catalog Card Number: 73-1005

THE LAW

In order to know what it is,
we must know what it has been,
and what it tends to become.

Oliver Wendell Holmes, Jr.
The Common Law (1881), p. 1

Contents

List of Figures

List of Tables

Acknowledgments

Many persons have contributed ideas and materials for this book. My thanks go first to Professor Lawrence E. Vredevoe, Emeritus, Graduate School of Education, UCLA, who introduced me to the subject of the courts and the schools, and to whom I owe the greatest debt of gratitude for his assistance and encouragement while writing this book. We had many valuable discussions of legal and educational subjects while I was pursuing graduate studies at UCLA and later when we taught courses on law and education together at California Lutheran College, Thousand Oaks, where the manuscript was revised for publication. His own textbook, *Discipline* (Dubuque, Iowa: Kendall/Hunt, 1971), is a study of legal principles and practical techniques as applied to the problem of classroom management and control.

I am also deeply grateful to Professors Clarence Fielstra, Harold Horowitz, Erick L. Lindman, and Svend Riemer, of the Schools and Departments of Law, Sociology, and Education at UCLA, who critiqued the text and who placed their imprimatures upon an earlier version of this work. Professor Mortimer D. Schwartz, School of Law, University of California, Davis, reviewed the manuscript in draft and additionally has kept the writer abreast of 1971-73 publications and developments in the fields of law and education.

Professor James S. Coleman, Johns Hopkins University, read the Introduction and the chapters on race and school finance in the early stages of the research and provided valuable comments which were incorporated in the text and footnotes.

Others who should be acknowledged for their ideas, materials, or encouragement include: Professor Claude W. Fawcett and Professor William H. Lucio, both of the Graduate School of Education, UCLA; Professor Morris D. Forkosch, the School of Law, Gonzaga University; Professor Lawrence A. Harper, Emeritus, Department of History, University of California, Berkeley; Professor Thompson Black, Jr., Los Angeles State College; Professor Raymond Fielding, Temple University; and my colleague Dr. Robert L. Wright, with whom I had frequent discussions of many topics contained herein. Mr. Frederick M. Wirt, formerly Director, Institute for Desegregation Problems, Department of Education, University of California, Berkeley, provided an early transcript of the Texas School finance case.

Mrs. Helen K. Wise, Customer Services, University Microfilms of Ann Arbor, Michigan, responded with the utmost courtesy and promptness to my request for a DATRIX search of bibliographical titles related to law and education. The results of that literature search began the study orginally.

Cynthia Hogan and her mother, Nancy, spent many tedious hours in 1971-72 in the UCLA Law Library and the Los Angeles County Law Library confirming legal citations and photocopying the law cases that are digested and discussed in this book.

In 1972 and 1973, graduate students in Education at California Lutheran College heard numerous lectures drawn from this book while it was still in manuscript, and the questions they raised during class discussions contributed in many ways to the writer's better understanding of his subject.

The chapters on race, wealth, and individual rights provided materials for the author's discussion of "The Courts and School Politics" at the Educational Policy Seminar, November 3, 1973, sponsored by the Graduate School of Education, University of California at Los Angeles.

Matters of form and style in preparing the manuscript for the press were left in the very capable hands of Mrs. Betty Martin (Student Service Center), West Los Angeles, Mrs. Virginia Atkinson of Manhattan Beach, and Mrs. Rae Clark of Santa Monica, and to all of them I am grateful for their part in producing this book.

And finally—to Mary Wienold, my personal secretary, who helped in innumerable ways with it all, a special thanks and my appreciation are due.

John C. Hogan

Santa Monica, California
November 1973

1 Introduction

Education and the Public Interest

The public interest served by elementary and secondary education has varied accordingly in different historical periods as the position of the family and the child in society has changed. Thus, when the family carried the responsibility for the welfare and education of its members from the cradle to the grave, the child received his training in the father's craftsman shop, in the fields, or in the home, where he was taught whatever was necessary to maintain the family as a self-perpetuating economic unit.[1] The law had no concern whatsoever with education at this time or even with the kind of work performed by children.[2] The public benefit from providing a child with an education beyond what was taught within the family was viewed as essentially nil.

With the coming of the industrial revolution, however, major changes occurred in the family's functions, both as an economic unit and as the training grounds for children. As work organizations developed outside of the family, children became occupationally mobile and sought employment in manufacturing, commercial, or business enterprises. Just as families lost much of their self-sustaining productivity function, so also they lost many of their welfare functions, including the primary responsibility for training children. As a result of these societal developments, the education and training a child received came to be of interest to all of the people in the community, not just to his prospective employers, for without an *adequate education* he might someday become dependent upon them for his support. Few people in these early times ever thought of an "equal educational opportunity"; rather, the need was for a "general educational opportunity" that provided adequate training or schooling to enable the child in later life to perform some productive and self-supporting role in society. In sum, the public interest served by education emerged when children and men began to employ their labor outside the family, and this "paved the way for public education."

The Concept of "Educational Opportunity"

The recognition of the public benefits from having a system of universal education for all children was preceded by private education, which developed with the expansion of the mercantile class.[3] The notion that it was in the public interest to have a "general educational opportunity for all children arose only in

1

the nineteenth century." In the United States, this came to mean public, tax-supported, "free" schools, *common schools*[4] *under the control of the state*, attended by children of all social classes and providing a common educational experience.

The law entered the picture, and education in such schools eventually became compulsory, except for "those upper-class children in private schools, those poor who went to no schools, and Indians and Southern Negroes who were without schools."[5] This led to the establishment of a kind of monopolistic or socialized[6] system of education in the United States whereby the public schools became the principal dispensers of knowledge and learning, except for the private schools, which remained in large part beyond the reach of the state. The old saw "leaving education to educators" developed, and for over one hundred years school-teachers and administrators enjoyed much autonomy in the classroom and in running their schools. So long as the schools provided a "general educational opportunity," the public interest was thought served, and the law and public policy would not intervene.[7]

The concept of a "general educational opportunity" has served the public interest both in the United States and elsewhere in the industrial world. In our country, however, largely because of the adoption of the Fourteenth Amendment to the United States Constitution in 1868 and the courts' interpretation of the equal protection clause of that amendment to apply to education, this concept was enlarged to include a special meaning that has focused on "equality" in the schools.

The first stage in the evolution of the concept of equality of educational opportunity was the notion that all children must be exposed to the same curriculum in the same school. A second stage in the evolution of the concept assumed that different children would have different occupational futures and that equality of opportunity required providing different curricula for each type of student. The third and fourth stages in this evolution came as a result of challenges to the basic idea of equality of educational opportunity from opposing directions. The third stage can be seen at least as far back as 1896 when the Supreme Court upheld the southern states' notion of "separate but equal" facilities. This stage ended in 1954 when the Supreme Court ruled that legal separation by race inherently constitutes inequality of opportunity. By adopting the "separate but equal" doctrine, the southern states rejected assumption three of the original concept, the assumption that equality depended on the opportunity to attend the same school. This rejection was, however, consistent with the overall logic of the original concept *since attendance at the same school was not an inheret part of that logic.* The underlying idea was that opportunity resided in exposure to a curriculum; the community's responsibility was to provide that exposure, the child's to take advantage of it.[8]

Equality, Education, and the Law

Once loosed, the idea of Equality is not easily cabined. Cox, 80 *Har. L. Rev.* 91 (1966)

The concept of "equality" in educational opportunity flows not from constitutional language about education or schooling, but rather from the more general constitutional provisions about equal protection or equal treatment under the law; thus, the "right or duty of education is not mentioned or referred to in the Federal Constitution, though most of the other fundamental principles are."[9] *The concept of "equality" in education, therefore, was in its origin judge-made law "derived" by the courts from the Equal Protection Clause of the Fourteenth Amendment and applied by them to the schools, and the first cases involved racial discrimination in the schools.*[10]

This is also true in the states.[11] In California, for example, the concept of "equality" in educational opportunity is drawn not from the constitutional language about education itself (Article IX), but from the more general provisions of the state constitution requiring equal treatment of all persons through "uniform general laws" and the prohibition against the granting of special "privileges and immunities,"[12]

All laws of a general nature shall have a uniform operation (Art. I, Sec. 11).

No special privileges or immunities shall ever be granted which may not be altered, revoked, or repealed by the Legislature; nor shall any citizen, or class of citizens, be granted privileges or immunities which, upon the same terms, shall not be granted to all citizens (Art. I, Sec. 21).

In making this connection between the general constitutional provisions about "equality" and the more specific constitutional provisions about the responsibility of the state to provide all of its children with a "general educational opportunity," the courts, beginning about 1950, have referred to the great public interest that is served by schooling today.[13]

Thus, in 1954, the Supreme Court of the United States, in *Brown v. Board of Education of Topeka,*[14] established the precept that has been adopted whole-heartedly by federal and state courts in most education cases decided ever since, namely, that the public interest is broadly served by education:

Today, education is perhaps the most important function of state and local governments. Compulsory school attendance laws and the great expenditures for education both demonstrate our recognition of the importance of education to our democratic society.[15]

The public benefits of education were also noticed: "It is required in the performance of our most basic public responsibilities, even service in the armed forces. It is the very function of good citizenship."

This precept has been embellished upon by other courts; thus, education is a "priceless commodity"[16] and a "fundamental right" of every citizen; it is "vital and, indeed, basic to civilized society,"[17] so fundamental as to be "fittingly considered the cornerstone of a vibrant and viable republican form of democracy."[18] For some courts, it seems beyond argument that "the right to receive a public school education is a basic personal right,"[19] "a substantial right implicit in the 'liberty' assurances of the Due Process Clause,"[20] and it has even been said (and so held) that the right to an *equal educational opportunity* is "a fundamental right, a legal right, a species of property, equal to, if not greater than, other tangible property rights, it being the right to be a human being."[21] This theme of an abiding respect for the vital role of education in our society has been echoed in numerous other decisions of the justices, but it reached its pinnacle in the case of *Serrano v. Priest*, (1971), wherein the Supreme Court of California declared: "We are convinced that the distinctive and priceless function of education in our society warrants, indeed, compels our treatment of it as a 'fundamental interest.' "[22]

At that high point, however, the precept was shot down by the Supreme Court of the United States itself in *San Antonio Independent School District v. Rodriguez* (1973):[23] "the importance of a service performed by the State does not determine whether it must be regarded as fundamental for purposes of examination under the Equal Protection Clause." Without detracting in any way from the grave significance of education to the individual and to society and affirming that, in the context of a racial discrimination, *Brown v. Board of Education of Topeka* "has lost none of its vitality with the passage of time," the Supreme Court declared: "Education, of course, is not among the rights afforded explicit protection under our Federal Constitution. Nor do we find any basis for saying it is implicitly so protected."[24] Education, per se, is not a federal matter;[25] it was one of the powers left to the states, or to the people, when the Constitution was adopted. The states are thus, constitutionally, the custodians of the public interest in maintaining a public school system that, as a minimum, provides "each child with an opportunity to acquire the basic minimum skills necessary for the enjoyment of the rights of speech and of full participation in the political process."[26] According to *Rodriguez*, the public interest is not served when the federal courts intervene in a school matter that does not involve infringement of a legitimate constitutional right.

The chapters that follow examine trends in court decisons that have affected the organization, administration, and programs of the public schools, primarily for the historical period since 1950; the cases are grouped for analysis in three broad areas: race, wealth, and individual rights. It will be shown how the law courts have come to share in the making of educational policy decisions with the school authorities in these areas; and how, after one-hundred years of laissez faire, the courts discovered the schools and thus set about establishing rights for children.

2

Changing Conceptions of the Role of the Courts in Education

Introduction

United States Court of Appeals Judge J. Skelly Wright, in the case of *Hobson v. Hansen,*[1] decided in 1967, concluded his opinion with the following "Parting Word":

It is regrettable, of course, that in deciding this case this court must act in an area so alien to its expertise. It would be far better indeed for these great social and political problems to be resolved in the political arena by other branches of government. But these are social and political problems which seem at times to defy such resolution. In such situations, under our system, the judiciary must bear a hand and accept its responsibility to assist in the solution where constitutional rights hang in the balance.

This statement might better have been labeled a "Prologue to the Future," because of its incisive description of things that were soon to come about in education.

The Divisions of Educational Jurisprudence

Five stages in the evolution of the role of the courts in education are discernible.

1. *The stage of strict judicial laissez faire.* From 1789 to about 1850 the federal and state courts ignored education. Federal courts viewed it as a state and local matter, and state courts were rarely called upon to intervene in a school matter.

2. *The stage of state control of education.* During the period 1850 to about 1950, state courts asserted that education was exclusively a state and local matter. Few cases affecting education were presented to the Supreme Court of the United States, and consequently a body of case law developed at the state level which permitted,[2] if not actually sanctioned, educational policies and practices that failed to meet federal constitutional standards and requirements.

3. *The reformation stage.*[3] Beginning about 1950 (and continuing until today), the federal courts, the Supreme Court in particular, recognized that educational policies and practices as they had developed under state laws and state court decisions were not in conformity with federal constitutional

requirements. This is the period of federal court infusion of constitutional *minima* into existing educational structures.

4. *The stage of "education under supervision of the courts."* Concurrent with the "reformation stage," there has been a discernible tendency of the courts, federal and state, to expand the scope of their powers over the schools (e.g., intervention in matters affecting the administration, organization, and programs of the schools; retaining jurisdiction over cases until their mandates, orders, and decrees have been carried into effect;[4] etc.). It is therefore clear that a new judicial function is taking place.

5. *The stage of "strict construction."* Beginning March 21, 1973, there has been a further development that will affect the role of federal courts in education: the landmark decision in the school finance case, *San Antonio Independent School District v. Rodriguez,*[5] wherein the Supreme Court of the United States declared: "Education is not among the rights afforded explicit protection under our Federal Constitution. Nor do we find any basis for saying it is implicitly so protected."[6] This "strict construction" posture of the Nixon Court is bound to affect the trend of federal court decisions concerned with the organization, administration, and programs of the public schools which has so clearly marked the period since about 1950.[7]

The Estimate of Court Decisions Affecting Education

The divisions of educational jurisprudence set forth above are supported by the data on numbers of court decisions presented in Table 2-1 below. It is estimated that approximately 40,000 court cases affecting the organization, administration, and programs of the schools were decided between 1789 and 1971.[8] This includes decisions reported by state courts, federal courts, and the Supreme Court of the United States. The total number of federal court cases affecting education has increased in every period shown since 1897, with sharp increases for the periods beginning in 1956 and in 1967.[9] On the other hand, the total number of state court decisions affecting education, while still substantial, has decreased since 1956.[10]

The Classical View of the Courts and Education

The State and Education

What may be called the "classical view" of the role of the courts in education endured until about 1950; it was a period for over one hundred years when education was viewed as a state and local matter—but not exclusively and

Table 2-1

State and Federal Court Cases Which Have Affected the Organization, Administration, and Programs of the Schools[a] (1789 through 1971)

Periods	Total Cases	State Court Cases	Federal Court Cases
1789-1896[b]	3,096	3,046	50
1897-1906	2,304	2,289	15
1907-1916	3,060	3,038	22
1916-1926	4,464	4,420	44
1926-1936	6,324	6,257	67
1936-1946	5,544	5,456	88
1946-1956	7,203	7,091	112
1956-1966	4,420	3,691	729
1967-1971[c]	3,510	2,237	1,273
Totals	39,925	37,125	2,800[d]

[a]Estimated.

[b]One-hundred and seven year period.

[c]Five year period (incomplete because 1971 cases were still being reported).

[d]Includes cases decided by the lower federal courts and the Supreme Court of the United States.

Source: *The American Digest System* (Century Edition, and 1st, 2nd, 3rd, 4th, 5th, 6th, and 7th Decennial Editions, and General Digest (Fourth Series), 1658-1971; *The Federal Cases*, 30 Vols., 1789-1, 1880; *United States Supreme Court Digest*, Vol. 12 and Pocket Part, 1754-1971; *Federal Digest*, Vol. 57 and Pocket Part, 1754-1960; *Modern Federal Practice Digest*, Vol. 44 and Pocket Part, 1939-1971; Clark Spurlock, *Education and the Supreme Court*, 1955; and *Official Reports of the Supreme Court of the United States*, 1789-1971.

(As of January 1, 1972)

entirely free from federal involvement. The argument was sometimes put in this form: the states control public education because the Constitution of the United States does not mention education as a function delegated to the general government. Under the Tenth Amendment, those "powers not delegated to the United States by the Constitution, nor prohibited by it to the States, are reserved to the States respectively, or to the people." Court interpretations of this language were consistent: education is a state function and the power over the public schools is vested exclusively in the state. Thus:

Schools "are matters of State, not local jurisdiction."[11]
"Education belongs to the State."[12]
"Today, education is perhaps the most important function of State and local governments."[13]
Although "the responsibility for public education is primarily the concern of

the States ... such responsibilities ... must be exercised consistently with federal requirements as they apply to State action."[14]

The General Government and Education

While the "classical view" held that the state controls public education, it also recognized that the general government was empowered to tax and spend money for educational purposes. This federal power was implied from the broad language of the "general welfare" clause of the Constitution: "The Congress shall have Power to lay and Collect Taxes, Duties, Imposts, and Excises, to pay the Debts and provide for the common Defense and general Welfare of the United States" (Art. 1, Sec. 8, cl. 1). This was interpreted by the courts to mean that Congress was not limited in the expenditure of money to direct or express grants of legislative powers found elsewhere in the Constitution.[15] Hence, Congress might tax and spend money in aid of public education (for "general welfare"). However, state control of public education and the power of the general government to spend money for educational purposes, as noted above, were to be exercised subject to constitutional requirements and limitations. Thus, state or federal actions affecting education, in theory at least, must be consistent with the general provisions of the Constitution.

The most distinguishing characteristic of the "classical" period was the laissez faire attitude of the courts towards the schools, which is epitomized by the phrase "leaving education to the educators." It was this disinterested, hands-off attitude which resulted in the development of a body of state case law which permitted state and local educational policies and practices that failed to meet minimum constitutional requirements under the First and Fourteenth Amendments and which first attracted federal court attention to the schools.

Federal Court Jurisdiction Over Education

Two means for obtaining federal court jurisdiction in cases affecting education are: by questioning the validity of a state or federal statute under the United States Constitution, or by alleging that some constitutionally protected right, privilege, or immunity of the individual has been violated.[16] Otherwise, the case will normally be decided in the state courts. The "classical view" allowed for cases to be raised under the first means, and in fact most of those decisions by federal courts before 1950 involved the validity of a state statute; it was only toward the end of the period that federal court cases involving the schools were brought on the basis of an infringement of constitutionally protected individual rights.[17]

This change was made possible, in part, by a Supreme Court interpretation that made the Bill of Rights applicable to the states.

A New Role for the Bill of Rights

Whereas, originally, the first ten amendments (the Bill of Rights) applied only to the federal government (*"Congress* shall make no law respecting. . . ."), and this was so held by the Supreme Court,[18] beginning in 1925, the freedom of speech and freedom of the press provisions of the Bill of Rights were absorbed into the Fourteenth Amendment and made applicable not only to Congress but to the states as well.

For present purposes we may and do assume that freedom of speech and of the press—which are protected by the First Amendment from abridgment by Congress—are among the fundamental personal rights and "liberties" protected by the Due Process clause of the Fourteenth Amendment from impairment by the states.[19]

Other provisions of the Bill of Rights respecting the rights of individuals were subsequently made applicable to the states through the Fourteenth Amendment.

Thus, a broad new area was opened up for the federal courts to regulate, and it included education: student and teacher rights and other school activities that violated any of the first ten constitutional amendments. But because of the laissez faire attitude courts had traditionally held toward education and the schools, federal court activity in this area was only nominal until the 1950s.

Education Under Supervision of the Courts

The Modern Trend

The modern trend in decisional law is toward "education under supervision of the courts." A new judicial function is clearly emerging: it involves supervision of the schools by the courts to assure that constitutional *minima* required by the First and the Fourteenth Amendments are met. At least one United States Court of Appeals judge, James P. Coleman, made this point quite clear when he said: "As a matter of fact, most of the school districts now before us, if not all of them, *have been under the supervision of the federal courts for as much as five years.* I think it is quite clear what this proves."[20] Not only do the courts today decide more cases affecting the schools, but when they issue mandates, orders, and decrees they retain jurisdiction over the cases to assure that their orders are effectively carried out.[21]

One need only compare the extent of court involvement in education in the 1940s with court involvement in the schools as it existed in 1973 to appreciate what significant change has occurred. The roots of this new judicial function can be traced to about 1950, when erosion of the "classical view" of education as exclusively a state and local function began and when the federal courts, the Supreme Court of the United States in particular, recognized that certain policies and procedures of the public schools failed to meet constitutional requirements of the First and Fourteenth Amendments.

That basic changes are taking place in judicial thinking about the role of the courts in education is shown by some cases that have been concerned with:

the power of courts to reopen schools closed to avoid desegregation

the power of courts to require levying of taxes for support of schools

the power of courts to assign teacher and students to specific schools to achieve racial balance

the power of courts to require special programs for the underprivileged

the power of courts to enforce student and teacher rights of freedom of expression.[22]

The changing role of the federal courts in education, particularly in the southern states, is further illustrated by a few specific examples:

1. A federal court ordered the appointment of a Black assistant principal at a Louisiana high school where the student body was two-thirds white, and the order was upheld on appeal.[23]

2. A federal court ruled that a state in integrating its school systems should make provisions for a plan governing the assignment and dismissal of teachers and said that such a plan should establish objective, nondiscriminatory *standards and procedures for evaluating teachers*; the plan should contain definitions and instructions for the application of standards to given teachers and should set forth methods by which teaching is to be evaluated.[24]

3. There are numerous examples of federal courts ordering student and faculty assignments, such assignments to be made according to a plan that complies with the principles of Supreme Court decisions.[25]

4. There are federal court decisions that restrict the transfer of students and that hold that where there is a scarcity of space in the schools being desegregated, majority to minority transfers have priority over other transfers.[26]

5. Federal courts have ordered that formerly segregated school districts must operate as "unitary systems" for several years before students may be assigned within the system on the basis of *achievement test scores.*[27]

6. Per pupil expenditures and teachers' salaries have also come under scrutiny by the federal courts; thus, where the district's elementary school had 74 percent of the white enrollment, had 15.5 percent smaller teacher-pupil ratio, had 9.7 percent greater average teacher cost, and had 26.7 percent greater teacher expenditure per pupil than did elementary schools with 98 percent of the black enrollment, it was contended by the school authorities that such discrepancies were random and were due to technological reasons beyond the school board's control. Held: the right to an equal educational opportunity was

being denied to the black children. Ordered: per pupil expenditures for teachers' salaries and benefits in any elementary school must not deviate—except for adequate justification—more than 5 percent from the mean per pupil expenditure for such salaries, etc., at all elementary schools in the district.[28]

However, a federal district court "is not concerned with *nonconstitutional questions* or with matters lying properly within administrative judgment and discretion of local school authorities."[29]

As the above summary shows, there is already a considerable body of federal decisional law that affects the organization, administration, and programs of the public schools, primarily and at the moment, directed mainly at southern schools and southern school districts, and for the purpose of disestablishing "dual school systems" that discriminate, but which could have applicability to education in the North and in the West as the federal judiciary continues to consider *de facto* school desegregation situations outside of the South.[30]

Judges and Lawyers

There are roughly 6000 to 8000 judges in the United States assigned to federal and state courts which have jurisdiction over cases involving the schools and education;[31] not all of these judges, however, have ever participated in the decision of such a case. A very small minority of the judiciary and an even smaller minority of the total lawyers[32] in the country are making the decisions that call for sweeping changes in the operation of the public schools. Their power stems, in great part, from earlier (post-1950) decisions of the Supreme Court of the United States which support and sanction and, in some instances, require their activity.

The Supreme Court and Education

While education as such has never been the central issue in a case decided by the Supreme Court of the United States,[33] that Court since about 1950 and until 1973 has adopted an "activist posture" toward education by accepting and deciding cases that have an impact on the schools, and it is logical to conclude from the great stress placed on education in the first *Brown*[34] decision, and in subsequent cases, that this has not been entirely coincidental, but rather that it reflects a changing conception the Supreme Court itself has of its role in education.

When this tendency of the Court to involve itself with educational matters first became visible, there were justices who warned about the possible problems of the Supreme Court becoming a "super school board" supervising all of the schools and school districts in the country. Thus, as long ago as 1948, Supreme Court Justice Jackson referred to the zeal shown by the Court for its own ideas of public school instruction and the danger of becoming a super board of education:

To lay down a sweeping constitutional doctrine as demanded by complainant and apparently approved by the Court, applicable alike to all school boards of the nation . . . is to decree a uniform, rigid and, if we are consistent, an unchanging standard for countless school boards representing and serving highly localized groups which not only differ from each other but which themselves from time to time change attitudes. It seems to me that to do so is to allow zeal for our own ideas of what is good in public instruction to induce us to accept the role of a super board of education for every school district in the nation.[35]

And Justice Black, in 1968, warned about the problems inherent in Supreme Court supervision of the public school curriculum:

However wise this Court may be or may become hereafter, it is doubtful that, sitting in Washington, it can successfully supervise and censor the curriculum in every public school in every hamlet and city in the United States. I doubt that our wisdom is so nearly infallible.[36]

The first Justice Harlan, in *Cumming v. Board of Education* (1899), observed that education in the public schools,

is a matter belonging to the respective states, and any interference on the part of Federal authority with the management of such schools cannot be justified except in the case of a clear and unmistakable disregard of rights secured by the supreme law of the land.[37]

Other members of the Supreme Court, however, at other times have obviously felt otherwise, as the trend in decisions until 1973 clearly shows.

The apparent willingness of certain individuals and groups to accept greater involvement of the courts in the educational process is evident; perhaps it is because of the growing financial and other crises in public education, that there is a general agreement that a major reform is needed in the way we operate our schools.

Educators, both teachers and administrators, seem powerless as individuals to do very much about it, even unable to provide sound educational inputs to court decisions affecting the schools.[38] They have, in general, accepted the new role of the courts in education but not without voicing complaint and some have welcomed it in such areas as desegregation and student discipline.

Local school boards, many of which in the 1950s vigorously resisted the implementation of court orders (i.e., desegregation), by the mid-1960's were in compliance with the letter, if not always the spirit, of the court decisions. The year 1966 represented a major turning point in southern school district compliance with court orders.[39] It shows a willingness of school boards, even if under compulsion, to accept the new role of the courts in education.

Some local boards in the West, unable to obtain desired reform in their schools in the normal manner, have turned to the courts for help and do not appeal to the Supreme Court of the United States cases decided to their liking.[40]

State educational agencies suddenly are quick to issue general directives ordering local districts to remake their policies and procedures to conform to court mandates.[41]

Other groups (ACLU, NEA, etc.) have adopted the practice of instigating new suits or filing briefs *amicus curia* in support of pending suits seeking to change the policies and procedures of the schools.[42]

Some political leaders (e.g., George Wallace and other southern politicians) have many times voiced strong opposition to the changing role of the courts in education. President Nixon is on record as opposing compulsory busing to achieve racial balance in the schools.[43] Numerous other political leaders, however, are strong supporters of the new role of the courts in education.

The general public, especially those parents with children in schools that are under court orders to bus pupils to achieve desegregation, is another group that has voiced considerable dissatisfaction with the new role of the courts in the educational process, but that complaint has been primarily for the reason cited, namely busing of pupils and the consequent abolition of the "neighborhood school" concept. Otherwise, the general public seems to be satisfied with the schools.[44] Because it is less aware of court decisions in other areas that affect the schools, the public appears to be disinterested and unconcerned whether or not students and teacher rights to "freedom of expression" (*Tinker*), etc. are enforced by courts on school campuses.

According to George Gallup, who surveyed public attitudes towards the schools,

The major problem facing the public schools in 1970 and in 1969, in the opinion of the American people, was discipline. In 1971, finance—how to pay for the schools—is cited most often as the biggest problem with which local public schools must deal.[45]

In the 1972 "Fourth Annual Gallup Poll of Public Attitudes Towards Education," discipline again ranked as the number-one problem of the public schools in the mind of the public:

1. lack of discipline
2. lack of proper financial support
3. integration-desegregation problems
4. difficulty in getting "good" teachers
5. large school, too large classes

6. parent's lack of interest
7. lack of proper facilities
8. poor curriculum
9. use of dope, drugs[46]

A major reform has been taking place in the way public schools operate, and there is a willingness on the part of some individuals and groups to accept as one solution to the problem greater court control over the management of the public schools.[47]

3 Race and Education

The Constitutional Aspects

The main thrust of educational jurisprudence since about 1950 has been concerned with enforcing the constitutional *right of individuals* to receive education on equal terms irrespective of their race; there is also a corresponding constitutional *duty imposed on the state* to provide such educational opportunity:

The constitutional *duty* of a state to provide an equal educational opportunity did not originate with the *Brown* decision. It was the basis of the many decisions rendered by the Supreme Court and by lower federal courts in the three generations following *Plessy v. Ferguson.*[1]

At least until 1938, courts said that this *duty* was satisfied if the state provided *separate* schooling for whites and for other races.[2] The Fourteenth Amendment speaks of "equal protection of the laws," and the *duty* it imposes upon the state is that it not deny to any person within its jurisdiction such protection. Federal and state courts have construed this as a clear constitutional command to eliminate *state*-imposed segregation from public schools.

The Fourteenth Amendment

The Anatomy of the Amendment

The Fourteenth Amendment contains five sections, one that pertains to enforcement (Sec. 5) and three that are essentially of historical interest (Secs. 2, 3, and 4). The first section has the greatest applicability to education and has been described as "probably the greatest single source of the rights of persons and of limitations upon the states that exists in the entire Constitution and all of the other Amendments."[3] This section consists of two sentences: one concerns "citizenship and naturalization" and the other contains three clauses: *privileges and immunities, due process,* and *equal protection.* It is this latter clause which courts apply in cases affecting education: "No state shall . . . deny to any person within its jurisdiction the equal protection of the laws." This language is prohibitory on the states; it has been said however, to "contain a necessary implication of a positive immunity, or right, most valuable to the colored

15

race."[4] It has been customary to say that the equality guaranteed by the Fourteenth Amendment is: equal treatment of persons similarly situated, or that all persons within a class must be treated alike.

Interpretation of the Amendment

In the Supreme Court's first interpretation of the Fourteenth Amendment, the language was strictly construed to apply solely to situations involving *discrimination against Negroes*; this, the Court said in the *Slaughter-Houses cases*[5] was the only "evil to be remedied by this clause."

We doubt very much whether any action of a state not directed by way of discrimination against the Negroes as a class, or on account of their race will ever be held to come within the purview of this provision. It is so clearly a provision for that race and that emergency, that a strong case would be necessary for its application to any other.

Strauder v. West Virginia (1880) referred to the above interpretation: "If this is the spirit and meaning of the Amendment, whether it means more or not, it is to be construed liberally, to carry out the purposes of its framers."[6]

However, another interpretation maintains that the equal protection concept was inserted as a clause in the Fourteenth Amendment to assure equal rights and procedures regardless of a person's race or color; hence, many nonracial situations were early adjudicated under it.[7]

Does historical evidence support either the one or the other of these interpretations of the Fourteenth Amendment's equal protection clause?[8]

The Supreme Court of the United States explored evidence of the original understanding and meaning of the language of the clause at the 1953 reargument of *Brown v. Board of Education of Topeka.* In their briefs and on oral argument, counsel were requested to address the following questions:

1. What evidence is there that the Congress which submitted and the State legislatures and conventions which ratified the Fourteenth Amendment contemplated or did not contemplate, understood or did not understand, that it would abolish segregation in public schools?
2. If neither the Congress in submitting nor the States in ratifying the Fourteenth Amendment understood that compliance with it would require the immediate abolition of segregation in public schools, was it nevertheless the understanding of the framers of the Amendment
   (a) that future Congresses might, in the exercise of their power under section 5 of the Amendment, abolish such segregation, or
   (b) that it would be within the judicial power, in light of future conditions, to construe the Amendment as abolishing such segregation of its own force?
3. On the assumption that the answers to questions 2(a) and (b) do not dispose of the issue, is it within the judicial power, in construing the Amendment, to abolish segregation in public schools?

4. Assuming it is decided that segregation in public schools violates the Fourteenth Amendment
    (a) would a decree necessarily follow providing that, within the limits set by normal geographic school districting, Negro children should forthwith be admitted to schools of their choice, or
    (b) may this Court, in the exercise of its equity powers, permit an effective gradual adjustment to be brought about from existing segregated systems to a system not based on color distinctions?[9]

"Inconclusive" was Chief Justice Warren's summation of the findings of the reargument; after review of all the pertinent sources, he said: "This discussion and our own investigation convince us that, although these sources cast some light, it is not enough to resolve the problem with which we are faced. At best, they are inconclusive."[10]

The late Mr. Justice Harlan, in *Oregon v. Mitchell*, reviewed the history of the Fourteenth Amendment, and expressed "complete astonishment at the position of some of my Brethren that the history of the Fourteenth Amendment has become irrelevant."[11] Harlan's astonishment was evoked by Justice Douglas's statement:

In *Harper v. Virginia Board of Elections* . . . we stated: "Notions of what constitutes equal treatment for purposes of the Equal Protection Clause *do* change." That statement is in harmony with my view of the Fourteenth Amendment, as expressed by my Brother BRENNAN: "We must therefore conclude that its framers understood their amendment to be a broadly worded injunction capable of being interpreted by future generations in accordance with the vision and needs of those generations." *Hence the history of the Fourteenth Amendment tendered by my Brother HARLAN is irrelevant to the present problem.*[12]

It is quite possible that the Fourteenth Amendment, the point at which it started and that at which it has arrived today, through successive court interpretations, are on entirely different planes. Some would say that the equal protection clause was returned by the Supreme Court to its historic purpose and function with the 1954 *Brown case*. Others disagree,[13] saying that our historical understanding of the meaning, purpose, and intent of the Fourteenth Amendment no longer supports the Supreme Court's interpretation of the language of the equal protection clause. Inquiry and disagreement about the original meaning intended for the Amendment is thus far from settled.

The "State Action" Concept

The language of the Fourteenth Amendment is a limitation on "state action," whether legislative, judicial, or executive, and is not directed toward private acts of individuals unsupported by state authority.[14] Formerly, it was thought that the amendment could be infringed only by affirmative "state" as distinguished from "private" action.[15] Thus, in the *Civil Rights cases* (1883), it was said:

The first section of the Fourteenth Amendment is prohibitory in its character, and prohibitory upon the states. . . . It is state action of a particular character that is prohibited. Individual invasion of individual rights is not the subject matter of the Amendment. It has a deeper and broader scope.[16]

Specifically, the Amendment "nullifies and makes void" all state laws, legislation, and "state action" of every kind (e.g., acts of boards of education, school administrators, teachers, etc.) that deny to citizens of the United States "equal protection of the laws." Although the principle was established in the *Civil Rights cases* that the Fourteenth Amendment refers to "state," as distinguished from "private," action, the Supreme Court of the United States has subsequently in many situations applied the corollary principle that the restrictions on "state action" apply to the manner in which a state regulates legal relations between "private" persons. Harold Horowitz maintains that in these corollary situations there is state action, and that the sole issue is whether the particular state action determining legal relations between private persons is constitutional.[17]

The Supreme Court of the United States has never devised a precise "formula" for ascertaining the contents and limits of the state action concept. It is said that this would be an "impossible task."[18] *The nonobvious involvement* of the state in private conduct becomes apparent only by "sifting facts and weighing circumstances."[19] Since absolutely private conduct with no state involvement whatsoever probably rarely exists, some nexus of the state with private conduct will usually be found.

The "Public Function" Doctrine
and Public and Private Schools

In the 1940s the Supreme Court of the United States began to open up and expand the concept of state action. Certain private actions, if they constituted a "public function," were subjected to state regulation. Justice Black, in *Marsh v. Alabama*, articulated the "public function" doctrine:

Ownership does not always mean absolute dominion. The more an owner, for his advantage, opens up his property for use by the public in general, the more do his rights become circumscribed by statutory and constitutional rights of those who use it.[20]

Privately owned bridges, ferries, turnpikes, and railroads are "built and operated primarily to benefit the public, and since their operation is essentially a public function, it is subject to state regulation." Company towns, shopping centers—

and in 1970, a private park left in trust to be used by "white people only," all were brought under the public function concept. What about private schools and colleges? Can they be brought within this reasoning?

The late Justice Harlan, dissenting in *Evans v. Newton* (the private park case), points to these possible future educational applications of the public function doctrine:

More serious than the absence of any firm doctrinal support for this theory of state action are its potentialities for the future. Its failing as a principle of decision in the realm of Fourteenth Amendment concerns can be shown by comparing—among other examples that might be drawn from the still unfolding sweep of governmental functions—the *"public function" of privately established schools* with that of privately owned parks. Like parks, the purpose schools serve is important to the public. Like parks, private control exists, but there is also a very strong tradition of public control in this field. Like parks, schools may be available to almost anyone of one race or religion but to no others. Like parks, there are normally alternatives for those shut out but there may also be inconveniences and disadvantages caused by the restriction. Like parks, the extent of school intimacy varies greatly depending on the size and character of the institution.

For all the resemblance, the majority assumes that its decision leaves unaffected the traditional view that the Fourteenth Amendment does not compel private schools to adapt their *admission policies* to its requirements, but that such matters are left to the States acting within constitutional bounds. I find it difficult, however, to avoid the conclusion that this decision opens the door to reversal of these basic constitutional concepts, and, at least in logic, jeopardizes the existence of denominationally restricted schools *while making of every college entrance rejection letter a potential Fourteenth Amendment question.*

While this process of analogy might be spun out to reach privately owned orphanages, libraries, garbage collection companies, detective agencies, and a host of other functions commonly regarded as nongovernmental though paralleling fields of governmental activity, the example of schools is, I think, sufficient to indicate the pervasive potentialities of this "public function" theory of state action. It substitutes for the comparatively clear and concrete tests of state action a catch-phrase approach as vague and amorphous as it is far-reaching. [21]

However, it has been noted that outside of the South, the

need for imposing the requirements of equal protection on private schools is far from pressing, for two reasons . . . most of these schools and virtually all those which are particularly sought after because of their reputation have shown little disposition to exclude Negroes. Furthermore, the interest of most Negroes in private education is now indeed academic, because high costs erect a barrier nearly as severe as the racial barrier. Substantial integration in private education will have to wait until desegregation in employment and in public education provides the means for Negroes to attain higher economic status. [22]

In July 1973 however, two private schools in Virginia were ordered to integrate by a United States district court judge, who cited a provision of the 1866 Civil

Rights Law to support his ruling that private schools cannot deny admission to Blacks because of their race.[23] Judge Albert V. Bryan, Jr. ordered two suburban Virginia schools, Bobbe's School in Arlington and the Fairfax Brewster School in Fairfax County, to cease discrimination against Blacks in their admissions policies. One a nursery school and the other an elementary school with classes through the sixth grade, neither school receives any public funds either directly or indirectly through tax exemptions.

Judge Bryan's ruling is based on the provision of the 1866 civil rights law, which says that all persons have a right to "make and enforce contracts."[24]

This is about the most important freedom decision ever made. It is so fundamental it affects the entire country.[25]

... a breakthrough for eliminating discrimination and some of the practices of these Southern white academies that flourish in the South.[26]

There is no longer a place of refuge for any group.[27]

The "twilight of state action" seems to be at hand, argues Jerre Williams, who reaches these conclusions about court decisions affecting matters of public and private concern:

1. The sun is setting on the concept of state action as a test for determining the constitutional protections of individuals. Through developments concerning "color of state law," state inaction, private groups and organizations becoming sufficiently oriented to public concern to justify public control, and judicial enforcement of private agreements, state action is so permeating that it is present in virtually all cases.
2. A kind of analysis which resembles the state action analysis is still properly used in those cases which evaluate the extent to which a private group or organization has become oriented to public concern. But the purpose of this analysis is not to determine whether there has been state action or not, but rather to determine whether the state's compulsory constitutional interest in the elimination of discrimination is overbalanced by the desirability of permitting a private right to engage in personal discrimination.
3. Personal freedom to discriminate lessens as the personal role becomes lessened, either through lack of personal interest . . . or the public's concern as the person moves into a relationship with the public generally. . . .
4. There is no formula. Each case must turn upon its own facts, although stare decisis will give a measure of predictability to similar cases.
5. The elimination of state action as a controlling concept does not eliminate the role of the courts. Rather, it broadens it.[28]

The state action concept is still a very important element in Supreme Court decisions affecting the schools, and where the Fourteenth Amendment is involved, the Court looks for purposeful state action, be it the action of the state legislature or of the school authorities themselves acting under the authority of the legislature. Sometimes it has been called "state action" and othertimes the *de jure/de facto* distinction,[29] yet the search for some form of state involvement continues to be of paramount importance. This is clearly shown in the discussion of the federal and state cases on race and education that follows.

The Beginnings of Equality in Education

The involvement of federal courts in education has come about primarily because of the race question; the old "separate but equal" doctrine and the modern concept of "equal educational opportunity" both had their origins in the racial discrimination cases, the latter being "derived" by the courts from the equal protection clause of the Fourteenth Amendment. Racial discrimination in the public schools led ultimately to the new role of courts in education.

In *Roberts v. The City of Boston* (1849), Chief Justice Shaw summarized the facts that gave rise to the case: Sarah Roberts, aged five, had been excluded from the public school nearest her home solely because she was Black and had been forced to attend a more distant school made up of children of her own race, which school was said to be equal in all respects to the school from which she was excluded. Shaw then asked: "Under these circumstances, has the plaintiff been unlawfully excluded from public school instruction?"[30] The legal answer was that obviously she had not.

Thus was born the doctrine of "separate but equal," which reigned in educational jurisprudence thereafter for more than one hundred years. This also was the beginning of the end of the "neighborhood school" concept for minority race children, for Sarah had been excluded by the highest court in Massachusetts from the school nearest to her home.

But did not Chief Justice Shaw ask (and did not the decision of the Court answer) the *wrong* question? History has shown that under this set of facts, the proper question before the Massachusetts court was not whether the girl had been "unlawfully excluded from public school instruction," but rather "whether she had been denied equal protection of the laws." (The Fourteenth Amendment, of course, did not exist in 1849.) Accordingly, Shaw decided the case on the basis of state law. The Massachusetts constitutional provision that all persons regardless of color, etc. are "equal before the law," Shaw said, is but a statement of a broad general principle suitable for inclusion in declarations of rights and in constitutions, but when that principle comes to be applied in actual practice, we must look elsewhere in the law to find rights of the individual to which it applies.

The statement of the principle itself creates no new rights, nor does the constitutional provisions that the legislature and the magistrates of Massachusetts should "cherish" public schools and grammar schools. There was no provision of law—state, constitutional, or otherwise—establishing a right of the individual to receive an education. Such a right was expressly repudiated by the court:

Had the legislature failed to comply with this injunction, and neglected to provide public schools in the towns or should they so fail in their duty as to repeal all laws on the subject, and leave all education to depend on private means, strong and explicit as the direction of the constitution is, it would afford no remedy or redress to the thousands of the rising generation who now depend on these schools to afford them a most valuable education, and an introduction to useful life.[31]

There was no right to demand a public education: the state might close all public schools, if it so chose, and leave education to wholly private means.

The *Roberts case* approved of a classification drawn on the basis of race for educational purposes. This was in keeping with the thinking of the time. (Since then the courts have generally held—but not more recently[32]—that constitutional requirements of equality are satisfied so long as there is a "reasonable basis" for the classification.) Not only the classification—Blacks and whites educated in separate schools—but the increased burden that classification placed on the Black child was deemed reasonable and not illegal:

The increased distance, to which the plaintiff was obligated to go to school from her father's house, is not such, in our opinion, as to render the regulation in question unreasonable, still less illegal.[33]

The *Roberts case* set the course for judicial thinking about race and education which was to continue for about one hundred years to come:

1. Education is a state matter, and cases affecting it are to be disposed under state law.

2. The "neighborhood school" concept does not apply to Negroes (and other minorities).

3. The state may close its public schools, if it chooses, thereby leaving all education to private means.

4. There is no *right* of the individual to demand a public education.

5. The Massachusetts constitutional provision that "all persons . . . are equal before the law" is but a platitude—a principle—and we must therefore look elsewhere in the law to find out what rights of the individual it covers.

6. Educational classifications requiring separation of the races ("separate but equal") are *reasonable* and therefore permissible.

In 1896 there was set in motion a long line of race cases (*Plessy v. Ferguson*),[34] many of them affecting the public schools,[35] which perpetuated the notion that "separate but equal" facilities satisfy constitutional requirements of the equal protection clause of the Fourteenth Amendment, and which appeared to culminate in 1954 when the Supreme Court of the United States decided *Brown v. Board of Education of Topeka*,[36] a *de jure* segregation case. Reciting the harmful effects of racial segregation on the child, supported by modern sociological and psychological authority (the famous footnote 11), and declaring that "any language in *Plessy v. Ferguson* contrary to this finding is rejected," the Court announced: "We conclude that in the field of public education the doctrine of 'separate but equal' has no place. Separate educational facilities are inherently unequal."[37] By this language, *Plessy v. Ferguson* was not expressly overruled; it was repudiated with respect to the point recited above; nevertheless, the case was not overruled.[38]

In its origin and as it was first applied in education, the "separate but equal" doctrine was a cryptic statement of the white race's fear of *miscegenation* and sociological consequences it foresaw therefrom. In law, however, it was the statement of a right *and* a duty: a right (legally enforceable) to receive equal educational treatment in *separate* schools, and a duty imposed on the state to provide such treatment; however, the right depended upon a condition precedent: "That the state had previously established schools or in some other way had undertaken to provide its people with education." As such, it was a *right* enjoyed by whites and Blacks and all others.

The main thrust of Supreme Court race decisions from *Plessy* (1896) to *Gaines* (1938), so far as they affected the public schools, was on the power of the state to establish *separate* schools; the constitutional duty of the state to provide equal educational opportunity is mentioned, but whether the separate schools were in fact equal seems to have been of secondary significance to the decision of the cases (*Plessy*, especially pp. 544-45). Where this point was raised by counsel in *Cumming v. Richmond County Board of Education*[39] ("the vice in the common school system of Georgia was the requirement that the white and colored children of the state be educated in separate schools"), the Supreme Court said: "We need not consider that question in this case. No such issue was made in the pleadings."

In *Berea College v. Commonwealth of Kentucky*,[40] the fine was imposed (and upheld on appeal) for *not* maintaining separate schools for the races, while the central issue in *Gong Lum v. Rice*,[41] was color as the basis for separation of the races, not the matter of equality of the educational opportunity provided by the all-Black school to which the Chinese child was assigned. The plaintiff's argument, which raises the miscegenation issue, was thought provoking:

The white, or Caucasian, race, which makes the laws and construes and enforces them, thinks that in order to protect itself against the infusion of the blood of other races its children must be kept in schools from which other races are excluded. The classification is made for the exclusive benefit of the law-making race. The basic assumption is that if the children of two races associate daily in the school room the two races will at last intermix; that the purity of each is jeopardized by the mingling of the children in the school room; that such association among children means social intercourse and social equality. This danger, the white race, by its laws, seeks to divert from itself. It levies the taxes on all alike to support a public school system, but in the organization of the system it creates its own exclusive schools for its children, and other schools for the children of all other races to attend together.

If there is danger in the association, it is a danger from which one race is entitled to protection just the same as another. The white race may not legally expose the yellow race to a danger that the dominant race recognizes and, by the same laws, guards itself against. The white race creates for itself a privilege that it denies to other races; exposes the children of other races to risks and dangers to which it would not expose its own children. This is discrimination.

Color may reasonably be used as a basis for classification only in so far as it indicates a particular race. Race may reasonably be used as a basis. "Colored" describes only one race, and that is the negro.[42]

The Supreme Court, however, saw no legal denial of equal protection when the child of Chinese blood was classified for educational purposes with the "Colored" race.

A point of turning occurred in 1938 with the decision of *Missouri ex rel. Gaines v. Canada*;[43] and although the case dealt primarily with separation of the races, not equality of educational programs in the law schools (there being no Negro law school facilities then existing in the State of Missouri for comparison purposes), the Supreme Court began to talk about a "federal right" to equal education, "discrimination" in education, "substantially equal advantages" in education, and "equality of right" in education. The decision in this case contains clear enunciations of the *right of the individual to receive (and the duty of the state to provide) an equal educational opportunity*:

The question here is not the duty of the State to supply legal training, or of the quality of the training which it does supply, but of *its duty when it provides such training to furnish it to the residents of the State upon the basis of an equality of right....* The white resident is afforded legal education within the state; the negro resident having the same qualifications is refused it there and must go outside the State to obtain it. That is a denial of the equality of legal right to the enjoyment of the privilege which the state has set up. ... We find it impossible to conclude that what otherwise would be an unconstitutional discrimination, *with respect to the legal right to the enjoyment of opportunities within the State*, can be justified by requiring resort to opportunities elsewhere. ... the essence of the constitutional right is that it is a personal one.[44]

By 1950 the thrust of the Supreme Court's race decisions had clearly shifted from the "separate" aspects of education to the "equality" aspects. The *Sweatt* and the *McLaurin cases* addressed the question "To what extent does the Equal Protection Clause of the Fourteenth Amendment limit the power of a state to distinguish between students of different races in professional and graduate education in a state university?" Thus, in *Sweatt v. Painter*[45] Chief Justice Vinson made comparisons of the two Texas law schools and concluded that the separate law school established for Negroes was "not substantially equal" to that provided whites at the University Texas Law School, and that the equal protection clause of the Fourteenth Amendment requires that the Negro student be admitted to the all-white school. He said:

In terms of a number of the faculty, variety of courses and opportunity for specialization, size of the student body, scope of the Library, availability of Law Review and similar activities, the University of Texas Law School is superior.[46]

But more important, the University of Texas Law School "possesses to a far greater degree those qualities which are incapable of objective measurement but which make for greatness in a law school": reputation of faculty, experience of the administration, position and influence of alumni, standing in the community, traditions and prestige, etc. Said the Court: "Petitioner may claim his full constitutional right: legal education equivalent to that offered by the State to students of other races."[47]

In *McLaurin v. Oklahoma State Regents*,[48] it was put in this language: the Black graduate student pursuing studies and courses leading to the doctorate in education has a "personal and present right to the equal protection of the laws," and he "must receive the same treatment at the hands of the State as students of other races."[49]

The appellants in *Briggs v. Elliott*[50] alleged that "equal facilities are not provided for Negro pupils," and the district court ordered School District No. 22 of Clarendon County, South Carolina, "to proceed at once to furnish educational facilities for Negroes equal to those furnished white pupils." The U.S. Supreme Court, however, vacated the judgment of the district court and ordered the case remanded for further proceeding in light of a report filed by the school district on actions it had taken to carry out the district court's order.

Recall that the war years of the 1940s and the decade afterwards was a period of population growth and mobility in which far-reaching changes were taking place in the attitudes of society towards race and racial discrimination: in public accommodations, partly because of this mobility;[51] in private housing and neighborhood living patterns, attributable in part to this growth; in people's tacit acceptance of interracial personal relationships; and ultimately in the racial composition of the public schools. It was also a period in which law courts across the nation were striking down statutes (in fields other than education) which classified people on the basis of race. For instance, the California antimiscegenation law,[52] enacted in 1872, and amended in 1905 and 1933, was declared unconstitutional in 1948 (*Prez v. Sharp*)[53] and was removed from the books in 1959. The deplorable condition of some public schools in some parts of the country testified openly to the inequality in education.

The stage was thus set for an event that the careful observer of law, society, and the schools might have foreseen: *Brown v. Board of Education of Topeka*, wherein the Supreme Court of the United States in 1954 held:

Segregation of white and Negro children in the public schools of a State solely on the basis of race, *pursuant to state laws permitting or requiring such segregation*, denies to Negro children the equal protection of the laws guaranteed by the Fourteenth Amendment—even though the physical facilities and other "tangible" factors of white and Negro schools may be equal.[54]

The legal distinction the Court made between *de jure* and *de facto* segregation (the italics) has troubled school districts ever since; much of the ensuing argument over implementation and compliance with the *Brown* decision, first in the South and now in the great cities outside of the South, has involved this distinction, which is inherent in the language of the Fourteenth Amendment itself: "No State shall ... deny to any person within its jurisdiction the equal protection of the laws." Even if physical facilities and other "tangible" factors be equal, if there are *state laws* permitting or requiring segregation, then the equal protection clause of the Fourteenth Amendment is violated.

Whether a state-built and publicly financed freeway that effectively isolates Blacks from whites and results in a separate and predominantly Black high school; whether the actions of state planning groups that fashion and build the Black community around the school; whether realtors, licensed by the state, who keep "white property" white and "Black property" Black; whether banks, chartered by the state, which shaped the policies that handicapped Blacks in financing homes other than in Black ghettos; whether residential segregation, fostered by state-enforced restrictive covenants, and which therefore result in segregated schools; whether "any of these factors add up to *de jure* segregation in the sense of that state action we condemned in *Brown v. Board of Education* is a question not yet decided."[55] The Supreme Court of the United States has not yet (1972) decided a case in which school segregation results from such factors unaided by a *state law* expressly permitting or requiring segregation in the schools. The contours of state action that would—or would not—bring such a case within the confines of the *Brown* decision are still being drawn.

The 1971 decision *Swann v. Charlotte-Mecklenburg Board of Education*,[56] which authorized compulsory busing, among other means, for the dismantling of "dual school systems," made this point quite clear:

The constant theme and thrust of every holding from Brown I to date is that state-enforced separation of races in public schools is a discrimination that violates the equal protection clause. The remedy commanded was to dismantle dual school systems.

We do not reach in this case the question whether a showing that school segregation is a consequence of other types of state action, without any discriminatory action by the school authorities, is a constitutional violation requiring remedial action by a school desegregation decree. This case does not present that question and we therefore do not decide it.[57]

The Supreme Court's sole object has been "to eliminate from the public schools all vestiges of state-imposed segregation."[58]

A flood of court cases—United States Supreme Court, federal circuit, and district court decisions—followed *Brown*, and many of these were concerned with implementation and securing compliance with that decision in the South; efforts of the courts to overcome balky school boards led to strong judicial pronouncements such as these: "with all deliberate speed" (*Brown II*, 1955);

the "interpretation of the Fourteenth Amendment enunciated by this Court is the supreme law of the land" (*Cooper v. Aaron*, 1958); and the "clock has ticked the last tick for tokenism and delay in the name of 'deliberate speed' " (*U.S. v. Jefferson County Board of Education*, 1966).

In the name of securing compliance with the *Brown* decision, courts have exercised broad control over the organization, administration, and programs of the public schools, including the power to reopen schools closed by local districts to avoid desegregation and the power to prohibit the closing of schools for the same reason; the power to order state taxation for support of schools; the power to order assignment of pupils and teachers to specific schools to achieve racial balance and to order special remedial programs; the power to order studies made of school district desegregation plans, involving the hiring of additional personnel and mandating that the costs thereof be paid by the state board of education—and the power to order *busing to achieve racial balance.*

Racial Imbalance in Public Schools—The California Doctrine

In *Guey Heung Lee v. David Johnson* (1971),[59] in denying Americans of Chinese ancestry a stay of a desegregation order, Justice Douglas referred to California statutory history affecting children of Chinese ancestry as the classical example of *de jure* segregation, and then quoted as above from the *Swann* case, and said that no evidence had been shown since *Brown I* that San Francisco had ever redrawn a school attendance line for purpose of eliminating *racial imbalance*. He added:

Brown v. Board of Education was not written for Blacks alone. It rests on the Equal Protection Clause of the Fourteenth Amendment, one of the first beneficiaries of which were the Chinese people of San Francisco. The theme of our social desegregation cases extend to all racial minorities treated invidiously by a state or any of its agencies.[60]

In this situation involving the Chinese of San Francisco, Douglas seems to have discovered the "clavical in the cat"[61]—*racial imbalance* as a vestige of state-imposed segregation existing from early times when California statutory law required the establishment of separate schools for Chinese.[62]

Such statutes have long been abolished, and the California Supreme Court as long ago as 1963, *Jackson v. Pasadena City School District*,[63] held that (on the basis of state law) *de facto* racial segregation in the public schools of the state is "an evil" and that school boards should take affirmative steps to eliminate *racial imbalance*, however created. Said the court:

It should be pointed out that even in the absence of gerrymandering or other affirmative discriminatory conduct by a school board, a student under some circumstances would be entitled to relief where, by reason of residential segregation, substantial racial imbalance exists in his school.[64]

The court, noting that so long as large numbers of Negroes live in segregated areas, school authorities will face the difficult situation of providing them with the kind of education they are entitled to have, since "residential segregation is in itself an evil which tends to frustrate the youth in the area and to cause antisocial attitudes and behavior." Further,

Where such segregation exists, it is not enough for a school board to refrain from affirmative discriminatory conduct. . . . The right to an equal opportunity for education and the harmful consequences of segregation require that school boards take steps, *insofar as reasonably feasible*, to alleviate racial imbalance in schools regardless of cause.[65]

This statement has been quoted and reaffirmed many times since as the law as it stands today in California. Not all state and federal courts, however, accept the California doctrine that school districts have an affirmative duty to eliminate "racial imbalance" in the schools.[66]

In *Winston-Salem/Forsyth County Board of Education v. Scott*,[67] Chief Justice Burger referred to the school board's apparent misunderstanding, that it was *required* to achieve a fixed racial balance that reflected the total composition of the school district, as "disturbing":

If we were to read the holding of the District Court to require, as a matter of substantive constitutional right, any particular degree of racial balance or mixing, *that approach would be disapproved and we would be obliged to reverse.* The constitutional command to desegregate schools does not mean that every school in every community must always reflect the racial composition of the school system as a whole.[68]

The determination of racial balance is an "obvious and necessary starting point" for courts to decide whether in fact any violation exists.

On the limits to the use of transportation (buses) to correct *state-enforced* racial school segregation, the Chief Justice quoted *Swann*:

The District Court's conclusion that assignment of children to the school nearest their home serving their grade would not produce an effective dismantling of the dual system is supported by the record. . . .

In these circumstances, we find no basis for holding that the local school authorities may not be required to employ bus transportation as one tool of school desegregation. Desegregation plans cannot be limited to the walk-in school.

An objection to transportation of students may have validity when the time or distance of travel is so great as to either risk the health of the children or significantly impinge on the educational process. . . .

It hardly needs stating that the limits on time or travel will vary with many factors, but probably with none more than the age of the students.[69]

In no prior case had the Supreme Court case dealt with busing of students "in this context of the limits on the use of transportation as part of a remedial plan, or with racial imbalancing."[70]

White "flight" to the suburbs has left many big city neighborhoods and schools mostly Black; hence, the proposal for abandonment of "geographical criteria" (school districts boundaries) and busing across existing school district lines. Thus,

The most radical approach to the problem of racial imbalance is to make integration rather than geographic proximity the fundamental determinant of the school a child attends. Such a plan would require transportation for white and Negro children.[71]

This "radical approach" was proposed in Virginia where a district court ordered the consolidation of the Richmond city schools with those of certain suburban counties. This was followed by President Nixon's March 1972 statement charging that, in some cases, the "courts have gone too far."[72] Declaring that busing is one of the most difficult issues of our times, the president noted that across the nation school districts have been "torn apart" over this issue and called for "action to stop it."

The reason action is so urgent is because of a number of recent decisions of the lower Federal Courts. *Those courts have gone too far*; in some cases beyond the requirements laid down by the Supreme Court in ordering massive busing to achieve racial balance.

Richmond

When U.S. District Judge Robert Merhige ordered the predominantly Black school district of Richmond, Virginia, to merge with the suburban districts of Henrico and Chesterfield Counties, a whole new legal dimension was added to the school desegregation picture: the possibility of integrating Black schools in the city with the white schools of adjacent counties and using school buses to do it. White exodus to the suburbs with its accompanying residential segregation had left such a predominance of Blacks in the Richmond schools that any plan limited to the city itself would render all city schools racially identifiable. Judge Merhige based his decision, *Bradley v. School Board of the City of Richmond, Virginia*,[73] on findings that these state-aided factors had contributed to the school desegregation: "history of private and governmental enforcement of segregation in schools and housing and reluctance by state and other authorities to desegregate, prior practices disregarding district boundaries for other purposes, and lack of discontinuity between city and suburbs."

The U.S. Fourth Circuit Court of Appeals (June 5, 1972) overturned Merhige's order, saying:

May a United States District Judge compel one of the States of the Union to restructure its internal government for the purpose of achieving racial balance in the assignment of pupils to the public schools? We think not, absent invidious discrimination in the establishment or maintenance of local governmental units, and accordingly reverse."[74]

Richmond, at this junction albeit belatedly, had done all it could do "to disestablish to the maximum extent possible the formerly state-imposed dual school system within its municipal boundary." In his concern for effective implementation of the Fourteenth Amendment, the district judge failed "to sufficiently consider, we think, a fundamental principle of federalism incorporated in the Tenth Amendment" and failed to consider the limitations (i.e., *Swann*) "on his power to fashion remedies in school cases." One of the powers reserved to the states under the Tenth Amendment is the power "to structure their internal government," and when a state exercises such power wholly within the domain of state interest, "it is insulated from federal judicial review."

Because we are unable to discern any constitutional violation in the establishment and maintenance of these three school districts nor any unconstitutional consequence of such maintenance, we hold that it was not within the district judge's authority to order the consolidation of these three separately political subdivisions of the Commonwealth of Virginia."[75]

The Supreme Court of the United States, May 21, 1973, in a *per curiam* decision, said of the Richmond case: "The judgment is affirmed by an equally divided Court. Mr. Justice Powell took no part in the consideration or decision of these cases."[76] The permissibility of crossing school district boundaries for purposes of desegregation, therefore, has been left for a later decision—possibly Detroit. (See Figure 3-1.)

Detroit

Elsewhere, in Michigan, U.S. District Judge Roth ordered (June 14, 1972) a busing plan for the city of Detroit, described as "the largest yet ordered by a federal court." Having first deferred a motion to join "contiguous suburban" school districts, Roth then concluded that "it was necessary to consider a metropolitan remedy for desegregation" and appointed a panel, charging it with the responsibility for preparing and submitting an effective desegregation plan.[77] The panel subsequently recommended, and Roth so ordered, that Michigan purchase 295 buses and begin the plan, which would require the consolidation into one attendance area of fifty-three separate school districts and approximately 780,000 students. The U.S. Sixth Circuit Court of Appeals (July 21) granted a stay and, following arguments in August 1972, delivered its decision by a unanimous three-judge panel.

The appeals court panel ruled (December 9) that the state must share the blame for racial segregation in Detroit's public schools and that a merger of the city schools with the suburban districts is a proper cure for the problem.[78] The panel referred to the holding of the court of appeals in the Richmond case, saying: "We respectfully decline to follow that decision."

The panel called for new district court hearings with the participation of adjacent school districts which might be annexed, the purpose of which would be to work out the precise shape of a new "metropolitan" district. The case

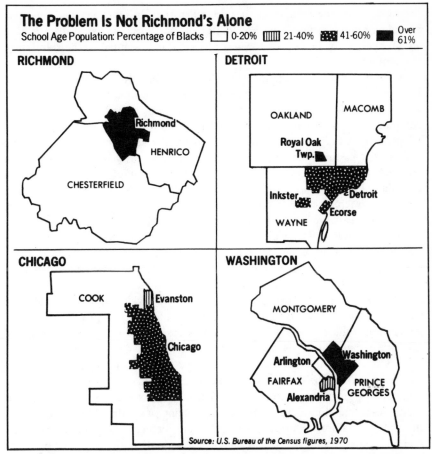

Figure 3-1. The Problem is Not Richmond's Alone. "Also potentially involved are cities where court cases are not pending. Washington, D.C., for example has a school-age population of 178,500 that is 86 percent black. But most of the surrounding suburbs in Virginia and Maryland have schools that are more than 80 percent white. And in Chicago, the city's school-age population of 851,800 is 43 percent black, while, except for some pockets such as Evanston, the schools in the rest of Cook county are more than 90 percent white." Source: Warren Weaver, Jr., "Busing: The Suburbs May Be Called Out of Bounds," *New York Times*, May 27, 1973. © 1973 by The New York Times Company. Reprinted by permission.

"calls up haunting memories of the now long-overruled 'separate but equal doctrine,'" the panel said. "We should not have one law for the South and a different one for the North" nor can constitutional rights of Black children be "hemmed in by the boundaries of a school district. It is obvious that some plan for desegregation beyond the boundaries of the Detroit school district is both within the equity powers of the district court and essential to the solution of this problem."[79]

A Detroit-only desegregation plan "will lead directly to a single, segregated Detroit school district, overwhelmingly black in all of its schools, surrounded by a ring of suburbs and suburban school districts overwhelmingly white in composition in a state in which the racial composition is 87 percent white and 13 percent black." Big-city school systems for Blacks surrounded by suburban school systems for whites, the panel said, does not satisfy the equal protection requirements of the Fourteenth Amendment. The panel referred to state control over the school districts within its borders: the state "has not treated its school districts as sacrosanct" but rather has used them entirely as "creatures of the state," frequently realigned them to meet statewide objectives and kept them securely controlled financially and administratively from the state capitol. The state and the Detroit school board had engaged in discriminatory practices which were "significant, pervasive, and causally related to the substantial amount of segregation in the Detroit school system."[80]

Acknowledging that Michigan has a public policy against racial discrimination and that the *underlying* problem might be "rooted in private residential segregation," the panel said the state took steps that, while "a bit more subtle than the compulsory segregation statutes of Southern cities . . . were nonetheless effective." These state actions included: state involvement in school construction plans which helped cause or maintain attendance patterns caused by residential segregation, exclusion of Detroit from some state transportation funds, discrimination against Detroit in financing of capital improvements, and the state legislature's intervention to block city desegregation moves. The panel said the state, under the U.S. Constitution's Fourteenth Amendment, is the body that must not deny equal protection of the laws.

This court never before has been confronted with a finding that any less comprehensive a solution than a metropolitan area plan would result in an all-black school system immediately surrounded by practically all-white school systems in a region which is predominantly white.[81]

Then, in an "extraordinary move," the full nine members of the Sixth U.S. Circuit Court of Appeals nullified (February 8, 1973) the above-described decision of the three-judge panel and began to hear arguments anew in the Detroit case.

On June 12, 1973, the court of appeals upheld the principle of including predominantly white suburban school districts in the integration of predominantly Black metropolitan school systems, but set aside the Detroit plan for interdistrict busing mandated by Judge Roth and ordered new hearings in the case because the fifty-two suburban school districts involved had not been allowed to make their objections known in court.[82] The court of appeals agreed with Roth that discriminatory practices of both the state of Michigan and the Detroit school board had perpetuated segregation in the Detroit city schools and that a "Detroit only" desegregation plan would result in a single segregated city school district overwhelmingly Black in all of its schools. The Detroit case is expected to be appealed to the Supreme Court; however, the high court might refuse to review the case at this stage and wait until after there have been further district court hearings at which the suburban school districts are allowed to present their views.

The Detroit decision presents complex political, legal, and sociological issues; the political issue is *federal v. state rights*: the power reserved to the states under the Tenth Amendment to structure their own internal political borders (school district lines) as against the power of the federal courts to restructure such borders in the name of the equal protection clause of the Fourteenth Amendment; the broader issue is whether school segregation "rooted in private residential segregation" is included in the kind of state action that the Supreme Court has condemned; whether state involvement in school construction "which helped cause or maintain attendance patterns caused by residential segregation" is included within that kind of state action disapproved by the 1954 *Brown case*.

Other Court Decisions

Distinguishable fróm the Richmond and Detroit cases because of their unique factual situations, these cases have looked at crossing *school district boundary lines* for purposes of *desegregation*, by busing of pupils and teachers, or *equalization of financing*, by merger or consolidation of school districts.

In Indiana (*United States v. Board of School Commissioners of Indianapolis*),[83] a school desegregation action was brought by the United States against a common school corporation that controlled the central part of a former city that has been consolidated with the county into a "metropolitan government" under a state statute that expressly provided that no school corporation would be affected by the consolidation.

The defendant School Board . . . controls all of the public elementary and high schools within a geographical area known as the School City of Indianapolis (hereinafter "School City"), as required by Indiana law. The shape of School City resembles that of a trussed fowl, with its head to the north, its bound feet to the south, and its flapping wings extending east and west. The east-west wingspread, at its greatest, is about 16 miles. The north-south dimension of the School City is about 13 miles.[84]

The district court ordered joinder of other municipal and school corporations in the county so that it could be determined whether the aforementioned statute "was unconstitutional as tending to cause segregation or inhibit desegregation."

The court of appeals (February 1, 1973) affirmed, holding that the evidence of both "segregative intent and causation" was substantial enough to support the district court's finding that the school board had been following a course of *de jure* segregation.

In Massachusetts (*School Committee of Boston v. Board of Education*),[85] the city school committee sued the Commonwealth Board of Education for withholding state school funds under the Massachusetts "racial imbalance" law and the board counterclaimed to require the committee to file a plan to eliminate racial imbalance in the schools, which it did:

The "First Stage Plan" (Short Term Relief)

Metco is a "privately administered, publicly funded program called Metropolitan Council for Educational Opportunity (a voluntary *intercity* program). This plan is designed to reduce racial imbalance within the Boston schools by identifying non-white students in the City of Boston school system who volunteer to participate and placing them voluntarily in metropolitan or suburban school systems. The city or town cooperating with Boston must, of course, volunteer to do so."[86]

The "Fourth Stage Plan"

This plan contained a lengthy proposal for "metropolitanization" which implies the combination of urban and suburban school systems. This was to be accomplished by an "ascription plan" under which a number of non-white Boston students would be absorbed by the schools of seventy-four communities lying within a radius of twenty miles of Boston. *"The most obvious of several difficulties with this proposal is that not only does the board lack statutory power to enforce such a plan, but it also ignores the racial imbalance law's prohibition against long haul busing."*[87]

The Supreme Judicial Court then held on appeal that the withholding of the funds "was arbitrary and an abuse of Board's discretion."

In New Jersey, in *Spencer v. Kugler,*[88] the district court dismissed a suit brought by Blacks who charged that racial imbalance in the schools, *caused by New Jersey statutes that established municipal boundaries as school district lines*, violated the Fourteenth Amendment:

In none of the schools of which the plaintiffs complain is any black pupil "segregated" from any white pupil.... Nowhere in the drawing of school district lines are considerations of race, creed, or national origin made.... A continuing trend towards racial imbalance caused by housing patterns within the various school districts is not susceptible to federal judicial interference.[89]

The Supreme Court of the United States agreed with the dismissal.

In Maryland (*Starr v. Parks*),[90] white parents of children attending schools in the city of Baltimore sued to compel admission of their children to schools in the neighboring counties.

The all-white plaintiffs have become disenchanted with the fact that most City schools are now, by dint of a process of re-segregation mostly black. . . . Indeed, the plaintiffs seem to be contending . . . that the open-door policies of the Baltimore City schools in an effort to comply with federal court decisions in the integration area from *Brown v. Board* on down, have resulted in a system overloaded with blacks, which the plaintiffs now want to escape.[91]

The district court dismissed the complaint because the existence of a predominantly Black city school district and adjacent predominantly white county school districts does not violate the Maryland Constitution or Annotated Code where, *inter alia*, the situation is one of *de facto* segregation arising from school district boundaries dating back to the nineteenth century.

In Wyoming (*Sweetwater County Planning Committee for the Organization of School Districts v. Henkle*),[92] on an appeal by the county planning committee from a lower court decision reversing the state committee's approval of the county's modified unified school districts plan, the state supreme court held that *the joinder of an affluent school district with a poorer district* "so as to provide equivalent [educational] opportunities to all students" is not a satisfactory solution to the financial problem—and the matter, with specific suggestions, was referred to the state legislature.

In Kentucky (*Clark v. Board of Education of Shelbyville, Kentucky*),[93] on an action against the county board of education by parents of Black children attending schools operated by a single district to compel merger with the remaining county schools operated by the board, the district court held that the factual allegations of the complaint were neither "nebulous and/or conclusory," that the board operated all county schools except those in this single district, *that the district was unable to raise revenue comparable to that raised by the remainder of the county*, and that despite recommendations of the Department of Education, the county refused to merge with the district; however, the relief sought—an order compelling merger—was described as "legislative in nature."

In Connecticut, the city of Hartford sued the state in the district court, the "first time a city has taken this step,"[94] charging that Hartford's constitutional rights, due process, and equal protection of the laws were violated by state school districting laws that gave the city increasingly segregated and deteriorating public schools.

In Georgia, an ACLU (Margie Hames) suit, proposed a five-county metropolitan desegregation plan, which would merge the schools of Atlanta with those of predominantly white suburban counties.[95]

Atlanta

The Atlanta school desegregation case, now in its fifteenth year before the courts, was filed in 1958 as *Calhoun v. Members of the Board of Education, City of Atlanta*,[96] an action by Negro children for injunctive relief to compel operation of the public schools without racial discrimination. Said the district court at that time: "The custom and practice of maintaining separate schools for Negroes and whites has existed in this state for many years, with the approval of the highest courts of the land, and it cannot be rapidly and suddenly ended."[97]

The case has since been heard by every level of the federal judiciary, including the Supreme Court of the United States (1964),[98] which described Atlanta's efforts towards school desegregation as "commendable." Yet the schools of Atlanta are still segregated, and the case is still undecided.

After many rehearings, the court of appeals (June 10, 1971)[99] ordered that the school board be required to implement a "student assignment plan" that complies with the principles of *Swann*; on remand the district court (July 28, 1971) set forth the following statement of the facts:[100] whereas in 1958, Atlanta had a pupil ratio of 70 percent white and 30 percent Black, by 1971 this had reversed itself to 70 percent Black and 30 percent white, with the white students concentrated at the extreme northern and southern ends of the district, which is sixteen miles long and fourteen miles wide: the vast middle is industry and high-density Black housing. "The line between these areas is steadily creeping towards the ends." Resegregation is the result of "factors completely beyond the control of school authorities. . . . White flight to the suburbs and private schools continues." In the face of these evolutional *de facto* changes, "The problem is no longer how to achieve integration, but how to prevent resegregation."

The only device that could effect a significant change in the pupil ratio is mass busing—but Atlanta has no buses, no drivers, and no funds with which to acquire them, and the

Atlanta Transit System is in dire straits itself. . . . Atlanta now stands on the brink of becoming an all-black city. A fruit-basket turnover through busing to create a 30% white-70% black uniformity would unquestionably cause such results in a few months time. . . . The remedy of mass busing under these circumstances is rejected. . . . If the premise of *Brown* is correct and education in an all-black system is injurious then certainly the results here would impinge the educational process for the children remaining. . . . Atlanta's *de jure* status has long since been removed by board action and by successive court decrees. There is absolutely no evidence of any affirmative action by the board to increase segregation.

Whereupon the Atlanta system was "judicially declared unitary, and a dismissal will be directed on January 1, 1972." In a "Comment" appended to the opinion, the court noted that *consolidation* of the Atlanta school system with the Fulton County system should be studied without delay.[101] On appeal (October 21), however, the dismissal was vacated and the plaintiffs allowed time to present an "alternative and superior" desegregation plan; the district court was directed to explore school districts consolidation as put forth in the above-mentioned "Comment."[102]

In June 1972 the ACLU (Margie Hames) "merger suit" was filed,[103] and the district court certified (June 23) its findings to the court of appeals wherein it rejected the "alternative and superior" plan and again declared the Atlanta school system unitary. The possibility of a settlement of this long-pending litigation then appeared likely and led to a prehearing conference (September 26), followed by the court of appeals' order (October 6, 1972) "issued to authorize and guide such settlement negotiations."[104] One settlement proposal—the first "compromise plan"—was filed on November 17, but class and representation complications negated the court's acceptance of the proposal.

On November 24 the court of appeals again vacated the district court's findings that the Atlanta school system was nondiscriminatory and unitary; the case was remanded to the district court for determination of the status of the class or classes in the litigation, and for an order requiring the school system to prepare and submit a comprehensive desegregation plan.[105] Since that time, the issue of who represents the plaintiff has been resolved, a second "compromise plan" prepared, and the ACLU "merger" suit is still "hanging in the wings."[106]

The "Atlanta Compromise" (the second plan) was accepted early in 1973 by the district court, but with several groups promising appeals to come; it provides for a Black superintendent, a 50 percent Black administration, and a minimum of busing (2765 students).[107] Opposing views of this outcome are:

What you may be seeing in Atlanta at this moment in history is a change—maybe a subtle one—in the thrust of desegregation in America.[108]

There aren't enough whites in the city system to go around, and integration can only be achieved if the courts order desegregation across county lines.[109]

In time metropolitan desegregation is inescapable.[110]

Denver

Keyes v. School District No. 1, Denver Colorado,[111] decided June 21, 1973, the first school desegregation case to reach the Supreme Court of the United States involving a city outside the South, is of considerable interest as an indication of how the high court may be expected to rule on future cases involving segregation in school districts in the North and West.

The original action was brought in June 1969 in the District Court for the District of Colorado by parents of Denver schoolchildren (hereinafter called simply, Keyes),[112] who sought first to desegregate the Park Hill area schools in Denver. Upon securing an order from the district court that granted that relief, Keyes expanded his suit to include desegregation of all the schools in the Denver school district, particularly those located in the "core city" area; the district court, however, denied this further relief, holding that *deliberate* racial segregation of the Park Hill schools did not prove a like segregation policy addressed specifically to the "core city" schools. Keyes, the district court said, was required to prove *de jure* segregation for each new area of the Denver school district that he sought to have desegregated by court order.

However, the district court did find that the segregated "core city" schools were inferior to the so-called "white" schools located elsewhere in the district; relying on the Supreme Court holding in *Plessy v. Ferguson* (1896)[113] that "separate but equal" facilities satisfy constitutional requirements, the district court ordered the Denver school authorities to provide *substantially equal facilities* for the "core city" schools.

This latter relief was reversed by the Tenth U.S. Court of Appeals, which affirmed the Park Hill ruling and agreed with the district court that the Park Hill segregation, even though deliberate, proved nothing regarding the school district's overall policy of segregation.[114]

The Supreme Court of the United States, in a majority opinion written by Justice Brennan, held:[115]

1. The district court, for purposes of defining a "segregated" core city school, erred in not placing Negroes and Hispanos in the same category, since both groups suffer the same educational inequities when compared with the treatment afforded Anglo students.

2. The district court and the court of appeals both did not apply the correct *legal standard* in dealing with Keyes's contention that the school board had a policy of deliberately segregating the core city schools.

    a. Proof that the school authorities have pursued an intentional segregative policy in a substantial portion of the school district will support a finding by the trial court of the existence of a dual system, absent a showing that the district is divided into clearly unrelated units.

    b. On remand the district court should decide initially whether the school board's deliberate segregative policy respecting the Park Hill schools constitutes the whole Denver school district, a dual school system.

    c. Where, as in this case, a policy of intentional segregation has been proved with respect to a significant portion of the school system, the burden is on the school authorities (regardless of their claims that their "neighborhood school policy" was racially neutral) to prove that their actions as to other segregated schools in the system were not likewise motivated by a segregative intent.

The judgement of the court of appeals was modified to vacate (rather than reverse) the parts of the Final Decree that concerned the core city schools, and the case was remanded to the district court for further proceedings.[116]

That the decision in the Denver case failed to go as far as some observers of the Supreme Court and school desegregation in the North had hoped for is shown by this commentator's analysis of the results in the case:

The Denver school case, viewed before hand as the ultimate test of desegregation outside the South, proved anticlimatic. In a murky decision fully endorsed only by one Nixon justice, Blackmun, the court said Denver will probably have to integrate, set down complicated rules for judging Northern segregation, and indicated it is not going to be as hard on the rest of the country as it was on the South.

The ruling was so mild that it evoked nothing more than a yawn from antibusing forces in the White House and Congress, but Justice Rehnquist still dissented. Powell wrote a denunciation of busing and Burger, explicitly withholding his approval of the decision, concurred only in its application to Denver. Their views may be the key to future school cases.[117]

A close look at each of the decisions written in the case—Brennan's, Powell's, Douglas's and Rehnquists's—will reveal just how much of this is true.

Mr. Justice Brennan (For the Court)

What is a "Segregated" School? Denver is a tri-ethnic, as distinguished from a bi-racial, community, consisting of the Anglo, Negro, and Hispano[118] parties to this suit. The Court said:

What is or is not a segregated school will necessarily depend on the facts in each particular case. In addition to the racial and ethnic composition of the school's student body, other factors such as the racial and ethnic composition of faculty and staff and the community and administrative attitudes toward the school must be taken into consideration.[119]

The district court recognized these specific factors, but erred in separating Negroes and Hispanos for the purpose of defining a "segregated" school. Hispanos are an identifiable class for purposes of the Fourteenth Amendment; schools with a predominance of Negroes *and* Hispanos are "segregated" schools. Compare with this, however, Justice Powell's contour of "An Integrated School System."[120]

School Board Practices Which are Prohibited. All parties agreed that the Denver school system was never operated under a constitutional or statutory provision which mandated or permitted racial segregation in public education. The court identified the "gravamen" of this action (as alleged by Keyes in the original complaint):

that respondent School Board alone, by use of various techniques such as the manipulation of student attendance zones, school site selection and a neighborhood school policy, created or maintained racially or ethnically (or both racially and ethnically) segregated schools throughout the school district, entitling petitioners to a decree directing desegregation of the entire school district.[121]

The board had rescinded three resolutions (Nos. 1520, 1524, and 1531) previously adopted to desegregate the Park Hill area schools, replacing them with a "volunteer student transfer program." The district court ordered the Park Hill schools desegregated through implementation of these resolutions. Presumably, this would undo the segregative effects of such past school board practices as "gerrymandering" attendance zones, use of "optional zones," excessive use of "mobile classrooms," etc. Such practices, if a result of a purposeful and systematic program of racial segregation, are illegal.

Where the plaintiffs prove that the school authorities have carried out a systematic program of segregation affecting a *substantial portion* of the students, schools, teachers, and facilities within the school system, said the Court, it is only "common sense" to conclude that there exists a predicate for finding of the existence of a "dual" school system. In support of this conclusion, the Court recited the following considerations:

First, it is obvious that a practice of concentrating Negroes in certain schools by structuring attendance zones or designating "feeder" schools on the basis of race has the *reciprocal* effect of keeping other nearby schools predominantly white. Similarly, the practice of building a school . . . to a certain size and in a certain location, "with conscious knowledge that it would be a segregated school" . . . has a substantial *reciprocal* effect on the racial composition of other nearby schools. So also, the use of mobile classrooms, the drafting of student transfer policies, the transportation of students and the assignment of faculty and staff, on racially identifiable bases, have the clear effect of earmarking schools according to their racial composition, and this, in turn, together with the elements of student assignment and school construction, may have a profound *reciprocal* effect on racial composition of resident neighborhoods within a metropolitan area, thereby causing further racial concentration within the schools.[122]

In short, "common sense" dictates the conclusion that "racially inspired" school board actions have an "impact beyond the particular schools that are the subjects of those actions."

An exception to this *reciprocal* effect is that rare case in which the "geographical structure of or the natural boundaries within" a school district have the effect of dividing the district into "separate, identifiable and unrelated units." Such a determination, however, is a *question of fact* to be resolved by the trial court. "In the absence of such a determination, proof of state-imposed segregation in a substantial portion of the district will suffice to support a finding by the trial court of the existence of a dual system."[123]

Accordingly, the district court, on remand, must decide first whether the Denver school board's policy of *deliberate* racial segregation with respect to the

Park Hill schools constitutes the entire Denver school system a "dual" school system. The record suggests, says Brennan, that the "official segregation" in Park Hill affected the racial composition of schools throughout the district. But this is a *factual question* for resolution on remand.

Legal Standard—Shifting of the Burden of Proof. A finding of intentional segregation as to a portion of a school system has *probative value* in assessing the school authorities' intent with respect to other parts of the same school system; indeed, it is highly relevant to the issue of the board's intent with respect to other segregated schools in the system. In support of this, the Court relied on these evidentiary principles, which are applicable either to civil or criminal cases:

1. The prior doing of other similar acts, whether clearly a part of a scheme or not, is useful as reducing the possibility that the act in question was done with innocent intent.[124]

2. Evidence that similar and related offenses were committed ... tend[s] to show a consistent pattern of conduct highly relevant to the issue of intent.[125]

3. A finding of illicit intent as to a meaningful portion of the item under consideration has substantial probative value on the question of illicit intent as to the remainder.[126]

Applying these evidentiary principles in the special context of school desegregation, the Court declared:

We hold that a finding of intentionally segregative school board actions in a meaningful portion of a school system, as in this case, creates a *presumption* that other schooling within the system is not adventitious. It establishes, in other words, a *prima facie* case of unlawful segregative design on the part of school authorities, and *shifts to those authorities the burden of proving* that other segregated schools within the system are not also the result of intentionally segregative actions.[127]

This is true even if different areas of the school district are viewed independently of each other—because there is a "high probability" that similar impermissible considerations have motivated the school board's actions in other areas of the system too: "We emphasize that the differentiating factor between *de jure* segregation and so-called *de facto* segregation ... is *purpose* or *intent* to segregate."[128] Where an *intentionally* segregative policy is practiced in a "meaningful or significant segment" of a school system, it is both reasonable and fair to require that the school authorities bear the burden of showing that their actions as to other segregated schools within the system were not also motivated by segregated intent.

Declaring that this "burden-shifting principle" is neither new or novel,[129] the Court said there are no hard and fast standards governing who bears the burden of proof in every situation. Rather, the issue becomes a question of "policy and fairness based on experience in the different situations." In the context of racial segregation, courts have recognized a variety of situations in which "fairness" and "policy" require *the state authorities to bear the burden of explaining actions or conditions which appear to be racially motivated.*

Thus, be it a statutory dual system or an allegedly unitary system where a meaningful portion of the system is found to be intentionally segregated, the existence of subsequent or other segregated schooling within the same system justifies a rule imposing on the school authorities the burden of proving that this segregated schooling is not also the result of intentionally segregative acts. . . . Their burden is to adduce proof sufficient to support a finding that segregative intent was not among the factors that motivated their actions.[130]

Here, the school authorities practiced *de jure* segregation in a meaningful portion of the school system through manipulation of the "neighborhood school" concept.

Justice Brennan concludes the opinion of the Court by setting forth the details of precise steps to be taken by the district court on remand:[131]

I. The school board must be allowed to prove its contention that the Park Hill Area is "a separate, identifiable and unrelated section" of the Denver school district which should be treated in isolation from the rest of the district.

FAILING TO PROVE THIS:

II. The District Court will determine whether the board's conduct since 1960 in carrying out the policy of *deliberate* racial segregation in the Park Hill schools "constitutes the entire school system a dual school system."

    1. If the Court finds that the Denver system is a "dual" school system, the school board is then under an "affirmative duty" (*Green v. County School Board*) to desegregate the entire system "root and branch."

    2. HOWEVER, if the Court determines that the Denver system is *not* a "dual" school system, THEN:

III. The District Court must allow the school board the opportunity "to rebut petitioners' prima facie case of intentional segregation in the core city schools raised by the finding of intentional segregation in the Park Hill schools."

    1. The school board's burden, at this point, would be to show that its policies and practices with respect to:

        school site location,
        school size,
        school renovations and additions,
        student attendance zones,
        student assignments and transfer options,
        mobile classroom units,

transportation of students,
assignment of·faculty and staff,
etc.,

considered together and premised on the "neighborhood school" concept, were not taken in the effectuation of a policy to create or maintain segregation in the "core" city schools; OR:
2. If unsuccessful in that effort, the board must show that such policies and practices were *not* factors in causing the existing condition of segregation in the "core" city schools.

IV. If the school board fails to rebut the petitioners' prima facie case, the district court must—as in the case of Park Hill—order "all-out desegregation" of the "core" city schools.

Brennan concluded the opinion of the Court by observing that considerations of "fairness" and "policy" demand no less in light of the board's intentional segregative actions.[132]

Mr. Justice Douglas (Separate Opinion)

The school board is a state agency, said Justice Douglas, consequently:

the boundary lines it draws
the locations it selects for school sites,
the allocations it makes of students, and
the budgets it prepares,

are all "state action" for Fourteenth Amendment purposes.

Quoting from Judge Wisdom's opinion in a Texas case (*United States v. Texas Education Agency*, 467 F. 2d 848), Douglas says that some concepts in law are incapable of precise definition; these include:

(a) "the reasonable man,"
(b) "due care,"
(c) "causation,"
(d) "preponderance of the evidence," and
(e) "beyond a reasonable doubt."

Likewise is the "quantity" of state participation which is a prerequisite to a finding of a constitutional violation. The degree of such state involvement is incapable of precise definition—it must be defined on a case-by-case basis.

Said Douglas: " ... I agree with my Brother Powell that there is, for the purposes of the Equal Protection Clause of the Fourteenth Amendment as applied to the school cases, no difference between de facto and de jure segregation.... I think it is time to state that there is no constitutional difference between de jure and de facto segregation, for each is the product of state actions or policies." (37 L. Ed. 2d 567) State action in the constitutional sense is found in all of these situations:

restrictive convenants which result in "neighborhood" units created along racial lines.

the expenditure of public funds by urban development agencies to build racial ghettoes.

the segregation of the races in separate schools where the school district is racially mixed.

the assignment of Black teachers to almost exclusively black black schools.

the closing of existing schools in the fringe area and opening new schools in distant white areas.

the continuation of a "neighborhood" school policy at the elementary level.

All of these things are state action, but they "are of a kind quite distinct from the classical de jure type of school segregation. Yet calling them de facto is a misnomer. . . . " (37 L. Ed. 2d 568) The interest to be balanced in this, and in similar school segregation cases, is summed up by Justice Douglas as follows:

The Constitution and Bill of Rights have described the design of a pluralistic society. The individual has the right to seek such companions as he desires. But a State is barred from creating by one device or another ghettoes that determine the school one is compelled to attend. (37 L. Ed. 2d 568)

Mr. Justice Powell (Separate Opinion)

"The focus of the school desegregation problem has now shifted from the South to the country as a whole," said Justice Powell, who concurred in part and dissented in part and pointed to the narrowness of the holding in this case: "The Court has inquired only to what extent *Denver public school authorities* may have contributed to the school desegregation which is acknowledged to exist in Denver."[133]

The Court's opinion was *not* concerned with constitutional or statutory provisions that mandate or permit racial segregation in public schools, because no such enactments have ever existed in Denver.

The Court's opinion was *not* concerned with state legislative actions, such as zoning or housing laws, which may have contributed to the segregation in Denver's schools.

The Court's opinion was concerned only with *acts of the public school authorities* that may have contributed to the segregation in Denver's public schools.

Powell says that progress in school desegregation in nonsouthern cities has lagged because of the *de facto/de jure* distinction "nurtured by the courts and accepted complacently by many of the same voices which denounced the evils of segregated schools in the South."[134]

Powell would do away with the *de facto/de jure* distinction, which he describes as "a legalism rooted in history rather than present reality;" he says:

In my view we should abandon a distinction which long since has outlived its time, and formulate constitutional principles of national rather than merely regional application.[135]

I would not ... perpetuate the *de jure/de facto* distinction ... [136]

The principal reason for abandonment of the *de jure/de facto* distinction is that, in view of the evolution of the holding in *Brown I* into the affirmative duty doctrine, the distinction can no longer be justified on a principled basis.[137]

There is thus no reason as a matter of constitutional principle to adhere to the *de jure/de facto* distinction in school desegregation cases. In addition, there are reasons of policy and prudent judicial administration which point strongly toward the adoption of a uniform national rule.[138]

Rather than continue to prop up a distinction no longer grounded in principle ... , we should acknowledge that whenever public school segregation exists to a substantial degree there is prima facie evidence of a constitutional violation by the responsible school board.[139]

These are rather startling pronouncements, especially from the Supreme Court justice who authored the opinion in the school finance case, *San Antonio Independent School District v. Rodriguez*[140] wherein he said: "Education, of course, is not among the rights afforded explicit protection under our Federal Constitution. Nor do we find any basis for saying it is implicitly so protected."[141]

In that case, Powell refused to concede that education is a "fundamental interest" and hence entitled the strict protection afforded by the "new equal protection standard," because education is not afforded explicit or implicit protection under the language of the Constitution. Here, however, he would abandon the *de jure/de facto* distinction explicit in the language of the Fourteenth Amendment: "*No state* shall ... deny to any person within its jurisdiction the equal protection of the laws."

Powell's argument for abandonment of the "de jure/de facto" *distinction can be summarized as follows:*

The great contribution of *Brown I*[142] was its holding that the Fourteenth Amendment forbids state-compelled segregation in public schools. This holding was essentially negative: the state (*de jure*) may not force children to attend segregated schools; state "neutrality" was required with "freedom of choice" permitted.

The doctrine of *Brown I*, as amplified by *Brown II*,[143] did not long retain its original meaning. Through a series of Supreme Court decisions, 1954-71, the concept of "state neutrality" was transformed into constitutional doctrine requiring "affirmative state action" to desegregate *dual* school systems.[144] The landmark case in this evolution of constitutional doctrine was *Green v. County School Board* (1968),[145] wherein the Court said that school boards have "the affirmative duty to take whatever steps might be necessary to convert to a unitary system in which racial discrimination would be eliminated root and branch."[146]

In *Green*, the "freedom of choice" program was identified by the Court as a subterfuge and the "affirmative duty" was to convert a *dual* school system (with "a long history" of state imposed segregation) to a *unitary* system. New Kent County, Virginia, was a rural setting, and there was doubt whether the new constitutional doctrine was also applicable to urban school systems with large metropolitan areas.

The doubt as to whether the "affirmative duty concept" would become a new constitutional principle of general application, however, was laid to rest with the decision of *Swann*[147] in 1971, wherein the affirmative duty in *Green* was applied to the urban school system of metropolitan Charlotte, North Carolina. There, some 107 schools and some 84,000 students were subjected to the same remedy—elimination of segregation "root and branch"—which had been applied to New Kent County, where there were only two schools with about 1300 pupils.

In *Swann*, the Court further noted it was concerned only with States having "a long history" of officially imposed segregation and the duty of school authorities to implement *Brown I*. In so doing, the Court refrained even from considering whether the *evolution of constitutional doctrine from Brown I to Green/Swann* undercut whatever logic once supported the *de jure/de facto* distinction.[148]

The Court in *Swann* called upon southern school districts "to alleviate conditions which in large part did not result from historic state-imposed *de jure* segregation." The root cause of segregation in all metropolitan areas, North, South, East, and West, is essentially the same: segregated residential patterns and migratory patterns that have a racial impact in the composition of the public schools, often perpetuated by actions of school authorities. "This is a national, not a southern phenomenon. And it is largely unrelated to whether a particular State had or did not have segregatory school laws."

Whereas *Brown I* rightly decreed the elimination of state-imposed segregation in that particular section of the country where it did exist, *Swann* imposed obligations on southern school districts to eliminate conditions which are not regionally unique but are similar both in origin and effect to conditions of the rest of the country . . . the remedial obligations of *Swann* extended far beyond the elimination of the outgrowths of the state-imposed segregation outlawed in *Brown*.[149]

Whereas under *Brown I* and *II* the constitutional right being enforced was "as a minimum—that one has the right not to be compelled by state action to attend a segregated school system," in the evolutional process since 1954/1955 the decisions of the Supreme Court "have added a significant gloss to this original right."

Hence, the principal reason for abandonment of the de jure/de facto *distinction, says Powell, is that evolution of the holding in* Brown I *into the "affirmative duty doctrine" which makes the distinction no longer justifiable on a principled basis.*

Powell (a former school board member in Virginia) set forth some of his ideas about education:

1. Public school authorities are the "responsible agency of the state" in matters affecting education, and they have an *affirmative duty* to eliminate segregation in the schools.[150]

2. Such authorities, "consistent with the generally accepted educational goal of attaining quality education for all pupils," must make and implement their customary decisions with a view toward enhancing integrated school opportunities.[151]

3. An "integrated school system" does not mean—indeed cannot mean in light of the residential patterns in most major metropolitan areas—that *every* school must in fact be an integrated unit.[152]

4. A school that happens to be all or predominantly white or all or predominantly black is not a "segregated" school (in a constitutional sense) if the system itself is genuinely integrated.[153]

5. Public schools are creatures of the state, and whether the segregation is "state-created or state-assisted or merely state-perpetuated" is irrelevant.[154]

6. There are reasons of policy and prudent judicial administration "which point strongly toward the adoption of a uniform national rule" with respect to school desegregation cases.[155]

7. School boards have a duty to minimize and ameliorate segregated conditions by pursuing an affirmative policy of desegregation.[156]

8. Concerning "large-scale" or "long-distance" busing of students in metropolitan school districts: "I record my profound misgivings. Nothing in our Constitution commands or encourages any such court compelled disruption of public education."[157]

9. Reasonableness:

In school desegregation cases, as elsewhere, equity counsels reason, flexibility, and balance. I am aware, of course, that reasonableness in any area is a relative and subjective concept. But with school desegregation, reasonableness would seem to embody a balanced evaluation of the obligation of public school boards to promote desegregation with other equally important educational interests which a community may legitimately assert. Neglect of either the obligation or the interests destroys the evenhanded spirit with which equitable remedies must be approached. Overzealousness in pursuit of any single goal is untrue to the tradition . . . which this Court has always respected.[158]

10. Affirmative desegregation steps can be ordered by Courts, "without damaging state and parental interests in having children attend schools within a reasonable vicinity of home."[159]

11. "In a pluralistic society such as ours, it is essential that no racial minority feel demeaned or discriminated against and that students of all races learn to play, work, and cooperate with one another in their common pursuits and endeavors."[160]

12. The transportation of pupils between their homes and classrooms "is as old as public education, and in rural and some suburban settings, it is as indispensable as the providing of books."[161]

13. There is a significant difference between busing that is voluntarily initiated by local school boards for educational purposes and that imposed by a federal court: the former usually represents a necessary or convenient means of access to the school nearest home; but the latter often require lengthy trips for no purpose other than to further integration.[162]

14. The state, parents, and children all have at stake in school desegregation decrees legitimate and recognizable interests.[163]

15. "The personal interest might be characterized as the desire that children attend community schools near home." Citing James Coleman: "Most school systems organize their schools in relation to the residents by having fixed school districts and some of these are very ethnically homogeneous."[164]

16. The "neighborhood school" provides greater ease of parental and student access and convenience, greater economy in public administration; but there are "more basic grounds" for keeping the "neighborhood school" concept: such schools reflect the deep desire felt by citizens for a sense of community in their public education. Public schools have been a traditional source of strength to our nation, and that strength may derive in part from the identification of many schools with the personal features of the surrounding neighborhood. Community support, interest, and dedication to public schools may well run higher with a neighborhood attendance pattern:

Many citizens sense today a decline in the intimacy of our institutions—home, church, and school—which has caused a concomitant decline in the unity and communal spirit of our people. I pass no judgment on this viewpoint, but *I do believe that this Court should be wary of compelling in the name of constitutional law, what may seem to many a dissolution in the traditional, more personal fabric of their public schools.*[165]

17. The law has long recognized the parental *duty* to nurture, support, and provide for the welfare of children, and this includes their education. Citing *Pierce v. Society of Sisters,*[166] *Meyer v. Nebraska,*[167] and *Griswold v. Connecticut*[168] as examples of Supreme Court decisions upholding the *right* to educate one's children as one chooses, Powell declared:

I do not believe recognition of this right can be confined solely to a parent's choice to send a child to public or private school. Most parents cannot afford the luxury of a private education for their children, and the dual obligation of private tuition and public taxes. Those who may for numerous reasons seek public education for their children should not be forced to forfeit all interest or voice in the school their child attends. It would, of course, be impractical to allow the wishes of particular parents to be controlling. Yet the interest of the parent in the enhanced parent-school and parent-child communication allowed by the neighborhood unit ought not to be suppressed by force of law.[169]

In their "commendable national concern" for eliminating public school segregation, the courts may have overlooked

the fact that the rights and interests of children affected by a desegregation program are also entitled to consideration. *Any child, white or black, who is compelled to leave his neighborhood and spend significant time each day being transported to a distant school suffers an impairment to his liberty and his privacy.* . . . A community may well conclude that a portion of a child's day spent on a bus might be used more creatively in a classroom, playground, or some other extracurricular school activity. Decisions such as these, affecting the quality of a child's daily life, should not lightly be held constitutionally errant.[170]

18. On busing and biracial school districts—the Metropolitan Areas: "Extensive student transportation" used solely to further integration, says Powell, falls disproportionately on the schools districts of our country, depending upon their degree of urbanization, their financial resources, and their racial composition.

Educational "disruption" caused by busing will be small (or none at all) in some districts with little or no biracial composition, while others,

notably in large, biracial metropolitan areas, must at considerable expense undertake extensive transportation to achieve the type of integration frequently being ordered by district courts. At a time when public education generally is suffering serious financial malnutrition, the economic burdens of such transportation can be severe, requiring both initial capital outlays and annual operating costs in the millions of dollars. And while constitutional requirements have often occasioned uneven burdens, never have they touched so sensitive a matter as wide differences in the compulsory transportation, requirements for literally hundreds of thousands of school children.[171]

19. Does the remedy (extensive busing) exceed what is necessary to redress the constitutional evil (neighborhood school segregation)? Powell says: Assume a maximum discharge of constitutional duty by the school authorities over the past decades, yet the fundamental problem of residential segregation persists; then, it is a novel application of equitable power, a dubious extension of constitutional doctrine, "to require so much greater degree of forced school integration than would have resulted from *purely natural and neutral nonstate causes.* "[172]

Must segregation that results from "purely *natural and neutral nonstate causes*" be addressed by the courts? If school segregation is harmful to children and courts are dedicated to its elimination in the public schools, why does it matter that it results from purely natural and neutral nonstate causes? Is not this simply another manner of saying that *de facto* segregation in schools will be permitted while *de jure* segregation in the schools will not be permitted?

20. Compulsory transportation of students places the major burden of the remedial action not on the offending state officials or school authorities, but the full burden falls upon the students themselves, who did not participate in any constitutional violation.[173]

20. Courts, in requiring such a far-reaching remedy as student transportation solely to maximize integration, risk setting in motion unpredictable and unmanageable social consequences:[174]

To what extent will dismantling neighborhood schools hasten an exodus to private schools, "leaving public schools the preserve of the disadvantaged of both races?"

How much impetus does such dismantlement give to "the movement from innercity to suburb" and the further geographical separation of the races?

To what degree will this remedy destroy community and parental support of the public schools, "or divert attention from the paramount goal of quality in education to a perenially devisive debate over who is to be transported where"?

21. "There is nothing in the Constitution, its history or—until recently—in the jurisprudence of this Court that mandates the employment of forced transportation of young and teenage children to achieve a single interest, as important as this interest may be."[175]

In the balancing of interests so appropriate to a fair and just equitable decree, transportation orders should be applied with special caution to any proposal as disruptive of family life and interests—and ultimately of education itself—as extensive transportation of elementary age children solely for desegregation purposes. As a minimum, this Court should not require school boards to engage in the unnecessary transportation away from their neighborhoods of elementary age children. It is at this age level that neighborhood education performs its most vital educational role.[176]

There are reasons of "physical and psychological health" at these tender years which argue against such transportation, and at the elementary level "the rights of parents and children are most sharply implicated."

22. Concerning state action, Powell says:

There is, of course, state action in every school district in the land. The public schools always have been funded and operated by States and their local subdivisions . . . there is also not a school district in the United States, with any significant minority school population, in which school authorities—in one way or the other—have not contributed in some measure to the degree of segregation which still prevails.[177]

23. Powell refers to the "ambiguities of *Swann* and the judicial disregard of legitimate community and individual interests," saying that absent a more

51

flexible and reasonable standard than that which has been imposed by district courts after *Swann*, "the desegregation which will now be decreed in Denver and other major cities may well involve even more extensive transportation than has been witnessed up to this time."[178] Further, "THE SINGLE MOST DISRUP-TIVE ELEMENT IN EDUCATION TODAY IS THE WIDESPREAD USE OF COMPULSORY TRANSPORTATION, ESPECIALLY AT ELEMENTARY GRADE LEVELS."[179] Powell concluded by saying this has risked distracting and diverting attention from basic educational ends, dividing and embittering communities, and exacerbating rather than ameliorating inter-racial friction and understanding.

It is time to return to a more balanced evaluation of the recognized interests of our society in achieving desegregation with other educational and societal interests a community may legitimately assert. This will help assure that integrated school systems will be established and maintained by rational action, will be better understood and supported by parents and children of both races, and will promote the enduring qualities of an integrated society so essential to its genuine success.[180]

The "Constitutional Right" to an Education. What is the constitutional "right" being enforced by the courts in school desegregation cases?[181] Justice Powell says it is not easy to identify this "right" since the precedents have been far from explicit. In *Brown I*, after emphasizing the importance of education, the Supreme Court said: "Such an opportunity, where the state has undertaken to provide it, is the right which must be made available to all on equal terms."[182]

In *Brown II*, the Court identified the "fundamental principle" enunciated in *Brown I* as being the unconstitutionality of "racial discrimination in public education."[183]

Supreme Court decisions since 1954, however, have added "a significant gloss" to this original right. Justice Powell states his conception of the "right," although nowhere articulated in these terms, enforced by the courts in school desegregation cases as follows:

I would now define it as the right, derived from the Equal Protection Clause, to expect that once the State has assumed responsibility for education, local school boards will operate *integrated school systems* within their respective dis-tricts.[184]

This means that school authorities, consistent with the generally accepted educational goal of attaining quality education for all pupils, must make and implement their customary decisions with a view toward enhancing integrated school opportunities.

An "Integrated School System." Such a system, Powell says, has a total absence of any laws, regulations, or policies supportive of the type of "legalized" segregation prohibited by *Brown*; measured by constitutional standards, the system would be "integrated" if the school authorities had taken steps to:[185]

1. integrate faculty and administration;
2. scrupulously assure equality of facilities, instruction, and curricula opportunities throughout the district;
3. utilize their authority to draw attendance zones to promote integration; and
4. locate new schools close to old ones and determine the size and grade categories with this same objective in mind.

Where school authorities make the determination to use student transportation, this must also be done with integrative opportunities in mind.

The above list is neither definitive nor all-inclusive, says Powell, but rather the "contour characteristics of an *integrated school system*. . . . An integrated school system does not mean . . . that *every school* must in fact be an integrated unit," for a school which happens to be all or predominantly white or all or predominantly black is not a 'segregated' school in an unconstitutional sense if the system itself is a genuinely integrated one.

Mr. Justice Rehnquist (Dissenting)

Justice Rehnquist, dissenting, draws attention to the similarities and differences between *Brown* and *Keyes*, not only in the plaintiffs' claims, but also in the nature of the constitutional violation.[186]

Classicial De Jure School Segregation. In *Brown* and its progeny, the Court held unconstitutional state statutes that mandated that Negro and white children attend separate schools. No such state statutes ever existed in Colorado or in the City of Denver.

School Board Decisions as Constitutional Violations. In *Keyes*, the constitutional violation was the school board's use of various techniques, such as manipulation of zoning, school site selection policy, and a "neighborhood school" policy that took into account race "in such a way as to lessen that mixing of races that would have resulted from a racially neutral policy of school assignment."[187]

But the manipulative drawing of attendance zones in a school district the size of Denver "does not necessarily" result in a denial of equal protection to all minority students within that district. Thus, there are significant differences between the proof required in a *Keyes*-type desegregation case versus a *Brown*-type desegregation case, where in the latter total segregation has been mandated by state statute.

The Court's opinion in *Keyes*, argues Rehnquist, obscures this important fact and hence a difference from *Brown*: in the *Brown* cases and the latter ones decided by the Supreme Court, *the situation which had invariably obtained at one time was a "Dual" school system mandated by law, by a law which prohibited negroes and whites from attending the same schools.*[188] In that kind of a factual situation, the state automatically assumes the "affirmative duty" to effectuate a transition to a unitary nondiscriminatory system. But in a school district the size of Denver, it is quite conceivable that the school board did in fact intentionally gerrymander certain attendance lines, keeping Blacks and Hispanos in one school and thereby kept another school largely white. This was a constitutional violation, yet through an "evenhanded" policy in drawing other attendance lines for other schools, other minorities at these other schools would have suffered no violation of their constitutional rights.

It certainly would not reflect normal English usage to describe the entire district as "segregated" on such a state of facts, and it would be a quite unprecedented application of principles of equitable relief to determine that if the gerrymandering of one attendance zone were proven, particular racial mixtures could be required by a federal court for every school in the district.[189]

"Federal Receivership" for Offending School Districts. In Chapter 2, notice was made of increasing federal court participation in education and in the operation of the schools;[190] Justice Rehnquist makes the point quite plain when he observes:

Underlying the Court's entire opinion is its apparent thesis that a district judge is at least permitted to find that if a single attendance zone between two individual schools in the large metropolitan district is found by him to have been "gerrymandered," the school district is guilty of operating a "dual" school system and is *apparently a candidate for what is in practice a federal receivership.*[191]

Both the language of the Court in its opinion and its reliance on *Green* establish this, and presumably district courts could require transportation of pupils throughout school districts to and from schools whose attendance zones have not been gerrymandered. This is described as the product of "judicial fiat,"

Yet unless the Equal Protection Clause of the Fourteenth Amendment now be held to embody a principle of "taint," found in some primitive legal systems but discarded centuries ago in ours, such a result can only be described as the product of judicial fiat.[192]

Federal court involvement in transportation of students, where there is no constitutional basis for it, is a further indicium of the evolution toward the period described earlier as "education under the supervision of the courts."[193]

The Fact-Finding Process. Notwithstanding the majority opinion's criticism of the district court for having "fractionated" the claims regarding the core area schools and the Park Hill schools, Rehnquist said separate treatment of these two separate areas was "absolutely necessary if a careful factual determination, rather than a jumbled hash of unrelated event was to emerge from the fact-finding process."[194] The *intent* with which a public body acts is often difficult to ascertain, especially when that body is a board of education whose membership constantly changes because of elections.

> The Court's opinion totally confuses the concept of a permissible inference . . . with what the Court calls a "presumption" and what it calls a "shifting of the burden of proof" and a "shifting of the burden of going forward with the evidence." No case from this Court has ever gone further in this area than to suggest that a finding of intent in one factual situation may support a finding of fact in another related factual situation *involving the same actor.*[195]

If by the word *fractionated* the majority opinion meant that the district court treated together events that occurred during the same time period, and that it treated those events separately from other events that occurred at another time span, this is correct; it is the "approach followed by most experienced and careful finders of fact."

The alleged discriminatory acts in Park Hill occurred between 1960 and 1969, while those in the core area took place between 1952 and 1961; add to this the fact that the Denver School Board was a public body whose membership was constantly changing during these periods, and "intent" becomes most difficult to ascertain.[196]

The "Two-Court" Rule.[197] Rehnquist argues that it is contrary to the settled principles of the Supreme Court to upset a factual finding of a District Court which has been sustained by the court of appeals, citing the 1949 case of *Comstock v. Group of Institutional Investors* wherein it was said: "A seasoned and wise rule of this Court makes concurrent findings of two courts final here in the absence of very exceptional showing of error."[198]

Brennan, in the majority opinion, answered this argument by observing that the Court had no occasion here to review the factual findings concurred in by the two courts below, but rather the opinion addressed only the question whether these two courts had "applied the correct legal standard in deciding the case as it affects the core city schools."[199]

One reading of the language of Supreme Court in the Denver case suggests that a "frontier" has been reached in the school desegregation cases, a point beyond which the full Court is unwilling to go, namely, *de jure* segregation in the sense of "state action," which was condemned in *Brown v. Board of Education of Topeka* and which has been inherent in every school desegregation case decided by the high court since 1954. However, another reading of this same language suggests that the Court, in Denver, penetrated that "frontier" when it condemned acts of school authorities that result in segregated schools.

The Denver decision is significant in that it shows how the present majority of the Supreme Court of the United States can be expected to handle other similar cases involving school segregation outside of the South, where such segregation is the *result of action taken by school authorities*. The case does not address itself to school segregation that results from other forms of segregative action, i.e., legislative actions such as zoning or housing laws that may contribute to school segregation; that has been left for some later decision, as has the question of whether federal courts may order busing across school district lines to achieve desegregation.

In *Brown* and its progeny, the Court condemned state statutes that required separate schools for blacks and whites.

In *Keyes*, the Court condemned acts of school authorities that result in racially segregated schools.

Left for another time, therefore, are many unanswered questions concerning school segregation in the North, East, and West that result from *other* forms of "state action." Some of these questions have been developing in cases decided by the lower federal court and state courts, particularly in California, where there are a number of "path-making decisions" affecting the schools which have yet to be brought before the high court.[200]

Conclusions

State and federal court involvement in the organization, administration, and programs of the public schools has grown steadily since 1954 and largely because of racial discrimination, which denies "equal educational opportunity" to the races;[201] the issue of *de jure v. de facto* segregation in schools is still far from settled even in the South and much less in the great cities of the North, East, and West. Some "guidelines," however, have begun to emerge which state legislatures, school boards, and school administrators must follow and respect if they are to avoid court interference in the management of their schools. Two such "guidelines" are now clearly established by state and federal court decisions:

1. *State statutes and state laws which require separate schools for Blacks and whites violate the Fourteenth Amendment's equal protection clause and therefore are unconstitutional.*

2. *When school officials have made a series of educational policy decisions based wholly, or in part, on considerations of the race of students or teachers and which contribute to increasing racial segregation in public schools, there has likewise been a violation of the equal protection clause of the Fourteenth Amendment.*

It is also established that: *Be it a statutory dual school system in the South or an allegedly unitary school system in the North, where a meaningful portion of the system is found to be intentionally segregated, the existence of subsequent or other segregated schooling within the same system justifies shifting to the school authorities the burden of proving that this segregated schooling is not also the result of intentionally segregative acts.*

In the struggle for obtaining "equal educational opportunity," the Fourteenth Amendment is being called upon to carry a large burden[202] when it is used by the courts as their principal tool or weapon to prevent and eliminate racial discrimination in the public schools. How far the language of the equal protection clause can continue to be stretched and extended, by court interpretation, to accomplish this worthy objective without doing violence to the intent of the framers and ratifiers of this post-Civil War constitutional amendment remains to be seen; had the Supreme Court of the United States in *Brown v. Board of Education of Topeka*[203] grounded its decision on another section, article, or amendment to the Constitution,[204] or had there been a different Supreme Court interpretation in the 1973 case of *San Antonio Independent School District v. Rodriguez,*[205] it is quite possible that the troublesome *de jure/de facto* distinction would never have arisen.

4 Wealth and Education

Constitutional Background

"Education, of course, is not among the rights afforded explicit protection under our Federal Constitution. Nor do we find any basis for saying it is implicitly so protected." Thus, in *San Antonio Independent School District v. Rodriguez* (1973),[1] the Supreme Court of the United States rejected the argument that there is a federal constitutional basis for the "right-to-an-education" thesis put forth in several recent federal court cases challenging the constitutionality of school financing systems.[2] The Court refused to agree that education is a *fundamental right* not specified in the Constitution. "It is not the province of this Court," said Mr. Justice Powell, "to create substantive constitutional rights in the name of guaranteeing equal protection of the laws."[3] This strict-construction posture of the Nixon Court would appear to affect the trend of federal court decisions concerned with the organization, administration, and programs of the public schools which has so clearly marked the period since about 1950.[4] Absent arbitrariness, capriciousness, or unreasonableness, and absent discrimination against a well-defined class that bears the "traditional indicia of suspectedness," or absent a class saddled with such disabilities or subjected to such a history of "purposeful unequal treatment" or relegated to such a position of "political powerlessness as to command extraordinary protection against the majoritorian political process," the Supreme Court of the United States should henceforth not be expected to intervene.[5]

However, courts in California,[6] Michigan,[7] and *ab initio* New Jersey,[8] basing their decisions on *state* constitutional grounds, have said that education is a "fundamental interest" and is of such great importance as to command *strict scrutiny* and other preferred treatment by the courts. Courts in other states have refused to adopt the "fundamental interest" argument and refused to hold that education is entitled to extraordinary protection from the majoritorian political process.[9]

What do courts and constitutions mean when they use the words *right, fundamental interest*, or *power* with respect to education?

Education as a "Right" of the People

There is in jurisprudence a debate over whether a *right* is a *power* or an *interest*. Roscoe Pound says that the "word suggests both; a power to exact a certain act or forebearance ... and a particular interest on account of which the power exists. ... But the right in itself is power."[10]

It has been customary in educational jurisprudence to look to the language of the Tenth Amendment of the Federal Constitution and to conclude therefrom that, since education is not one of the powers delegated to the United States, it is a *power* reserved to the states respectively, or to the people.

An *interest* is a "demand or desire which human beings either individually or in groups seek to satisfy."[11] The law does not create interests: it classifies them, and recognizes some of them, and gives effect to those it recognizes. Roscoe Pound identified three classes of interests, which the legal order protects: individual interests, public interests, and social interests. All three classes seem to have a place for education; and some courts have held that education is a "fundamental interest."

An analogy is helpful in understanding the positions of rights, powers, and interests in the legal order.[12]

POWER

a *right* is related to an *interest*

as the *fortress* is to the *protected land.*

Simply put: a *right* is "an interest protected by law."[13] Courts similarly will protect a "fundamental interest."

Rights retained by the people are enumerated in the Ninth Amendment: "The enumeration in the Constitution of certain rights, shall not be construed to deny or disparage others retained by the people." "Obtaining an education" is not among the rights enumerated in the Constitution; hence it may be one of the *other rights* retained by the people of California under the Ninth Amendment.

The notion that "obtaining an education" is one of the fundamental rights retained by the people under the Ninth Amendment is novel;[14] there is dicta in *Palmer v. Thompson:*

Rights, not explicitly mentioned in the Constitution, have at times been deemed so elementary in our way of life that they have been labeled as basic rights. ... There is, of course, not a word in the Constitution ... concerning the right of the people to education or to work or to recreation by swimming or otherwise. Those rights, like the right to pure air and pure water, may well be rights "retained by the people" under the Ninth Amendment.[15]

Furthermore, the Ninth Amendment "shows a belief of the Constitution's authors that fundamental rights exist that are not expressly enumerated in the first eight amendments, and an intent that the list of rights included there not be deemed exhaustive."[16]

Rights specified in state and federal constitutions are said to be "constitutionally secured" and are given added protection by the courts; *interests* characterized as "fundamental" are likewise afforded this added protection. (Should not the unspecified rights retained by the people under the Ninth Amendment be entitled to the same protection?) The principal difference, therefore, between a constitutional *right* and a *fundamental interest* is that one is specified in the constitution while the other is not; the preferred treatment afforded both is essentially the same. This led Justice Harlan to protest the practice of judges who "pick out particular human activities, characterize them as 'fundamental,' and then give them added protection under an unusually stringent equal protection test"—even where such activities are not shown to be arbitrary or irrational and where they are *"not mentioned in the federal constitution."*[17]

Education as a "Power" of the State or the People

Those *powers* not delegated to the United States by the Constitution, nor prohibited by it to the States, are "reserved to the States respectively, or to the people." (U.S. Constitution, Amendment X).

The power over education is not one of the powers delegated by the Constitution to the United States, nor is it prohibited to the states; hence, it is one of the powers reserved to the states or to the people.

However, the *power* over education reserved to the people by the Tenth Amendment was granted, in part, by the people in California to the state to be exercised by the legislature:

Const. 1849, Art. IX, Sec. 3. The legislature shall provide for a system of common schools, by which a school shall be kept up and supported in each district at least three months in every year, and any district neglecting to keep and support such a school may be deprived of its proportion of the interest of the public fund during such neglect.[18]

Const. 1849, Art. IX, Sec. 2. The legislature shall encourage, by all suitable means, the promotion of intellectual, scientific, moral, and agricultural improvement.[19]

Power over education, independently of this grant by the people, may also have been reserved by the Constitution to the state (U.S. Constitution, Amendment X).

A *power* over education, emanating from the Tenth Amendment, explicitly retained by the people of California is that of election of the State Superintendent of Public Instruction:

Const. 1849, Art. IX, Sec. 1. The legislature shall provide for the election, by the people, of a Superintendent of Public Instruction.[20]

In short, education in California, except for the election of the State Superintendent of Public Instruction by the people, is a state matter to be exercised by the legislature.

Constitutional language[21] such as, the "legislature shall provide for a system of common schools, by which a school shall be kept up and supported in each district at least three months in every year" and the "legislature *shall encourage*, by all suitable means, the promotion of intellectual, scientific, moral, and agricultural improvement," signifies the legislature's *power* over education; it does not establish a substantive right of the people to obtain an education.[22]

Other rights of the people are mentioned, but nowhere in the California Constitution is "obtaining an education" specified as a *right* of the people afforded explicit protection:

Const. 1849, Art. I, Sec. 1. All people are by nature free and independent, and have certain inalienable rights, among which are those of enjoying and defending life and liberty; acquiring, possessing, and protecting property; and pursuing and obtaining safety, happiness, and privacy.[23]

Education as a "Fundamental Interest"

The conclusion reached by the Supreme Court of the United States in the *Rodriguez case* was not entirely unexpected;[24] as if to insure against this possibility and to foreclose federal court review,[25] the Supreme Court of California documented the 1971 *Serrano v. Priest* decision at footnote 11:

The complaint also alleges that the financial system violates article I, sections 11 and 21 of the California Constitution. . . . We have construed these provisions as "substantially the equivalent" of the equal protection clause of the Fourteenth Amendment to the federal Constitution. . . . Consequently, our analysis of plaintiff's federal equal protection contention is also applicable to their claim under these state constitutional provisions.[26]

This is the state constitutional grounds upon which the court's decision rests.

Because the California Constitution contains no clear language concerning "obtaining an education as a right of the people," and in order to provide a further *state* basis for the *Serrano* decision's holding, Assemblyman Alex P. Garcia has introduced the following constitutional amendment into the California Legislature:

SECTION 1. All people are by nature free and independent and have certain inalienable rights, among which are those of enjoying and defending life and liberty; acquiring, possessing, and protecting property; and pursuing and obtaining *an education*, safety, happiness, and privacy.[27]

This amendment would establish an explicit state constitutional basis for a court decision that "obtaining an education" is a right of the people of California.

What does it mean for education and the schools now that state supreme courts, particularly in California, but also in Michigan—basing their decisions on state constitutional laws—have characterized education as a fundamental interest?

One of the publicly stated goals of those who seek reform of the schools through the courts has been to have education characterized as a fundamental interest.[28] That goal was realized in the case of *Serrano v. Priest,*[29] wherein the California Supreme Court held that the state's system for financing public schools, which relies heavily on local property taxes and causes substantial disparities in per pupil revenue among individual school districts, invidiously discriminates against the poor and therefore violates the equal protection provisions of the federal and state constitutions.

The most important fact about the *Serrano case,* however, is not that the Supreme Court of California invalidated the state's system for financing public schools because it violates the equal protection provisions of article I, sections 11 and 21 of the state constitution, although that is certainly a fundamental and far-reaching conclusion. Rather, the foundation upon which the court rested its reasoning to arrive at that conclusion was a new principle of law: *"the right to an education in the public schools is a fundamental interest."*[30] In the course of its opinion, the California court made the following solemn declaration: "We are convinced that the distinctive and priceless function of education in our society warrants, indeed compels, our treating it as a 'fundamental interest.' "[31] The full significance of this statement is not immediately apparent. Clearly, it reaches far beyond the facts of the immediate case; it seems to encompass *all* aspects of education, not just methods for financing public schools.

One important ramification of characterizing education as a fundamental interest is the test, or "standard," that the courts will use to measure constitutionality. We know from recent decisions in areas other than education that courts require more than the traditional test of "reasonableness" in cases where a statute or policy touching on a fundamental interest is challenged. Instead, they use the *new equal protection standard* to measure constitutionality. In California, at least, the courts would now look with "active and critical analysis" at state statutes and educational policies and practices challenged under the above-mentioned constitutional provisions, subjecting them to *strict scrutiny*; and the schools (i.e., the state) must bear the burden of showing that continued use of such policies or practices is *necessary to achieve a compelling state purpose.*

There has thus been a major change in the analytical framework within which California courts would decide cases affecting the organization, administration, and programs of the schools. The implications of this for education appear to be more far-reaching than those of the 1874 *Kalamazoo case,*[32] which extended public financing to secondary education, or of the 1954 *Brown case,*[33] which prohibited state-enforced separation of the races in the public schools. This new principle of the *Serrano case,* if subsequently reaffirmed by the Supreme Court of California when the case is again heard on appeal, would mark the end of judicial laissez faire in California education. It would mean that hardly a thread in the educational fabric is immune to strict "judicial scrutiny."

In order to fully appreciate the significance for education of what the California Supreme Court did in its decision in the *Serrano case*, it is necessary to understand the analytical framework within which courts in general, and the United States Supreme Court in particular, decide cases involving the equal protection requirement. This involves examining some of the professional apparatus that judges use to arrive at their decisions, including such technical legal terms as *right, power,* and *interest* (see above), *classification*, the *traditional standard of reasonableness*, the *compelling interest doctrine, suspect criteria, strict scrutiny, burden of proof*, the *new equal protection standard*, etc.

The Traditional Standard of Reasonableness

Classification, which is widely used in education, is the "jugular vein" of equal protection.[34] It involves the categorization of people into different groups or classes for purposes of *unequal* treatment. It is the *basis* on which the categorization is made (not the end result) to which courts look when deciding whether a state statute or educational practice violates the equal protection requirement. "The right to legislate implies the right to classify."[35] The *equality* required by the law does not mean that all persons must be treated alike, but only those persons under "like circumstances" or who are "similarly situated." The nub of the question, therefore, in the equal protection cases is the basis of the classification (or the *classifying factor*) which is used.[36] Courts have said that

the classification must be reasonable, not arbitrary, and must rest upon some ground of difference having a fair and substantial relation to the object of the legislation, so that all persons similarly circumstanced shall be treated alike.[37]

This is a concise statement of the traditional standard of reasonableness which courts still use in some cases to measure the constitutionality of state statutes and educational practices when they are challenged as a violation of equal protection of the laws. Under this standard, the person who attacks the educational practice bears the burden of proving that it is "arbitrary, capricious, or unreasonable," and courts ordinarily will not question the "wisdom or expediency" that called for the practice in the first place.[38]

The New Equal Protection Standard

However, this long-established rule that a statute does not deny equal protection if it is rationally related to a legitimate governmental objective is subject to a significant exception.

The Compelling Interest Doctrine.[39] This doctrine, which is of relatively recent vintage, has two branches.

1. The first branch requires that classifications based on "suspect" criteria be supported by a *compelling state interest.* This branch of the doctrine apparently had its genesis in racial classifications, which are regarded as inherently "suspect." (The criterion of *wealth* has since been added to the list of suspects.)

2. The second branch of the doctrine holds that a statutory classification is subject to the *compelling state interest* test if the result of the classification touches on a "fundamental right," regardless of the basis of the classification.

Two other aspects of the compelling interest doctrine must be noticed: *strict scrutiny* and who bears the *burden of proof.*

In cases involving "suspect classifications" or touching on "fundamental interests," the court has adopted an attitude of active and critical analysis, subjecting the classification to *strict scrutiny* . . . the state bears the burden of establishing not only that it has a *compelling* interest which justifies the law but that the distinctions drawn by the law are *necessary* to further its purpose.[40]

Whereas under the traditional standard the person attacking the educational practice has the burden of proving that it is "arbitrary, capricious, or unreasonable," under the new equal protection standard the burden of proof is shifted to the state (i.e., the school) which must show that continued use of the practice is necessary to achieve a compelling state purpose (Figure 4-1).

The new equal protection standard has been described as the Supreme Court's "favorite and most far-reaching tool for judicial protection of 'fundamental' rights not specified in the Constitution."[41] In their book on *Private Wealth and Public Education*, Coons, Clune, and Sugarman tell how the Court has carved out from among the various equal protection (discrimination) issues seeking its attention

an *inner circle* of cases to be given special scrutiny on substantive grounds . . . race cases still stand in the bull's-eye of the inner circle as the archetype of special or "invidious" discrimination. Hovering about this racial nucleus . . . are specimens of discrimination ranging from dilution of franchise to discrimination by wealth. The decisions are relatively few in number, and the rules they establish are fewer yet.[42]

Among the "special interests" (Figure 4-2) which have qualified for the *inner circle*, education is now an "outsider," at least so far as the Supreme Court of the United States is concerned[43] –but state courts in California and Michigan have characterized it as a "fundamental interest" and thus have admitted it to the circle.

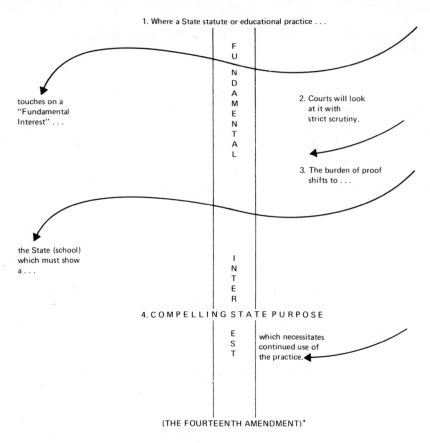

Figure 4-1. The New Equal Protection Standard.

The Constitutionality of Public School Financing Schemes

The Forerunners to Serrano v. Priest

Whereas in the race cases, as we saw in the previous chapter, the doctrine of "separate but equal" dates from the early beginnings of widespread public education in this country, *circa* 1849, the cases challenging state school financing statutes under the equal protection clause of the Fourteenth Amend-

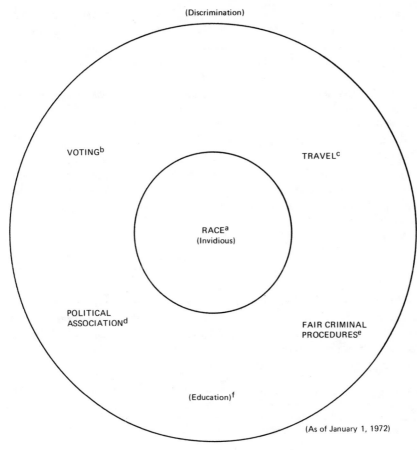

a. *Brown v. Board of Education of Topeka* (1954).
b. *Kramer v. Union Free School District No. 15* (1969).
c. *Shapiro v. Thompson* (1969).
d. *Williams v. Rhodes* (1968).
e. *Griffin v. Illinois* (1956).
f. *Serrano v. Priest* (1971), California Supreme Court.

Figure 4-2. The "Inner Circle" of Equal Protection.

ment or under similar state constitutional provisions are of fairly recent origin.[44] Since 1968 there have been more than forty lawsuits[45] filed with federal and state courts in some twenty-seven states attacking the constitutionality of public school financing statutes. There was a clearly discernible trend in the decisions toward invalidation of the statutes. Because of the Supreme Court's holding in the *Rodriguez case*, as discussed above, those cases that are successful will rest on *state* constitutional grounds alone.

The immediate forerunners of *Serrano v. Priest*, those school finance cases decided before August 30, 1971, when the California Supreme Court delivered its landmark decision, were all federal court cases, namely: *LeBeauf v. State Board of Education of Louisiana*,[47] *McInnis v. Shapiro*,[48] *Burruss v. Wilkerson*,[49] and *Hargrave v. McKinney*.[50] These decisions have been discussed extensively elsewhere;[51] in three of the cases—*LeBeauf, McInnis,* and *Burruss*—the courts upheld the state school financing statutes, notwithstanding the inequalities in the allocation and distribution of revenue that resulted from use of the local property tax base. In the *Hargrave case*, however, on remand, the three-judge court invalidated the Florida "millage rollback" statute because there was no rational basis for its discriminatory effect. On appeal, the Supreme Court of the United States vacated this decision (on other grounds) and indicated that on remand the lower court should thoroughly explore the equal protection issue.[52]

Whereas in the *Serrano case* the California Supreme Court used the new equal protection standard as the test for measuring the constitutionality of the California statute, in *McInnis* the court applied the traditional test of *reasonableness* and found that the Illinois legislation "is neither arbitrary nor does it constitute an invidious discrimination. It therefore complies with the Fourteenth Amendment."[53] In *Hargrave*, the court also applied the traditional test of reasonableness, but found the statute was unconstitutional. Asked by the plaintiffs to regard education as a "fundamental interest" and to apply the new, more strict standard, the court said:

Having concluded that there is no rational basis for the distinction which the legislature has drawn, we decline the invitation to explore the fundamental right-to-an-education thesis, and thus we do not reach the more exacting "compelling interest" approach.[54]

In *LeBeauf*, where the central thrust was a suit against the state board of education to bring about immediate desegregation of all public schools in the state, the court held that the provision of the Louisiana statute for allocation and distribution of funds to local school boards on a *per educable* basis (with an equalization factor being applied) did not violate the Constitution.[55]

In *McInnis*, no cause of action was stated, for these reasons: the Fourteenth Amendment does not require that public school expenditures be made only on the basis of pupils' *educational needs*; and the lack of judicially manageable standards makes the controversy nonjusticiable.[56] The term *educational needs*[57] was described as a "nebulous concept," presumably, a "conclusory term" reflecting the interaction of such factors as: the quality of teachers; the students potential; prior education; environmental and parental upbringing; and the school's physical plant. "Evaluation of these variables necessarily requires detailed research and study, with concomitant decentralization so each school and pupil may be individually evaluated."[58]

The "educational needs" theory was also unacceptable in *Burruss*, because courts have

neither the knowledge, nor the means, nor the power to tailor public monies to fit the varying needs of these students throughout the state. We can only see to it that the outlays on one group are not invidiously greater or less than that of another. No such arbitrariness is manifest here.[59]

Such, in brief, was the state of the case law on this subject when the first decision was rendered in *Serrano v. Priest*[60] in September 1970 by the California Court of Appeal, Second District. The *Serrano* complaint alleged that under the California school financing scheme, money spent per pupil varied from district to district according to the wealth of the pupil's parents and the district in which the pupil resided, not according to his educational needs. The court held that the complaint failed to state a cause of action under the equal protection clause of the Fourteenth Amendment. The plaintiffs appealed.

Serrano v. Priest (1971)[61]

The single most significant aspect of this decision, as noted above, has been the adoption of the new equal protection standard as a sort of "protective canopy" thrown over education. School policies and practices, all of which obviously touch upon this "fundamental interest," would be subjected to active court intervention—*strict scrutiny* and the "compelling purpose" doctrine—whenever they are challenged in court. School financing is just one such matter that touches on education.

Noting that the California system for financing the schools from local district property taxes results in wide disparities in revenue between school districts, the court said:

We have determined that this funding scheme indiviously discriminates against the poor because it makes the quality of a child's education a function of the wealth of his parents and neighbors. Recognizing as we must that the right to an education in our public schools is a fundamental interest which cannot be conditioned on wealth, we can discern no compelling state purpose necessitating the present method of financing.[62]

The court noted wide disparities in revenue per child devoted to education in certain districts, such as Baldwin Park ($577.00) as compared with Beverly Hills ($1,232.00). This, of course, was *not* new knowledge.[63] Moreover, said the court, "Affluent districts can have their cake and eat it too; they can provide a high quality education for their children while paying lower taxes. Poor districts, by contrast, have no cake at all."[64]

Discarding the argument that the case involved at most *de facto* discrimination, the court reiterated the California rule that is applied in racial discrimination cases:

Even assuming arguendo that defendants are correct in their contention that the instant discrimination based on wealth is merely *de facto*, and not *de jure*, such discrimination cannot be justified by analogy to *de facto* racial segregation. Although the United States Supreme Court has not yet ruled on the constitutionality of *de facto* racial segregation, this court eight years ago held such segregation invalid, and declared that school boards should take affirmative steps to alleviate racial imbalance, however created. *Jackson v. Pasadena City School District*, 59 Cal. 2d 876, 881. (1963). *San Francisco Unified School District v. Johnson*, 3 Cal. 3d 937. Consequently, any discrimination based on wealth can hardly be vindicated by reference to *de facto* racial segregation, which we have already condemned. In sum, we are of the view that the school financing system discriminates on the basis of the wealth of a district and its residents.[65]

The court said that the "indispensable role" that education plays in the modern state has two significant aspects. It is a major determinant of an individual's chances for "economic and social success in our competitive society"; and it is unique in its influence on a child's development as a citizen and his future participation in political and community life. Thus, education becomes "the lifeline of both the individual and society."[66]

The classic quotation from *Brown v. Board of Education*[67] is repeated:

"Today, education is perhaps the most important function of state and local governments. Compulsory school attendance laws and the great expenditures for education both demonstrate our recognition of the importance of education to our democratic society. It is required in the performance of our most basic public responsibilities, even service in the armed forces. It is the very foundation of good citizenship. Today it is a principal instrument in awakening the child to cultural values, in preparing him for later professional training, and in helping him to adjust normally to his environment. In these days, it is doubtful that any child may reasonably be expected to succeed in life if he is denied the opportunity of an education. Such an opportunity, where the state has undertaken to provide it, is a right which must be made available to all on equal terms."[68]

The "twin themes" of the importance of education to the individual and to society are traced through decisions of California cases, including *Piper v. Big Pine School District*[69] where it was said:

The common schools are doorways opening into chambers of science, art, and the learned professions, as well as into fields of industrial and commercial activities. Opportunities for securing employment are often more or less dependent upon the rating which a youth, as a pupil of our public institutions, has received in his school work. These are rights and privileges that cannot be denied.

The court then made this significant pronouncement: "We are convinced that the distinctive and priceless function of education in our society warrants, indeed compels, our treating it as a 'fundamental interest.' "[70]

In further support of this novel decisional principle, the court referred to these points which establish the great significance of education in today's world:[71]

1. *Democracy:* Education is essential in maintaining "free enterprise democracy"—that is, preserving an individual's opportunity to compete successfully in the economic marketplace, despite a disadvantaged background.

2. *Relevancy:* Education is universally relevant.

3. *Time:* Public education continues over a lengthy period of life—between ten and thirteen years. Few other government services have such sustained, intensive contact with the recipient.

4. *Personality:* Education is unmatched in the extent to which it molds the personality of youth. Public education actively attempts to shape a child's personal development in a manner chosen not by the child or his parents but by the state.

5. *Compulsory:* Education is so important that the state has made it compulsory—not only in the requirement of attendance but also by assignment to a particular district and school.

The court examined the question of continued "local control" and concluded that no matter how the state decides to finance its schools, it can still leave the decision-making power in the hands of the local districts.

The question of "territorial uniformity" was disposed of as follows:

. . . two lines of recent decisions have indicated that where fundamental rights or suspect classifications are at stake, a state's general freedom to discriminate on a geographical basis will be significantly curtailed by the equal protection clause. . . . The first group of precedents consists of the school closing cases, in which the Supreme Court has invalidated efforts to shut schools in one part of a state while schools in other areas continued to operate. . . . In the second group of cases, dealing with apportionment, the high court has held that accidents of geography and arbitrary boundary lines of local government can afford no ground for discrimination among a state's citizens. Specifically rejecting attempts to justify unequal districting on the basis of various geographic factors, the court declared: ". . . . The fact that an individual lives here or there is not a legitimate reason for overweighting or diluting the efficacy of his vote." If a voter's address may not determine the weight to which his ballot is entitled, surely it should not determine the quality of his child's education.[72]

Education, stated the court, is unique among public activities; education must respond to the command of the equal protection requirement. Hence: "If the allegations of the complaint are sustained, the financial system must fall and the statutes comprising it must be found unconstitutional."[73]

The judgment dismissing the case was reversed; the cause was remanded to the trial court with directions to overrule the demurs and to allow the defendants a reasonable time within which to answer. In other words, the case must go to trial. That is where the matter stands as of this date.[74] (Mr. Justice McComb dissented.)

It is clear that the state school financing system was just a convenient "vehicle" used by the Supreme Court of California to make its momentous pronouncement that education is a "fundamental interest," henceforth subject to the "compelling interest" doctrine and the stricter requirements of the new equal protection standard.

In summary, the scholarly debate over whether a child's education can or cannot be made to depend upon the wealth of his family and neighbors can be traced through these early sources:

Arthur Wise, Associate Dean, The Graduate School of Education, University of Chicago, first advanced this thesis in "Is Denial of Equal Educational Opportunity Constitutional?" 13 Administrator's Notebook, No. 6 (University of Chicago, Feb. 1965). He elaborated upon it in *Rich Schools, Poor Schools* (Univ. of Chicago Press, Chicago, 1968). It was his contention that the present system of funding education of all states except Hawaii (which is funded entirely out of general state revenues) denies the equal protection of the laws. A similar thesis has been advanced by Coons, Clune and Sugarman, in "Educational Opportunity: A Workable Constitutional Test for State Financial Structures," 57 Cal. L. Rev. 305 (1969), and in *Private Wealth and Public Education* (The Belknap Press of Harvard University Press, Cambridge, 1970). It is this thesis that has been adopted by the California Supreme Court in *Serrano, supra*, and by the federal courts in *Van Dusartz* and *Rodriguez*.[75]

Post-Priest *Decisions on Public School Financing*

Four post-*Priest* decisions on school financing that preceded the 1973 Supreme Court of the United States decision in the *Rodriguez case* were: *Van Dusartz v. Hatfield*,[76] *Spano v. Board of Education of Lakeland Central School District #1*,[77] *Robinson v. Cahill*,[78] and *Rodriguez v. San Antonio Independent School District*.[79]

The Robinson decision was by a state court (New Jersey), Spano by the Supreme Court of New York, while the other two decisions were by federal district courts (Minnesota and Texas).

Although the case has since been dismissed as a consequence of the Supreme Court decision in *Rodriguez*, the district court in *Van Dusartz*[80] follows *Serrano* with approval, saying that pupils in publicly financed schools enjoy a *right* under the equal protection clause of the Fourteenth Amendment to have the level of spending for their education unaffected by variations in the taxable wealth of their school districts or of their parents. The court concluded "that *such a right indeed exists and that the principle announced in* Serrano v. Priest *is correct."*[81] The virtue of the *Serrano* principle is that "the state remains free to pursue all imaginable interests except that of distributing education according to wealth."[82]

In *Spano v. Board of Education of Lakeland Central School District # 1,*[83] decided January 17, 1972, the Supreme Court of New York dismissed for failure to state a cause of action a complaint attacking as unconstitutional the New York legislative and constitutional provisions for levying and distributing school taxes, noting that

the applicable law, pronounced within the last two years by paramount judicial authority, the United States Supreme Court, is that the prevailing State and local legislative patterns of levying and disbursing taxes to defray the cost of public education . . . are not unconstitutional.[84]

Said the court, in referring to the previously decided cases on this subject,

Serrano, supra and the more recent *Van Dusartz v. Hatfield* . . . , seem to me to be exercises in a forensic "game plan." I must confess an almost irresistible urge to join the fray by penning paeans of praise for public education and to dilate upon the inequities of existing modalities for financing public school education. It takes little ingenuity to illustrate such disparities, reduced to the last mill.[85]

In *Robinson v. Cahill,*[86] decided January 19, 1972, the Superior Court of New Jersey, adopted the "fundamental interest" thesis and held that the New Jersey system of public school financing violates the requirement for equality contained in both the state and federal constitutions.[87] Two main contentions were at issue in the case:

1. The fact that a "thorough and efficient" education (as required by the state constitution) was afforded some pupils in New Jersey but denied to others, discriminated and therefore violated equal protection of the laws, and

2. The other, that the present system of school financing "*also discriminates against property owners* who are taxed at different rates throughout the State for the same public purpose."[88]

While the court disagreed that "unequal expenditures do not necessarily prove unequal education," it did say:

The Attorney General disputes the conclusion that mere differences in dollar expenditures prove differences in the quality of education. *He doubts the ability of the court to grapple with an issue as large and complex as the public school system; and there is some merit to both of these contentions.* However, based on probabilities and expert opinion, in this as well as other kinds of cases, some conclusions can be drawn. As might be expected, there is a correlation between dollar expenditures and input (such as teachers and facilities), and between input and output (results).[89]

This reference to the inability of courts to grapple with complex school issues reflects the sentiment expressed in Justice Wright's "Parting Word" in *Hobson v. Hansen.*[90]

The Court disputes the argument, often advanced, for local control over schools:

To what extent local control is real or mythical has been detailed in this case. . . . There is evidence to indicate that as much as 90% of some current budgets are composed of costs that are more or less fixed or recurring. . . . School boards in poor districts cannot opt to institute special services when their budgets do not include adequate funds even for essentials. In this sense local control is illusory. It is control for the wealthy, not for the poor.[91]

On appeal, however, the Supreme Court of New Jersey took a somewhat different view of the case, namely, that the New Jersey system of financing schools violates the state constitutional provision requiring a "thorough and efficient" system of public education for all school-age children; the court refused to pursue the equal protection argument, saying:

This court hesitates to turn this case upon the equal protection clause of the state constitution. The equal protection clause may be unmanageable if it is called upon to supply categorical answers in the vast area of human needs. . . . The Court will not pursue this equal protection issue in the limited context of public education.[92]

The district court in *Rodriguez*, which followed *Serrano* (and cited *Van Dusartz* with approval), invalidated the Texas method of financing public schools as a violation of the equal protection clause of the Fourteenth Amendment. "More than mere rationality is required"; said the court: "The crucial nature of education for the citizenry lies at the heart of almost twenty years of school desegregation litigation."[93] To the argument that equalized school financing is "socialized education," the court replied: "Education, like the postal service, has been socialized, or publicly financed and operated almost from its origin. The *type* of socialized education, not the question of its existence, is the only matter currently in dispute."[94]

To the charge that courts cannot act as a "super-legislature," the court replied that "the judiciary can always determine that an act of the legislature is violative of the Constitution."[95]

This case was appealed directly to the Supreme Court of the United States; in a landmark decision delivered on March 21, 1973, the Court, in *San Antonio*

Independent School District v. Rodriguez,[96] applying "strict construction" to the language of the U.S. Constitution, reaffirmed that education is a state matter and held that school financing systems that raise their revenue by means of local district property taxes do not violate the equal protection clause of the Fourteenth Amendment. As discussed above, the Supreme Court refused to characterize education as a "fundamental interest"; the decision has clearly limited the kinds of future cases involving the schools which will be decided by federal courts under the U.S. Constitution.[97] The decision, however, does not affect rights of individuals or groups *explicitly or implicitly protected* by the language of the First and Fourteenth Amendments or any other provisions of the Constitution. Racial discrimination cases, "freedom of expression" cases, etc., whether on a school campus or elsewhere, will still receive such protection.

Henceforth, challenges to school financing systems can be expected to be brought on *state* constitutional grounds only; in addition to *Serrano v. Priest,* one such case is presently pending in Michigan. Basing its decision on state constitutional grounds, the Supreme Court of Michigan, in *Milliken v. Green,*[98] decided December 29, 1972, struck down the state's system of financing public schools because it denies equal protection of the laws guaranteed by the Michigan Constitution; the system meets neither the "compelling state interest" test nor the "rational classification" test. Said the court:

In light of the People's concern and direct provision for education in the Constitution, this Court is compelled to recognize education as a fundamental interest under the Michigan Constitution requiring close scrutiny of legislative classifications concerning the distribution of educational resources. . . .

In passing for those who fear recognizing education as a fundamental interest because it can open a Pandora's box of other functions as fundamental interests, there are at least two important observations. The right to an education in Michigan is a *specifically enumerated* constitutional *mandate.* Second, education is *sui generis* and this Court has recognized its uniqueness.[99]

As if to further help relieve such fears, the court carefully defined the "limits" of its decision: school financing is complicated and involves several statutes, not all the provisions of which are called into question by this decision; the opinion does not require absolute equality in the distribution of state educational resources in all cases; and the opinion does not relate to *local control,*

The opinion relates only to the State's obligation "to maintain and support" public schools financially under Const. 1963, art. 8, sec. 2. . . . none of the matters relating to the exercise of local control is in question in this opinion.[100]

In an "Addendum" to the opinion of the court, Justice Brennan lamented the last-minute haste, in this case that had been permitted "to hang fire for five months," to issue the majority opinion; he said:

Nonetheless, they have the votes. In the Supreme Court, four votes seems to be the name of the game . . .

The majority opinion is not good law.

It is not even law at all.

It is a political position paper, written and timed to encourage action by the state legislature through the threat of future court intervention.

The majority concede that the question presented is moot. It is against every precept of good constitutional law for a supreme court to decide a constitutional question upon a moot case. . . .

Consider the fuzziness of this pronouncement: " . . . equal protection . . . may . . . be effectuated by state-wide distribution of all public school funds on an appropriate basis."

And what, pray tell, is *appropriate*?

The conclusion is inescapable that when this court says *"appropriate,"* it means "judicially declared to be appropriate."

How long will the people permit such judicial meddling in the affairs of the state?

How long will the legislature tolerate such pompous interference with their duties?

And when—

When, in the name of all that is sacred in the administration of justice will the members of this court turn a deaf ear to the siren call of executive and legislative politics, and come home to the dignity of judicial scholarship, judicial decisions, and judicial restraint?[101]

In February 1973, the Michigan Supreme Court granted a rehearing in this case and the opinion was subsequently vacated.[102]

Implementation and Securing Compliance

The problems encountered by the courts in the implementation of *Brown v. the Board of Education* (1954) in the South[103] called forth such strong judicial pronouncements as: "with all deliberate speed" (*Brown II*, 1954), the "interpretation of the Fourteenth Amendment enunciated by this Court is the supreme law of the land" (*Cooper v. Aaron*, 1958), and the "clock has ticked the last tick for tokenism and delay in the name of 'deliberate speed'" (*U.S. v. Jefferson County Board of Education*, 1966). Perhaps it is because of this experience with the race cases that the courts took a different approach to securing compliance with the wealth decisions.

No specific school financing plan was mandated by any of the above court decisions, although in *Robinson*, the court said that if a nondiscriminatory system of taxation was not enacted by January 1, 1973, then "from and after that date no state monies shall be distributed to any school district" or be distributed by state officials "in a manner that will [not] effectuate as far as possible the principles expressed herein."[104]

The district court in the *Van Dusartz case* cited three works the legislature might want to examine for their "explication of some of the numerous school financing systems available which meet the equal protection standard,"[105]

Guthrie, Kleindofer, Levin and Stout, *Schools and Inequality* (1971);

Coons, Clune, and Sugarman, *Private Wealth and Public Education* (1970);

"Educational Opportunity: A Workable Constitutional Test for State Financing Structures," 57 *Cal. L. Rev.* 305 (1969).

Although state authorities would have "freedom to choose" among various fiscal plans, securing compliance in this area would be less difficult than in the race cases—the courts could always seize the "pursestrings" and mandate how the money would be spent, if that became necessary.

Criteria for a Constitutionally Acceptable
School Financing Plan

What are the elements of a constitutionally (state) acceptable school financing plan? What *criteria* did the courts set forth in their decisions that could be used in developing such a plan? Some of the criteria the courts said could be used by legislatures and school authorities for a fiscal plan that meets minimum requirements are summarized in the accompanying table.

Table 4-1
Criteria for School Financing Plans

The following criteria were extracted from recent court decisions for use in judging whether a school financing plan meets the minimum constitutional requirements of the equal protection clause:

- Allocation and distribution of funds on a *per educable basis*, with an equalization factor being applied, does not violate the Federal Constitution.[a]
- The Fourteenth Amendment does not require that school expenditures be made *only* on the basis of "pupils' *educational needs*."[b]
- The lack of "judicially manageable standards" will invalidate a school financing plan.[c]
- The *manner* in which the plan operates may be crucial to the decision of the equal protection question.[d]
- The plan must be "uniform and consistent."[e]
- There is no requirement that the school system be uniform as to . . . *money spent per pupil*; rather, the system must be uniform in terms of courses of study offered and educational progression.[f]
- Even though the plan operates "uniformly and consistently," it may violate the equal protection clause if its effects are discriminatory.[g]
- The plan must not "invidiously discriminate" against the poor.[h]
- A plan which relies heavily upon local property taxes and causes substantial disparities among school districts in the amount of revenue available per pupil invidiously discriminates against the poor and therefore violates the equal protection clause.[i]

Table 4-1 (cont.)

— The quality of public education may not be made a function of wealth, other than the wealth of the State as a whole.[j]

— The classifying factor must not be *race*.[k]

— Lines drawn on the basis of wealth or property, like those of race, are traditionally disfavored.[l]

— Discrimination in legislative classifications on the basis of wealth is unconstitutional, regardless of whether it is the result of purposeful and intentional discrimination or *de facto* or unintentional classification.[m]

— "Territorial uniformity" in financing schools *may* be constitutionally required.[n]

— Courts will look at the *fiscal system as a whole* to see how it generates revenue.[o]

— To withstand an attack under the Fourteenth Amendment, the fiscal system as structured must be necessary to achieve a compelling state purpose.[p]

— Courts have neither the knowledge, means, nor power to tailor public moneys to fit the *varying needs* of pupils throughout the state.[q]

— *Federal funds* cannot be employed as a substitute for performance by a state of its constitutional obligation to equalize differences.[r]

— *Fiscal neutrality* is constitutionally required in school financing.[s]

— By itself, discrimination by wealth is not necessarily decisive. "No court has so held."[t]

— *Absolute uniformity* of school expenditures is not constitutionally required.[u]

— A fiscal system discriminates against *property owners*, if they are taxed at different rates throughout the state for the same public purpose.[v]

— There is no legitimate legislative purpose for giving rich districts "state aid," so long as some districts are underfinanced.[w]

— "Minimum aid" and "safe-harmless" aid is, in some cases, *political*.[x]

— In a certain sense, "local control" is illusory; it is control for the wealthy, not the poor.[y]

— Distribution of school resources according to the *chance location* of pupils cannot be tolerated.[z]

— It is clear that some kind of uniform, statewide tax can be adopted by the state to finance "thorough" education without relying on a real property tax.[aa]

— There is no compelling justification for making a taxpayer in one district pay a tax at a higher rate than a taxpayer in another district, so long as the revenue serves the common state educational purpose.[bb]

— Education serves too important a function to leave to the "mood" of the taxpayer.[cc]

— Equalizing tax burdens can be accomplished by known means—but no purpose is served by simply "bidding-up" the costs of the *same services* without the expectation of improvements.[dd]

---

[a]*LeBeauf v. State Board of Education of Louisiana*, 244 F. Supp. 256 (1965).

[b]*McInnis v. Shapiro*, 293 F. Supp. 327 (1968).

[c]Ibid.

[d]*Askew v. Hargrave*, 401 U.S. 476 (1970).

[e]*Burruss v. Wilkerson*, 310 F. Supp. 572 (1969).

[f]*Serrano v. Priest*, 10 Cal. App. 3d 1110 (1970).

[g]*Hargrave v. Kirk*, 313 F. Supp. 944 (1970).

[h]*Serrano v. Priest*, 96 Cal. Rptr. 601 (1971).

Table 4-1 (cont.)

[i]Ibid.

[j]*Rodriguez v. San Antonio Independent School District*, U.S. District Court, Western District of Texas, 1971.

[k]*Hobsen v. Hansen*, 269 F. Supp. 401 (1967).

[l]*Harper v. Virginia State Board of Elections*, 383 U.S. 663, 668 (1966).

[m]*Serrano v. Priest*, 96 Cal. Rptr. 602 (1971).

[n]*Serrano v. Priest*, 96 Cal. Rptr. 603, 621 (1971).

[o]*Serrano v. Priest*, 96 Cal. Rptr. 611 (1971).

[p]*Serrano v. Priest*, 96 Cal. Rptr. 620 (1971).

[q]*Burruss v. Wilkerson*, 310 F. Supp. 572, 574 (1969).

[r]*Rodriguez v. San Antonio Independent School District*, 377 F. Supp. 280 (D.C. Tex. 1971), Transcript, p. 7.

[s]*Van Dusartz v. Hatfield*, 334 F. Supp. 870, 872, 876-77 (1971).

[t]*Van Dusartz v. Hatfield*, 334 F. Supp. 876 (1971).

[u]*Van Dusartz v. Hatfield*, 334 F. Supp. 876-77 (1971).

[v]*Robinson v. Cahill*, 287 A. 2d 187 (1972).

[w]Ibid., p. 211.

[x]Ibid.

[y]Ibid., p. 212.

[z]Ibid., p. 214.

[aa]Ibid., p. 215.

[bb]Ibid., p. 216.

[cc]Ibid.

[dd]Ibid., p. 217.

Conclusion

There have been at least a dozen decided law cases,[106] at all levels of the state and federal judiciaries, in which judges have examined the problem of equal financing for public schools, yet in none of these have the courts been able to come up with a satisfactory solution; perhaps the Attorney General of New Jersey had a good point when he expressed doubts about the "ability of courts to grapple with an issue as large and complex as the public school system."[107] Judge Wright's observation, in *Hobson v. Hansen*, is also worth reconsidering, namely, that it would be "far better indeed for these great social and political problems to be resolved in the political arena by other branches of government."[108] It has also been said that:

"One scholar, one dollar"—a suggested variant of the "one man, one vote" doctrine proclaimed in *Baker v. Carr* . . . —may well become the law of the land. I submit, however, that to do so is the prerogative and within the "territorial imperative" of the Legislature or, under certain circumstances, of the United States Supreme Court.[109]

The Supreme Court of the United States, however, has made it quite clear that it will not be the final arbiter in this dispute.

78

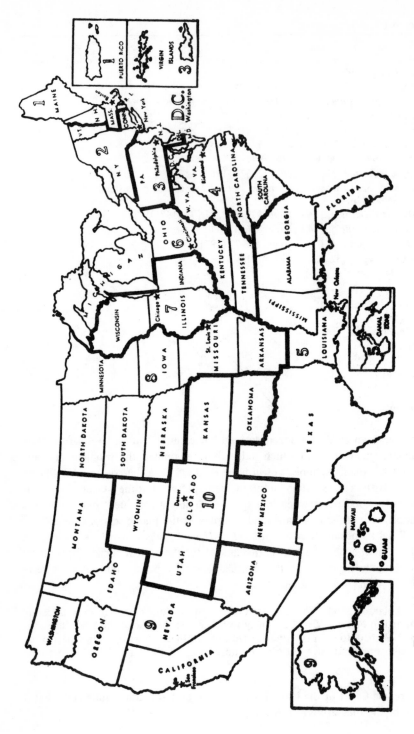

Figure 4A. The Eleven Federal Judicial Circuits. See 28 U.S.C.A. § 41. Reproduced with permission of the copyright owner, West Publishing Company, St. Paul, Minnesota.

5

Individual Rights and Education

Introduction

This book would not be complete without mention of certain parallel developments that have occurred in recent years in the expanding area of student[1] and teacher[2] rights under the First and Fourteenth Amendments. These developments have involved attempted regulation by school authorities of personal "liberties" of students and teachers. Courts have been asked to review the constitutionality of school rules and practices pertaining to "freedom of expression" (pure speech and symbolic expression), hair-styles and grooming, behavior and campus discipline, pregnancy, corporal punishment, admission and graduation requirements, suspension, expulsion, and so forth. School district use of test scores for pupil placement and teacher employment and promotion purposes, a long-standing educational practice, has been successfully challenged in the courts. Because of the long period of laissez faire and the apparent lack of interest of state and federal judges in school matters,[3] there developed a body of decisional law at the state level which permitted school authorities to make rules and regulation governing student and teacher conduct but which failed, in many instances, to meet minimum constitutional requirements.[4] Much of the recent federal court activity in this area, therefore, has been to correct this situation.

The "analytical tools" the courts have used to make this correction involve the *standard of review* and who has the *burden of proof.*[5] Whereas formerly the party attacking the statute, educational practice, or school rule carried the burden, now, where a First Amendment or a Fourteenth Amendment right is alleged to have been infringed, the school authorities must carry the burden of proving that the "intrusion by the state is in furtherance of a legitimate state interest." Thus, a different level of scrutiny, which affords special protection to First Amendment rights, has evolved from the earlier jurisprudential talk about the "preferred position" of such rights.[6] Some courts, as shown in the cases discussed below, characterize a student's hair-style as a *personal liberty,*[7] and in the absence of an "inherent, self-evident justification," the burden is on the school authorities to justify regulation of that liberty. In the pregnancy cases, education itself is characterized as a *basic personal liberty or right,*[8] and school authorities bear the burden of justifying any rule or regulation limiting or terminating that right. School rules that place restrictions on student "freedom of expression," symbolic or otherwise, must likewise meet a stricter test, namely, that they are necessary to prevent conduct that would *materially and*

79

substantially interfere with the orderly operation of the school, and the burden of justifying such rules is placed on the school authorities. This has not always been the case, however.

The Pugsley Principles

From *Pugsley* (1923) until *Tinker* (1969), in school cases, the courts almost uniformly adopted the concept of "reasonableness" as the standard for measuring the constitutionality of an educational practice or a school rule. They refused to consider if such practice was wise or expedient, but asked only whether it was a *reasonable* exercise of the power and discretion of the school authorities. Where a school rule could not be shown by the plaintiff to be "arbitrary, capricious, or unreasonable," the courts would not interfere, leaving the matter to the educational judgment and discretion of the school authorities (Table 5-1). By 1969, however, this had changed, and the Supreme Court of the

Table 5-1
Traditional Standard of "Reasonableness"

A school rule must *not* be "arbitrary, capricious, or unreasonable."

I.	II.
COURTS WILL NOT CONSIDER:	COURTS WILL CONSIDER:
1. Whether the rule is	1. Oppression or humiliation of the pupil
— "wise or expedient"	2. Consumption of time in compliance
— "essential to the maintenance of discipline"	3. Expenditure of money in compliance
2. Whether there is a "valid reason" for the rule	4. School authorities
	— arbitrary exercise of discretion
	— refusal to perform a legal duty

III.

Classification

"... the classification must be reasonable, not arbitrary, and must rest upon some ground of difference having a fair and substantial relation to the object of the legislation, so that all persons similarly circumstanced shall be treated alike." *F.S. Royster Co. v. Virginia*, 253 U.S. 412, 415 (1920).

IV.

Burden of Proof

"... we will not annul a rule of this kind unless a valid reason for doing so is made to appear; whereas, to uphold it, we are not required to find a valid reason for its promulgation." *Pugsley v. Sellmeyer*, 158 Arkansas 247, 254 (1923).

United States announced that students and teachers do not shed their First (and Fourteenth) Amendment rights at the schoolhouse gate.

The classical view of the courts and student and teacher rights was set forth in a 1923 Arkansas case, *Pugsley v. Sellmeyer,*[9] wherein the following school rule was challenged by a female student: "The wearing of transparent hosiery, low-necked dresses or any style of clothing tending towards immodesty in dress, or the use of face-paint or cosmetics, is prohibited."[10] Miss Pugsley's defiant breech of the rule was viewed by the school board as a challenge to their authority: she was age eighteen, wore talcum powder on her face, and refused "to submit or to obey the rule," and hence she was denied admission to the school.

The Arkansas Supreme Court held that the rule was "reasonable" and that the school board had the right to make and enforce it. The control and management of the public schools is vested in local boards, which have broad discretion:

the educational interests and school affairs in each school district in the State are placed by statute under the control and management of the school directors, and . . . to effectively exercise this authority a broad discretion must be accorded them . . . while their authority is not without limit . . . courts will not interfere in matters of detail and government of schools, unless the officers refuse to perform a clear, plain duty, or unless they unreasonably and arbitrarily exercise the discretionary authority conferred upon them.[11]

The writer for *Ruling Case Law* sets forth a more general statement of the classical decisional law on this subject: "courts are usually disinclined to interfere with regulations adopted by school boards, and *they will not consider whether the regulations are wise or expedient*, but merely whether they are a reasonable exercise of the power and discretion of the Board."[12] The point was often made that courts have more important duties to attend to than to participate in the day-to-day regulation and management of the schools. The business of education will be left to educators.

Courts have other and more important functions to perform than that of hearing complaints of disaffected pupils of the public schools against rules and regulations promulgated by the school boards for the government of the schools.[13]

This laissez-faire attitude prevailed for over one hundred years and to some extent does even today.[14] As one federal judge recently put it, "In this suit, the Court is called upon to resolve *another* conflict between the Constitution and the campus."[15]

In *Pugsley*, it was said: "Courts have this right of review, for the reasonableness of such rules is a judicial question." Also at stake was, for the recalcitrant student, a lesson in "respect for constituted authority and obedience thereto," one of the essential lessons to be taught in school.

It will be remembered also that respect for constituted authority, and obedience thereto, is an essential lesson to qualify one for the duties of citizenship, and that the schoolroom is an appropriate place to teach that lesson.[16]

What constitutes in school rules *unreasonableness*? In *Pugsley*, the court looked for any element of "oppression or humiliation to the pupil" and asked whether "consumption of time or expenditure of money" was required to comply with the rule. Not being offensive in these respects, and since the rule imposed no "affirmative duty" upon the pupil, and since there was no showing that the talcum powder was a medicant or was used other than as a cosmetic, the court refused to annul the rule, "for we will not annul a rule of this kind unless a valid reason for doing so is made to appear; whereas to uphold it, we are not required to find a valid reason for its promulgation."[17]

The Pugsley principles of student rights can be summarized:

1. Education is a state matter: courts will not normally interfere in the management of the schools.

2. The state has delegated authority over the schools to local boards, and the actions thereof, in general, are immune to court scrutiny unless such boards fail to perform a clear duty or unless they act unreasonably.

3. *Reasonableness*[18] —not the wisdom or expediency—of school rules would usually discourage review by a state court. (The educational wisdom that called forth the rule in the first instance was presumed.)

4. Courts have more important functions to perform than to hear schoolboys' complaints about the government of their schools.

5. Obedience ("to submit to or obey the rules") and respect for constituted authority are appropriate lessons for teaching good citizenship in the classroom.

6. The measures of "unreasonableness" include: student oppression or humiliation; consumption of time or expenditure of money; imposition of an unusual affirmative duty; and medical reasons.

7. The *burden of proof* is on the party (student) challenging the school rule. A valid reason for annulling a school rule must be shown by the student attacking the rule, while no valid reason at all need be shown by the school board for the rule's promulgation in the first instance or for its validation by the courts.[19]

Whereas First and Fourteenth Amendment rights, therefore, were apparently not thought applicable to a school rule that prohibited a girl from wearing talcum powder on her face in 1923—times have changed. Thus, by 1969, the Supreme Court of the United States had ushered in a new era in student-teacher rights, or at least made it plain that constitutional rights of students and teachers, whether on the campus or elsewhere, are subject to a different level of scrutiny.

There are indications . . . that courts are widening the scope of review. Turn of the century cases can be found holding that the courts have no jurisdiction at all over the internal operations of a school system. Later cases have set forth a "reasonable relationship" test, but this appears to be more a proper incantation than an indication of rigorous analysis. Today, however, while fairly uncritical acceptance of educators' views on the connection between a regulation and a legitimate school goal is still the rule, the recent cases indicate an increasing tendency to scrutinize facts and to give something more than a cursory hearing to student claims.[20]

This change was foreshadowed in 1934 when, in *West Virginia State Board of Education v. Barnette*,[21] the Court declared:

The test of legislation which collides with the Fourteenth Amendment, because it also collides with the principles of the First, is much more definite than the test when only the Fourteenth is involved . . . freedoms of speech and of press, of assembly, and of worship may not be infringed on such slender grounds [i.e., "rational basis"]. They are susceptible of restriction only to prevent grave and immediate danger to interests which the State may lawfully protect.[22]

Outside the context of education, such had clearly been the trend of the Court's decisions on First Amendment rights at least since as early as 1938.[23]

The effect of recent court decisions, therefore, has been to place new restraints upon actions that school authorities may take in cases affecting student and teacher rights. In 1970 the National Association of Secondary School Principals identified ten areas of conflict involving courts and schools and formulated "defensible positions" that school administrators might take on these issues:[24]

1. freedom of expression
2. personal appearance of students
3. codes of behavior
4. student property
5. extracurricular activities
6. discipline
7. student government
8. the student press
9. the right to petition
10. the use of drugs.

At stake, in each area, have been First and Fourteenth Amendment rights of students and teachers and the power of school authorities to regulate conduct.

The Landmark "Tinker" Decision

The leading Supreme Court case that shows the changing[25] attitude of courts toward cases involving student and teacher "freedom of expression" is *Tinker v.*

Des Moines Independent Community School District,[26] decided in 1969, wherein certain public school pupils in Iowa were suspended for wearing black armbands to protest the government's Vietnam policy. The students were quiet and passive and were not disruptive. Under these circumstances, said the Court (Justice Fortas speaking), "their conduct was within the protection of the free speech clause of the First Amendment and the due process clause of the Fourteenth":

1. The lower court[27] recognized that the wearing of an arm-band for the purpose of expressing certain views is "the type of symbolic act" that is within the 1st Amendment.
2. The wearing of arm-bands in the circumstances of this case was entirely divorced from actually or potentially disruptive conduct by those participating in it. "It was closely akin to 'pure speech' which . . . is entitled to comprehensive protection under the First Amendment."
3. First Amendment rights, applied in light of the special characteristics of the school environment, are available to teachers and students.
    "It can hardly be argued that either students or teachers shed their constitutional rights to freedom of speech or expression at the school-house gate" (p. 506).[28]
4. Boards of education have important, delicate, and highly discretionary functions, *but none that they may not perform within the limits of the Bill of Rights.* (*West Virginia v. Barnette*, 319 U.S. 624, at p. 637.)
5. The case lies in the area where students in the exercise of First Amendment rights collide with the rules of the school authorities.
6. This case does *not* relate to the regulation of the length of skirts or the type of clothing, to hair style, or deportment. It does *not* concern aggressive, disruptive action or even group demonstrations. "There is here no evidence whatever of petitioners' interference, actual or nascent, with the schools' work or of collision with the rights of other students to be secure and to be let alone. . . . There is no indication that the work of the schools or any class was disrupted. Outside the classrooms, a few students made hostile remarks to the children wearing armbands, but there were no threats or acts of violence on school premises."
    "Our problem involves direct, primary First Amendment rights akin to 'pure speech.' The school officials banned and sought to punish petitioners for a silent, passive expression of opinion, unaccompanied by any disorder or disturbance on the part of petitioners." (p. 508)
    Accordingly, this case does *not* concern speech or action that intrudes upon the work of the schools or the rights of the other students.
7. Where there is no finding and no showing that engaging in the forbidden conduct would "*materially and substantially*" interfere with the requirements of appropriate discipline in the operation of the school, the prohibition cannot be sustained.[29]
    "In order for the state . . . to justify prohibition of a particular expression of opinion, it must be able to show that its action was caused by something more than a mere desire to avoid the discomfort and unpleasantness that always accompany an unpopular viewpoint. (p. 509)"[30]

The burden of proof, which in *Pugsley* was carried by the student attacking the "reasonableness" of the school rule, was thus shifted in *Tinker* to the school authorities, who now have to justify their actions by showing that the prohibitions they impose on freedom of expression are necessary because of conduct that interferes *materially and substantially* with school operations.

8. Schools are not "enclaves of totalitarianism," and school authorities do not possess "absolute authority" over their students.

Students in school as well as out of school are "persons" under our Constitution. They are possessed of fundamental rights which the State must respect, just as they themselves must respect their obligations to the State. In our system, students may not be regarded as closed-circuit recipients of only that which the State chooses to communicate. They may not be confined to the expression of those sentiments that are officially approved. In the absence of a specific showing of constitutionally valid reasons to regulate their speech, students are entitled to freedom of expression of their views.[31]

9. The principle set forth in this case is *not* confined to the "supervised and ordained discussion" which takes place in the classroom. An important part of the educational process occurs elsewhere.

A student's rights, therefore, do not embrace merely the classroom hours. When he is in the cafeteria, or on the playing field, or on the campus during the authorized hours, he may express his opinions, even on controversial subjects like the conflict in Vietnam, if he does so without "materially and substantially interfer[ing] with the requirements of appropriate discipline in the operation of the school" and without colliding with the rights of others. *Burnside v. Byars*, p. 749. But conduct by the student, in class or out of it, which for any reason—whether it stems from time, place, or type of behavior—materially disrupts classwork or involves substantial disorder or invasion of the rights of others is, of course, not immunized by the constitutional guarantee of freedom of speech. . . . We properly read [the Constitution] to permit reasonable regulation of speech-connected activities in carefully restricted circumstances. But we do not confine the permissible exercise of First Amendment rights to a telephone booth or the four corners of a pamphlet, or to supervised and ordained discussion in a school classroom.[32]

Justice Black dissented, declaring that this case marks the beginning of "an entirely new era in which the power to control pupils by the elected 'officials of state supported public schools . . . ' in the United States is in ultimate effect transferred to the Supreme Court."[33] And he added that if pupils in our schools can "defy and flout orders of school officials" to keep their minds on their own schoolwork, it is the beginning of a "new revolutionary era of permissiveness in this country fostered by the judiciary." We cannot ignore the plain fact that some of the "country's greatest problems are crimes committed by the youth" and that school discipline, like parental discipline, is an important part of training children to be good citizens, to be better citizens. Black concluded that

groups of students all over the land are already running loose, conducting break-ins, sit-ins, lie-ins, and smash-ins. . . . Turned loose with lawsuits for damages and injunctions against their teachers as they are here, it is nothing but wishful thinking to imagine that young, immature students will not soon believe it is their right to control the schools. . . . This case, therefore, wholly without constitutional reasons in my judgment, subjects all the public schools in the country to the whims and caprices of their loudest-mouthed, but maybe not their brightest, students. I, for one, am not fully persuaded that school pupils are wise enough, even with this Court's expert help from Washington, to run the 23,390 public school systems in our 50 States. I wish, therefore, wholly to disclaim any purpose on my part to hold that the Federal Constitution compels the teachers, parents, and the elected school officials to surrender control of the American public school system to public school students. I dissent.[34]

The Impact of the "Tinker" Decision on the Public Schools

Have recent school developments in the area of student and teacher liberties and rights tended to support Justice Black's thinking about this matter? Has there been any significant change in school management practices since the *Tinker* decision? What impact, if any, has the decision had upon the public schools?

One immediate consequence of this decision was the ruling in September 1970, by a three-judge federal panel, that the *California Education Code* provisions restricting student expression on school campuses were unconstitutional.[35] Following this determination, the California legislature[36] in 1971 repealed Sections 9012 and 9013 of the *Education Code* and added new sections (Secs. 10,611 and 24,425.5) dealing with the right of students to exercise free expression—with specified exceptions—on school campuses.[37]

Students of the public schools have the right to exercise free expression including, but not limited to, the use of bulletin boards, the distribution of printed materials or petitions, and the wearing of buttons, badges, and other insignia, except that expression which is obscene, libelous, or slanderous according to current legal standards, or which so incites students as to create a clear and present danger of the commission of unlawful acts on school premises or the violation of lawful school regulations, or the substantial disruption of the orderly operation of the school, shall be prohibited.

Each governing board of a school district and each county superintendent of schools shall adopt rules and regulations relating to the exercise of free expression by students upon the premises of each school within their respective jurisdictions, which shall include reasonable provisions for the time, place, and manner of conducting such activities. (Approved and filed Oct. 8, 1971.)

In the meantime, the California State Board of Education had developed "guidelines" conforming to the *Tinker* requirements for school districts.[38]

Sections 10,611 and 24,425.5 of the *Education Code* became California law on March 4, 1972.[39] Four days later, some students at University High School in West Los Angeles distributed and offered for sale on the school campus an underground tabloid-sized newspaper called *The Red Tide*, several issues of which were confiscated by the school authorities, who suspended the students involved for distributing literature "for sale" on the school property and for not first clearing the newspaper with the school's principal.[40] The students asked that all confiscated issues of the paper be returned to them, that the suspension be erased from their school records, and that the school administration recognize in the future their right to distribute the paper. The students charged that the action of the school authorities amounted to "prior restraint," which is prohibited under the new sections of the *Education Code*; legal counsel for the school, however, pointed out that under the above-mentioned code provisions the schools are empowered to set the "time, place, and manner" of distribution.[41] A guidebook, *Student Rights and Responsibilities*, was published in April 1972. This book, which contains freedom of expression "guidelines" adopted by the Los Angeles City school board in conformity with state law, declares: "Although a high degree of freedom is extended to the school newspaper staff, advisers and administrators retain the authority to censor when necessary.... [The principal] must retain final authority over the content, format, issuance, and other aspects of the publication."[42]

The publishers of *The Red Tide* maintained that, by requiring students to submit material to the principal before it could be distributed, board policy imposes "prior censorship," which denies them their constitutional right to publish and reach an audience; further they alleged that two school board publications, "The Local Board Policy for Student Rights and Responsibilities" and the handbook of *Student Rights and Responsibilities* are "vague, inconsistent, confusing, and overbroad."[43]

A school board regulation that places a *prior restraint* on freedom of expression in student publications, even publications produced without school sponsorship, may violate the First Amendment, unless certain safeguards are observed by the school authorities in drafting the regulation; thus, the Fourth Circuit Court of Appeals, in *Baughman v. Freienmuth*,[44] (1973), held that a school board regulation that requires principals to review and approve student publications produced without school sponsorship *prior to their general distribution in the school*, but which does not provide a time limit within which the principal must act, the method for review of the principal's decision, or precise definition of the term "distribution" is an unreasonable restriction of students' First Amendment rights. Challenged in this case was a school board regulation which read in pertinent part:

Under the following procedures, student publications produced without school sponsorship may be distributed in schools: ... A copy must be given to the principal for his review. If, in the opinion of the principal, the publication contains libelous or obscene language, advocates illegal actions, or is grossly insulting to any group or individual, the principal shall notify the sponsors of the publication that its distribution must stop forthwith or may not be initiated, and state his reasons therefor.

The court said this school regulation places a *prior restraint* on freedom of expression, which is denied to the government under the First Amendment. "In secondary schools, however, First Amendment rights of students are not coextensive with those of adults." However, there is a *presumption* in law against a school regulation such as this which places a *prior restraint* on freedom of expression; to overcome this presumption, said the court, the school regulation must come within the constitutional limits defined in the 1971 case of *Quarterman v. Byrd,*[45] where court had said:

School authorities may by appropriate regulation exercise prior restraint upon publications distributed on school premises during school hours in those special circumstances where they can reasonably forecast substantial disruption of or material interference with school activities on account of the distribution of such printed material. ... [There is a lack] of any criteria to be followed by the school authorities in determining whether to grant or deny permission, and of any procedural safeguards in the form of an expeditious review procedure of the decision of the school authorities.[46]

These two points are important for school authorities who must make the decision affecting students' rights of freedom of expression: there are no "criteria" to be followed in determining whether to grant or deny permission to distribute a student publication; and procedural safeguards must be provided for a review of the school's decision to deny freedom of expression.

As to procedure, said the court, this school regulation lacks the safeguard of a

specific and reasonably short period of time in which the principal must act. Moreover, it fails to provide a procedure for review of the principal's decision. In view of this lack of procedural safeguards, the regulation constitutes an unreasonable restriction on the First Amendment rights of school children.

The regulation's proscription against "distribution" was also described as unconstitutionally vague, and the court distinguished between two categories of material and the conditions necessary for "prior restraint" by school authorities:[47]

1. There may be no prior restraint of certain types of communicative material unless there is a disruption so substantial that it can be reasonably anticipated that the distribution would disrupt school operations.

2. With respect to other types of material, such as pornography, one copy may be the subject of what is legitimate prior restraint.

The challenged regulation's prohibition of material that advocates illegal actions or grossly insults any groups or individual seems to belong in the first category and thus goes beyond the permissible standard of forecasting substantial disruption.

Finally, there is always the danger that "criticism of the authorities or of their policies may be unconstitutionally choked off." Accordingly, "the use of terms of art such as 'libelous' and 'obscene' are not sufficiently precise and understandable by either high school students or administrators to be acceptable criteria."[48]

A superior court judge in California ordered the Oxnard High School to allow a seventeen-year old junior to run for a student body office without advance screening of his campaign material and platform by the school authorities. In *Berkowitz v. Oxnard Union High School District*, (1973),[49] the court issued a temporary restraining order requiring the school authorities to place the student's name on the ballot for the associated student body election or to postpone the election pending a full-scale hearing in the constitutionality of such "prior restraint." The complaint in the case stated:

The Oxnard Union High School has adopted a guideline for the student freedom of expression which provides that copies of any printed materials for distribution or posting should be submitted to the principal at least 48 hours in advance and that the principal will approve or disapprove within 24 hours thereafter, giving the reasons therefore. [*sic*] In the event of a denial by the principal the applicant may file a written appeal with the assistant superintendent of pupil personnel, whose decision shall be final.[50]

This is a total of seventy-two hours, and since the election in question was to be held within approximately twenty-four hours from the date of the filing of the complaint, it would "cause great and irreparable injury to the plaintiff in that he would be denied his right to campaign for the competitive elective office until after the election is held." Following issuance of the temporary restraining order, the school decided to proceed with the election; the student was allowed to run for office, and he won the student body presidency. Said the Oxnard High School principal, "The candidates were only asked, not required, to submit advance outlines of their speeches."[51]

Another consequence of the *Tinker* decision was the 1970 exchange of correspondence, excerpted below, between a California metropolitan school district and an attorney for the teachers in the district, which addressed itself to the question whether teachers, in order to express their opinions about national issues, might wear black armbands on the school campus. The attorney for the teachers, relying on the *Tinker case*, maintained that since students have the right to express political opinions, it would appear "that teachers have the same right of freedom of expression according to the First Amendment, so long as they do not take advantage of their position in class to indoctrinate students." The reply and interpretation by the school's attorney of the law as it applies to the right of teachers to wear armbands having political propaganda significance is set forth below:[52]

STATEMENT
(Attorney for the Teachers)

RE: Rights of Teachers
Tinker v. Des Moines School District

It has come to our attention that when teachers have, in order to express their opinion about national issues, chosen to wear black arm bands in the School System, they have been threatened with administrative action and have been charged with violation of Sec. 9013 and 9021 of the *Education Code*.

I hope that you have read the *Tinker v. Des Moines* case as decided by the U.S. Supreme Court stating that students have a right to express political opinions and it would seem to me that teachers have the same right of freedom of expression according to the First Amendment, so long as they do not take advantage of their position in the class to indoctrinate students.

We would appreciate your views on this before we decide to take any other action on behalf of the teachers involved or decide to make a test case out of it.

REPLY
(Attorney for the school district)

This school district generally has no objection to the display by elementary and secondary school teachers of armbands having political propaganda significance while such teachers are in the teachers' lunchroom, teachers' lounge or such other places on school grounds during the period beginning one hour before school opens and ending one hour after school closes, where they are not among, or within sight of, pupils. However, under the policy of this school district adopted pursuant to State Statutes, teachers may display neither armbands having political propaganda significance nor any other similar insigne while such teachers are in the classroom, corridors, libraries, play areas or such other places on school grounds during the period beginning one hour before school opens and ending one hour after school closes, while they are among, or within sight of, pupils.

This school district is of the view that the foregoing position is in consonance with law, including the holdings of: (a) the United States Supreme Court in *Tinker v. Des Moines Independent Community School District*, 89 S. Ct. 733 (1969), (b) the California Supreme Court in *Los Angeles Teachers Union v. Los Angeles City Board of Education*, 455 P (2d) 827 (1969), and (c) the California Appellate Court in *Dunbar v. Governing Board of Grosemont Junior College District*, 275 ACA (2d) (1969) and *Meyers v. Arcata School District*, 269 CA (2d) 549 (1969), as well as the clear intent and meaning of California Education Code sections 9012, 9013, and 9021.

This exchange of correspondence took place in 1970. Sections 9012 and 9013 of the *Education Code*, as noted above, were repealed in 1971.

Conduct Which "Materially and Substantially" Interferes with School Operations

An example of the dichotomy between student conduct that school officials may prohibit and student conduct that they must permit is shown by two cases decided by the United States Court of Appeals for the Fifth Circuit on the same day. In *Burnside v. Byars,*[53] students sought to wear buttons bearing the message "one man one vote" with "SNCC" inscribed in the center. School officials prohibited these buttons and suspended students who insisted on wearing them. The buttons were prohibited because of fear that they would cause a commotion and also because they had no bearing on the students' education. The school authorities believed that buttons would cause disruptions if passed around and discussed in the classrooms. There was evidence that the buttons did cause a "commotion" in the halls as students sought to see them. The court characterized the response of the students to the buttons, however, as "mild curiosity." The school authorities prohibited the wearing of so-called "freedom buttons," but permitted the wearing of other buttons of a political nature.

The court invalidated the school regulation prohibiting these buttons on the grounds that it was "arbitrary and unreasonable, and an unnecessary infringement on the students' protected right of free expression." While school officials have a substantial interest in providing for an orderly educational process and a wide discretion in prescribing rules of conduct, nevertheless:

The interest of the state in maintaining an educational system is a compelling one, giving rise to a balancing of First Amendment rights with the duty of the state to further and protect the public school system. The establishment of an educational program requires the formulation of rules and regulations necessary for the maintenance of an orderly program of classroom learning. In formulating regulations, including those pertaining to the discipline of school children, school officials have a wide latitude of discretion. But the school is always bound by the requirement that the rules and regulations must be reasonable. It is not for us to consider whether such rules are wise or expedient but merely whether they are a reasonable exercise of the power and discretion of the school authorities.

The court defined what is a "reasonable" regulation:

Regulations which are essential in maintaining order and discipline on school property are reasonable. Thus school rules which assign students to a particular class, forbid unnecessary discussion in the classroom and prohibit the exchange of conversation between students are reasonable even though these regulations infringe on such basic rights as freedom of speech and association, because they are necessary for the orderly presentation of classroom activities. Therefore, a reasonable regulation is one which measurably contributes to the maintenance of order and decorum within the educational system.

School authorities cannot infringe upon students' rights to free expression guaranteed by the First Amendment, unless the exercise of such rights "materially and substantially" interferes with the operations of the school.

But, with all of this in mind, we must also emphasize that school officials cannot ignore expressions of feelings with which they do not wish to contend. They cannot infringe on the students' right to free and unrestricted expression as guaranteed to them under the First Amendment to the Constitution, where the exercise of such rights in the school buildings and schoolrooms do not *materially and substantially* interfere with the requirements of appropriate discipline in the operation of the school.[54]

   The other case decided by the Fifth Circuit is *Blackwell v. Issaquena County Board of Education.*[55] The students also wore SNCC buttons. In addition to an inscription, these buttons depicted black and white hands joined together. In this case, the buttons occasioned disruptive conduct by the students: they passed them out in the corridors of the school and attempted to pin them on fellow students who did not want them; when told to remove the buttons, the students were belligerent and insulting; when asked to leave the school, they disrupted some classes. Told that they would be suspended unless they removed the buttons, a number of students did not, and they were suspended.

   The court in *Blackwell* held that the school regulation was reasonable, citing *Burnside*: a reasonable regulation is "one which is 'essential in maintaining order and discipline on school property' and 'which measurably contributes to the maintenance of order and decorum within the educational system.' "[56] The prohibition against buttons was reasonably related to the prevention of disruptive conduct.

A Few of "Tinker's" Prodigies

The aftermath of *Tinker* saw a large number of constitutional attacks in the federal courts (and in some state courts) on school rules restricting freedom of expression and on codes governing student dress and hair-styles.[57] Also at issue in these freedom of expression cases have been school athletic symbols, flags, school names and other such indicia expressing a viewpoint about controversial subjects, including desegregation.

   In *Guzick v. Drebus, Principal of Shaw High School*,[58] a student wore a button on his lapel and was suspended until he returned to school without the button. The school had an "informal" rule banning *all* emblems and insignia. The rule was never published,[59] but it had been applied uniformly and consistently for at least forty years. Because of fights and strong feelings existing among different groups at the school, tension was at an incendiary point. (Approximately 70 percent of the students were Black and 30 percent white.) Friction existed between the races and between students of the same race.

In upholding the school rule against buttons, the court distinguished the *Tinker case* wherein there was no threat of disruption, and said:

The button at issue in the instant case did not convey an inflammatory message. It does, however, portray the position of the wearer with respect to a political issue. Although there was evidence that the message conveyed in this particular button might be such as to inflame some of the students at Shaw High, the Court does not feel that such a result is likely.

Therefore, if this button were permitted, there would no longer be a rule prohibiting *all* emblems and insignia and the school authorities would have to decide whether to permit all buttons or to permit some, but not all, buttons. Hence,

any rule which attempts to permit the wearing of some buttons, but not others, would be virtually impossible to administer. It would involve school officials in a continuous search of the halls of students wearing the prohibited type of buttons. It would occasion ad hoc and inconsistent application. It would make the determination of permissible versus impermissible buttons difficult, if not impossible. . . .

A rule which permitted the wearing of some buttons but not others would itself be disruptive. . . . If a line is drawn between provocative and non-provocative buttons, the students most desiring to wear buttons, who desire to wear buttons of a provocative type, will feel discriminated against. . . . The wearing of buttons at Shaw High would greatly affect the discipline problem and will require that school administrators devote an even greater portion of their time to discipline. Buttons will raise the emotions of students at Shaw High, distract them from their educational pursuits, . . . the wearing of some buttons and not others will itself lead to disruptions of the educational process at Shaw. Similarly, the rule which permits the wearing of any button will occasion the wearing of provocative and inciting buttons and will also disrupt the educational process . . . the prohibition of buttons and other insignia at Shaw High significantly contributes to the preservation of peace and order, and . . . the blanket prohibition of buttons and other insignia is reasonably related to the prevention of the distractions and disruptive and violent conduct at Shaw High.

Thus the court concluded that the wearing of buttons at the school would add to the already incendiary situation and lead to material and substantial disruption of the educational process.

In this case, unlike *Tinker,*[60] there was more than an "undifferentiated fear" of a disturbance; there was a history of disturbances, and there was good reason to anticipate that disturbances would result in the future—if buttons were permitted. Therefore, the rule was reasonably related to the prevention of disruptive conduct at Shaw High School.

So also at a high school located near a military base where students wanted to protest the Vietnam War. *Hill v. Lewis*[61] held that the school's prohibition of armbands did not violate constitutional rights where more than one-third of the students were children of military personnel. Referring to *Tinker*, the court said:

First, "the wearing of an armband for the purpose of expressing certain views is the type of symbolic act that is within the Free Speech Clause of the First Amendment." ... Second, "undifferentiated fear or apprehension of disturbance is not enough to overcome the right to freedom of expression." ... Third, the burden of proof is on the school officials to demonstrate any facts which might reasonably have led them to forecast substantial disruption of or material interference with school activities. And fourth, conduct by the student, in class or out of it, which for any reason—whether it stems from time, place, or type of behavior—materially disrupts classwork or involves substantial disorder or invasion of the rights of others is, of course, not immunized by the constitutional guarantee of freedom of speech. ...

The Court in *Tinker* found that the wearing of armbands was entirely divorced from any actually or potentially disruptive conduct by those participating in it, under the circumstances of that case. ... The present case is factually distinguishable.[62]

In the *Hill case*, at least three different viewpoints were represented by the student groups, some with known antagonistic views. There had been active participation in organizing and advertising the demonstration, including marching in the school hallways, chanting, disrespect toward teachers, incidents of flag disrespect, and threats of violence. The order extended to *all* armbands, not just those with a particular symbol. The court refused to restrain the school authorities from suspending any pupil who participated in the anti-Vietnam War demonstration.

The *Tinker* decision was distinguished in *Melton v. Young*,[63] which involved the use of these symbols at a Tennessee high school: "Rebel," as the school's nickname; "Dixie," as the school's pep song; and impliedly, the Confederate flag as the school's banner. Integration of this formerly all-white high school was followed by disturbances, which led to the adoption of a code that prohibited "provocative symbols on clothing." A white student who wore a jacket with an emblem depicting the Confederate flag was suspended. The student charged that his First and Fourteenth Amendment rights had been violated; the court saw two questions involved here:

1. Did the regulation prohibiting "provocative symbols on clothing" violate free speech? Yes, was the answer. The regulation was unconstitutional because it failed to describe precisely the proscribed conduct and was thus "too vague, broad, and imprecise."

2. Could the student's suspension be sustained on the basis of the principal's statutory authority under state law which obligates him to maintain "such discipline and order within the school as will permit the educational process to be carried out?" Yes, again was the answer.

In *Tinker*, there was an absence of potential disruptive conduct, whereas here the school officials could reasonably believe that further disruptions would develop if plaintiff's conduct was not prohibited. "The evidence in this case is quite overwhelming that the Confederate symbol has been a cause of very serious, material and substantial disturbance in the school throughout the previous school year."[64]

Thus, the court upheld the student's suspension as constitutionally permissible, yet found the student conduct code was vague and overbroad and therefore invalid.

A southern school board, acting at the request of Negro students, ordered the high school to discontinue the use of the Confederate flag as a banner and the name "Rebels" for the school's athletic teams. This order was challenged by a parish resident, whose complaint was dismissed by the court, which said the board's decision was "an act relating to public policy within the domain of the general power of the board, and involving the public welfare of the community affected by it," and thus was *not subject to judicial review.*[65]

The order of a district court that a Confederate flag be removed from the office of an integrated school was affirmed by the court of appeals: "Under the facts of this case the [district court's] order banning symbols or indicia expressing the school board's or its employee's desire to maintain segregated schools . . . is fully warranted.[66]

The use of the Confederate flag as the school's symbol and "Rebels" as the school's official nickname was held to be unconstitutional in *Augustus v. School Board of Escambia County* (1973),[67] where the U.S. District Court issued an order prohibiting students from displaying the flag or using the nickname while attending school or participating in any school sponsored activity. Reasoning from *Brown v. Board of Education of Topeka* (1954), which ordered unitary school systems, the court said:

On the basis of its findings of fact, the court concludes, and holds, that the name "Rebels" and the use of the Confederate Battle Flag seriously interfered with the effective operation of a unitary school system at this school. . . . Removal of the symbols may not eliminate racial tension at the school. However, as long as the symbols remain, this tension will have a focal point. A unitary educational system cannot be maintained under such conditions.[68]

Citing the *Tinker case*, the court said it had the power to regulate certain types of expression in a situation such as presented in this case.

The language of a Texas school regulation, namely, "Any student who participates in a boycott, sit-in, stand-in, walk-out, or other related forms of distraction . . . shall by his action be subject to automatic suspension from school," was held in *Dunn v. Tyler Independent School District,*[69] to be constitutionally overbroad because it arbitrarily prohibited all such demonstrations without limiting itself to those which cause "*material and substantial* disruption of the educational environment.*" The regulation was vague, since it contained no precise definition of a disruption nor stated explicitly under what circumstances the automatic suspension provision would be applied. When constitutional liberties are involved, "precision of regulation is essential since the state may regulate in this area only with narrow specificity."[70]

The "Thicket" of Haircut Cases[71]

Courts across the country are not in agreement that school authorities may regulate the length of a student's hair,[72] nor do they all prohibit beards and moustaches from being worn by teachers or students. The Supreme Court of the United States has several times refused to review a haircut case.[73] The Court has denied certiorari in cases where the lower court sustained the school board, and it has also denied it in cases where the lower court overruled the school board.[74] The decisions, now many, involve both students and teachers, and they are about equally divided; almost half hold in favor of the students while the others hold for the school boards. Fewer state cases, however, have been litigated in

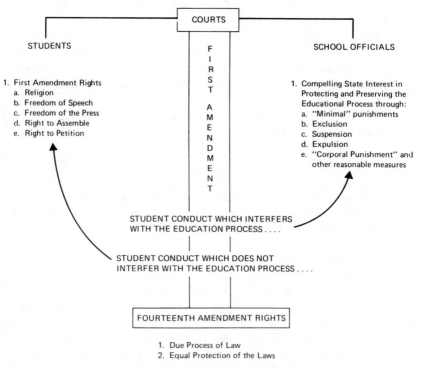

Figure 5-1. Balancing of Interests.

this area.[75] It is quite clear that the Supreme Court's ruling in *Tinker v. Des Moines Independent Community School District*[76] encouraged students to argue in the federal courts the right to wear their hair as they chose.[77]

There are two lines of reasoning courts follow in deciding haircut cases:[78] some courts see no constitutional merit in the students' claim and therefore uphold school board hair regulations simply on the basis of *reasonableness*, while other courts hold that a student's right to wear his hair as he pleases is *fundamental* and can be abridged only on a showing that the hair-style would disrupt the educational process. In these latter courts, students have generally prevailed; but there have been a number of cases in which school boards have demonstrated sufficient disruption.

Judicial responses to two key inquiries, then, provide the bases upon which "hair case" rulings have diverged: (1) does the student's interest in wearing long hair or a beard enjoy any special constitutional protection? and (2) if it does, what kind of showing must a school board make in order to override this interest?[79]

In some instances, students excluded from the public schools because of their hair have charged that this interferes with a *business interest*, i.e., they are "performers" who have developed a "public image" that depends upon long hair; however, wigs are common today. Thus, an early state case, *Leonard v. School Committee of Attleboro* (1965),[80] upheld the school committee's exclusion of a boy performer (who had actually appeared at the New York World Fair and at the Newport Jazz Festival) saying that the right to suspend a pupil because of the length of his hair is within the *discretionary powers* of school authorities and that the courts would not disturb those powers even where the pupil is a professional musician. Where three Dallas, Texas, students wore "Beatle-type" haircuts in violation of a school regulation and were thus excluded from the school, the court, in *Ferrell v. Dallas Independent School District*,[81] said: the state has "a paramount interest in maintaining an effective and efficient school system," and held that the rule against long hair was not unreasonable under state or federal constitutional laws.

Three Negro high school students who refused to shave when ordered by the school authorities to do so in conformity with a "good grooming rule" were suspended by action of the school superintendent.[82] The students filed a suit, seeking reinstatement to the school. The appellate court stated the applicable law as follows:

It was proper for school authorities to establish rules and regulations in the interest of school management and this included a hairstyle regulation. . . . Such regulations, and regulations which deal generally with dress and the like, are a part of the disciplinary process which is necessary in maintaining a balance as between the rights of individual students and the rights of the whole in the functioning of schools. The touchstone for sustaining such regulations is the demonstration that they are necessary to alleviate interference with the educational process.[83]

Evidence was presented which indicated that the failure of male students to shave has "a diverting influence on the student body," that the growth of hair on the plaintiffs' faces was extensive enough to make it "reasonable to require them to shave," that the plaintiffs were aware of the good grooming rule, and that no racial discrimination or denial of equal protection was involved in applying the rule to them. Therefore: "The rule in question is founded on a rational basis and . . . was not arbitrarily applied. It follows that no substantial federal constitutional question was presented." The court chose to treat the issue as one of disagreement over whether "the students have reached a point where they need to shave."

In *Finot*[84] a high school teacher was transferred from classroom teaching to home teaching because he wore a beard in violation of school policy; the California court said that a teacher has a constitutional right to wear a beard where a "good cause" for a school policy banning the beard is not shown. The benefit gained by the public from a restraint on the appearance of teachers must outweigh the right of the teacher to wear the beard, and such was not shown in this case.

In *Akin,*[85] where a sixteen-year-old boy refused to shave off his beard in conformity with the "good-grooming" policy of the Riverside School District and was expelled from school, the board was able to show that the wearing of a beard would be "definitely disruptive of the educational process" and have "adverse effect on the educational environment": two past instances where the wearing of moustaches by students had created school problems were cited. In deciding this case in favor of the school authorities, the California court said that the question of whether the school's grooming policy is an unreasonable infringement of the student's constitutional rights must be determined by these three criteria:

I. Whether the restraint imposed on the male students' freedom to grow a beard rationally and reasonably relates to the enhancement of a free public education.

II. Whether the benefits which the public gains by the restraint prohibiting a beard outweigh the resulting impairment of the students' right to grow a beard, and

III. Whether any alternative less subversive to the students' constitutional right is available.[86]

The court applied these criteria and found that the student's dismissal was justified. The "good grooming" regulation contributed to the "maintenance of order and decorum" in the educational system. The pupil was not denied equal protection of the law, since the school board uniformly applied the "good grooming" regulation to all male students.

Following the decision of this case, the Riverside Unified School District adopted in September 1969 the following campus dress and grooming policy, which recites the district's philosophy on dress and grooming, the requirements of state law, board policy, and administrative regulations to guide local school authorities in implementing the philosophy of the district.

RIVERSIDE UNIFIED SCHOOL DISTRICT
INSTRUCTIONAL SERVICES

DRESS AND GROOMING POLICY
Approved by the Board of Education September 8, 1969

PHILOSOPHY

The Dress and Grooming Policy is created in the belief that appearance has an effect in creating an atmosphere conducive to learning. Responsibility for achieving this atmosphere is shared by the student, his parents and school personnel. In view of the District's philosophy of encouraging and guiding individual schools to adapt the educational programs to meet the needs of the individual school community, it is appropriate that the district Dress and Grooming Policy provide some latitude within policy guidelines.

STATE LAW

1. *Adoption of Rules by Governing Board*
   Education Code 925—
   The governing board of each school district shall prescribe and enforce rules not inconsistent with law or with the rules prescribed by the State Board of Education, for its own government.
2. *Pupils to be Neat and Clean on Entering School*
   Article 7, Sec. 64 of California Adm. Code—
   All pupils who go to school without proper attention having been given to personal cleanliness, or neatness of dress, may be sent home, to be properly prepared for school or shall be required to prepare themselves for the schoolroom before entering. Every school building shall be provided with sanitary equipment for personal cleanliness.

BOARD POLICY

1. All students shall be required to dress and groom for school with attention to and emphasis upon the following:
   a. Neatness
   b. Cleanliness
   c. Modesty
   d. Decency
   e. Safety
   f. Personal and public health

2. Dress and grooming requirements and/or restrictions within any school shall be flexible and relate only to the criteria listed in number 1 above.
3. Any student whose manner of dress and/or grooming attracts undue attention to himself or causes a distraction to others within the school may be sent home to be properly prepared for school or shall be required to prepare himself for the schoolroom before entering.

ADMINISTRATIVE REGULATIONS

1. The respective schools are to use every necessary means of communication to inform parents and pupils of the Dress and Grooming Policy.
2. The interpretation and enforcement of the Dress and Grooming Policy is vested in the school principal although he may delegate it to a vice-principal, dean or director of Pupil Personnel Services.
3. The parents or guardians are to be notified whenever a pupil appears in violation of the Dress and Grooming Policy.
4. In cases of continued violation of the Dress and Grooming Policy, the principal of the school or his representative shall discipline the pupil according to the Code of Pupil Discipline of the Riverside Unified School District.
5. The parents or guardians shall be referred to the supervisor of Child Welfare and Attendance if further consultation is necessary.

Some school districts have no published policy with respect to the use of corporal punishment in the schools for disciplinary purposes, yet most districts do have student handbooks and guidelines concerning dress and grooming; in many cases, however, school policies on dress and grooming are new and have been developed since the *Tinker* decision in 1969 which opened up student rights.

In *Montalvo v. Madera Unified School District Board of Education,*[87] a school district regulation limiting the hair length of students was upheld upon the rationale that hair style, without more, is not *per se* an expression of speech within the protection of the First Amendment and not encompassed within the "liberty" umbrella of the Fourteenth Amendment.

However, in *Meyers v. Arcata Union High School District,*[88] a high school dress policy stating that "extremes of hair styles" were not acceptable was *unconstitutionally vague*, and the school could not expel a male student on the basis that his hair violated that policy. The words "extremes of hair styles are not acceptable," the court said, made the code vague and standardless:

Extremes of hair styles, however, are not facts: whether a given hair style is "extreme" or not is a matter of opinion, and the definitive opinion here rested in the sole—and neither controlled nor guided—judgment of a single school official. To him, an "extreme" style was "deviation from acceptable wear," but it was he alone who decided what was "acceptable" in the first instance and what was "deviation" in the next.[89]

Citing the *Akin case*, the court noted that because a long hair style is indistinguishable from a beard for constitutional purposes, a male effecting it in a school is entitled to the same protection. "Adulthood is not a prerequisite; the state must heed the constitutional rights of all persons, including schoolboys."[90] School authorities, nevertheless, may impose more stringent regulations upon the constitutional rights of minors than upon those of adults: "Where there is an invasion of protected freedoms . . . the power of the state to control the conduct of children reaches beyond the scope of its authority over adults." It, therefore, follows that not every limitation

upon the exercise of secondary students' constitutional rights by a school district governing board, is prohibited and, where there is empirical evidence that an aspect of a student's dress or appearance (such as hairstyle) has a disruptive effect within a school, the board may prohibit it.[91]

Accordingly, the school board could validly exercise its statutory rule-making power to require that the student wear his hair at a shorter length. But the dress policy as written is "vague and standardless," and hence the state cannot demand "compliance with an unconstitutionally vague standard of conduct."[92]

In *Davis v. Firment*,[93] a student was suspended because his long hair violated a school regulation, and the court found that the regulation served a necessary disciplinary purpose, since long hair had caused fights at the school. Said the court, quoting the school superintendent,

gross deviation from the norm does cause a disruption of the learning atmosphere and can create an undesirable separateness among students. Furthermore gross deviation can be and has been dysfunctional in the social adjustment of children.

However, in *Westley v. Rossi*,[94] where the school authorities argued that the school "must assume its share of responsibility for seeing to it that students dress neatly and appropriately and that they develop habits of cleanliness and good grooming," the court replied that on the contrary,

the rule is an attempt to impose taste or preference as a standard. The standard of appearance and dress of last year are not those of today nor will they be those of tomorrow. Regulation of conduct by school authorities must bear a reasonable basis to the ordinary conduct of the school curriculum or to carrying out of the responsibility of the school. No moral or social ill consequences will result to other students due to the presence or absence of long hair nor should it have any bearing on the wearer or other students to learn or to be taught.[95]

A "dress code" banning long hair on a college campus was held unconstitutional by a district court judge who described the code as arbitrary and in violation of the Constitution. The college had not shown that long hair interfered with the college educational process. The college code provided that: "Male students may not wear 'hair which falls below the eyebrows, or covers all or part of the ears or hangs directly over the collar of a dress shirt.' " On appeal, however, the code was upheld by the circuit court, which said:

> This is not a question of preference for or against certain male hair styles or the length to which persons desire to wear their hair. This court could not care less. It is a question of the right of school authorities to develop a code of dress and conduct best conducive to the fulfillment of their responsibility to educate, and to do it without unconstitutionally infringing upon the rights of those who must live under it. We do not believe that the plaintiffs have established the existence of any substantial constitutional right which is in these two instances being infringed. We are satisfied that the school authorities have acted with considera- tion for the rights and feelings of their students and have enacted their codes, including the ones in question here, in the best interests of the educational process. *A court might disagree with their professional judgment, but it should not take over the operation of their schools.*[96]

Referring to the "thicket of recent cases" concerned with the right of a student to wear long hair in a public school, the Court of Appeals for the First Circuit in *Richards v. Thurston*[97] documented its "pro-hair" decision with a summary of how the various courts have split in their decisions on the subject.[98] The case involved the suspension of a student who wore his hair "falling loosely about the shoulders" and who refused to have it cut. The court held that the suspension violated the student's "personal liberty" in the absence of "state justification" for the intrusion. In some of the decisions holding *against the student*, the courts rely on prior disruptions at the schools caused by unusual hair-styles and require the student to carry the burden of demonstrating the importance of the right he asserts; while in a few of the cases holding *for the student*, the courts disregard evidence of prior disruptions caused by unusual hair-styles. Thus: "the "pro-hair courts [have] held explicitly or implicitly that the school authorities failed to carry their burden of justifying the regulation against long hair."[99] Viewed in this analytical framework, the question of school authorities' power to regulate hair becomes one of *who must bear the burden of proof*—the school or the student?

What appears superficially as a dispute over which side has the burden of persuasion is, however, a very fundamental dispute over the extent to which the Constitution protects such uniquely personal aspects of one's life as the length of his hair, for the view one takes of the constitutional basis—if any—for the right asserted may foreshadow both the placement and weight of the evidentiary burden which he imposes on the parties before him.[100]

The court then determined that a "personal liberty" is at stake in the haircut cases: "We conclude that within the commodious concept of liberty, embracing freedoms great and small, is the right to wear one's hair as he wishes"—and hence the question becomes whether there is an "outweighing state interest"[101] that justifies the intrusion? The answer requires that courts must take into account: the liberty asserted, the context in which it is asserted, and the extent to which the intrusion is confined to the "legitimate public interest to be served. For example, the right to appear *au naturel* at home is relinquished when one sets foot on a public sidewalk."[102] So, too, the nature of a public school education "requires limitations on one's personal liberty in order for the learning process to proceed."

Finally, a school rule which forbids skirts shorter than a certain length while on school grounds would require less justification than one requiring hair to be cut, which affects the student twenty-four hours a day, seven days a week, nine months a year.[103]

The court concluded by saying that once a "personal liberty" is shown to be affected by a school rule, the burden of justifying the rule—in "the absence of an inherent, self-evident justification on the face of the rule"[104]—is on the school authorities.

There is no constitutional *right* for a student to wear his hair long in direct disobedience to a school rule or regulation, said the court in *Davis v. Firment*.[105] Plaintiff's contention was that First, Eighth, and Ninth Amendment rights were violated. The sole issue in the case, said the court, was whether the student has such a constitutional *right*; there being no such right, "the questions which therefore arise are whether the School Board had a legitimate interest in enforcing grooming regulations and whether this rule was a reasonable means of accomplishing this interest."[106] The school rule was a *reasonable means* of accomplishing a "legitimate interest" of the school board.

The Eighth Amendment argument, namely, that requiring a pupil to cut his hair constitutes "cruel and unusual punishment," was said to be "wholly without merit." The Ninth Amendment argument, however, was examined in detail.

Plaintiff's argument under the Ninth Amendment is entirely constructed around *Griswold v. State of Connecticut.* . . . In that case the Supreme Court held Connecticut's anti-contraceptive statute unconstitutional because its enforcement would violate the individual's right to privacy. Justice Douglas wrote the opinion of the Court and said that the particular provisions of the Bill of Rights have *"penumbras, formed by emanations from those guarantees that help give them life and substance."* The guarantees which Justice Douglas found to form the basis of the right of privacy were the right of association in the First Amendment, the prohibition against the compulsory quartering of soldiers "in any house" in time of peace in the Third Amendment, the protection against "unreasonable searches and seizures" guaranteed by the Fourth Amendment, the Fifth Amendment's Self-Incrimination Clause, which "enables the citizen to create a zone of privacy which government may not force him to surrender to his detriment," and the Ninth Amendment, which provides: "The enumeration in the Constitution, of certain rights, shall not be construed to deny or disparage others retained by the people."

Justice Douglas' only reference to the Ninth Amendment was to quote it, and plaintiff's strong reliance on this provision seems rather to be based on Justice Goldberg's concurring opinion, in which he said that the term "liberty" in the Fourteenth Amendment's Due Process Clause "embraces the right of marital privacy though that right is not mentioned explicitly in the Constitution." To justify this interpretation of liberty, Justice Goldberg asserted that the Ninth Amendment manifests the Framers' desire to give Constitutional protection to other fundamental rights not specifically mentioned in the Bill of Rights. . . .

Plaintiff contends that student Davis has a "fundamental personal right of free choice of grooming" and argues that such a right can be found under the reasoning of the *Griswold* case. But if this case is to fall within the ambit of *Griswold*, there must be some specific provision or provisions of the Bill of Rights from which student Davis' right of grooming emanates, or, if it is permissible to follow the approach of Justice Goldberg, the right must at least be "fundamental." The Court is of the opinion that this right is not of such a nature that it can be based on the guarantees provided in the Bill of Rights and, while the right of *privacy* may be so sacred as to be "fundamental," the same certainly cannot be said for the "right of free choice of grooming."[107]

The cases mostly involve male hair-styles; however, in *Susan Sims v. Colfax Community School District*[108] the plaintiff was a female student who challenged the constitutionality of a school rule that stated: "Hair must be kept one finger width above the eyebrows, clear across the forehead."[109] Noting that previous hirsute suits involved males and that, "to the court's knowledge," this was the first case involving a girl's hair length,[110] the court applied the test of "reasonableness," saying that the "appropriate analysis in determining reasonableness is that of weighing the individual's interest in engaging in the forbidden activity against the state's interest in circumscribing such activity."[111] Noting that the case law on student hair varies from place to place, the court offered this summary of the approaches other courts have used in these cases:[112]

1. Some courts have assumed that a student's interest in the selection of hair style is to be afforded the same degree of protection as that granted First Amendment rights such as free speech.[113] That becomes the basis of their decisions.

2. Other courts, however, state that a student's choice of hair style is at least a highly protected right though possibly *not* within the First Amendment.[114]

The courts described in (1) and (2) above have attached great importance to choice of hair-style by public school students and have held that the state is permitted to invade this interest only upon a showing of *compelling reasons* for so doing or upon a showing that if the forbidden conduct is allowed there would be a *material and substantial* interference to the educational system. Consequently, "hair rules have been upheld where the school demonstrated that long hair actually resulted in disruption of the school."[115]

However, where the school was unable to support the hair rule with incidents of disruption within the school, the rules have been found unreasonable and, therefore, unconstitutional.[116]

3. A few courts have adopted a different approach. These cases do not assign any particular importance to a student's right to wear any hair-style desired. They merely state that if the hair rule is reasonably calculated to prevent disruption or interference, the rule is constitutional.[117] These latter courts only "look to see whether the rule might prevent disruption and do not necessarily require the school to make an objective showing of disruption."

Two arguments were advanced by the school district for upholding the rule in this case, neither one of which was acceptable to the court: (1) support of the rule promotes good citizenship by teaching respect for authority and instilling discipline.[118] Recall that the same argument constituted one of the Pugsley principles (1923); this rationale was unacceptable in the present case, for to accept it, said the court, would mean that any rule made by a school authority, however arbitrary or capricious, could be justified by the schools. (2) The girl's typing instructor had complained that she was unable to "see the plaintiff's eyes during class," presumably because her hair hung down over her face, and "eye observation is necessary" for proper typing observation. Recognizing the pedagogical importance of eye observation in typing instruction, the court was "totally unconvinced that such a problem actually existed in this case."[119]

Thereupon, the school rule regulating the girl's hair was found to "unnecessarily and unreasonably circumscribe the student's constitutional rights under the Fourteenth Amendment."

Mr. Justice Black, speaking as a circuit justice from his chambers in Washington, D.C., on February 11, 1971 in the case of *Karr v. Schmidt*,[120] said the following.

I refuse to hold for myself that the federal courts have constitutional power to interfere in this way with the public school system operated by the States. And I furthermore refuse to predict that our Court will hold they have such power. It is true that we have held that this Court does have power under the Fourteenth Amendment to bar state public schools from discriminating against Negro students on account of their race but we did so by virtue of a direct, positive command in the Fourteenth Amendment, which, like the other Civil War Amendments, was primarily designed to outlaw racial discrimination by the States. There is no such direct, positive command about local school rules with reference to the length of hair state school students must have. And I cannot now predict this Court will hold that the more or less vague terms of either the Due Process or Equal Protection Clause have robbed the States of their traditionally recognized power to run their school systems in accordance with their own best judgments as to the appropriate length of hair for students. . . . Surely the federal judiciary can perform no greater service to the Nation than to leave the States unhampered in the performance of their purely local affairs. Surely few policies can be thought of that States are more capable of deciding than the length of the hair of school-boys. There can, of course, be honest differences of opinion . . . but it would be difficult to prove by reason, logic, or common sense that the federal judiciary is more competent to deal with hair length than are the local school authorities and state legislatures of all our 50 States. Perhaps if the courts will leave the States free to perform their own constitutional duties they will at least be able successfully to regulate the length of hair their public school students can wear.

Whereas the United States Supreme Court, in January 1972, without comment, refused to review a school "haircut" case, Mr. Justice Douglas, however, wrote a dissent.[121] Douglas declared that it "seems incredible that under our federalism" a state has the power to deny a public education to a student simply because his hair-style does not comport with the standards set by the school board: "Some institutions in Asia require their enrollees to shave their heads. . . . Would we sustain a public school regulation requiring male students to have crew cuts?" Noting that students are "persons" under our Constitution, in school as well as out, and that a student has a "full panoply of constitutional rights, though he is a minor," Douglas declared:

Hair style is highly personal, an idiosyncrasy which I had assumed was left to family or individual control and was of no legitimate concern to the state. It seems to me to be as such a purely private choice as was the family-student decision, sustained against a State's prohibition, to study the German language in a public school. Meyer v. Nebraska. . . . That family-student right, the Court held, was included within "liberty" as the word is used in the Fourteenth Amendment. . . . Opposed there—as in the present case—is the authoritarian philosophy favoring regimentation.

While the word *liberty* is not defined in the Constitution, the Supreme Court said in the *Griswold case*[122] that "it includes at least the fundamental rights 'retained by the people' under the Ninth Amendment."[123] Douglas then compares one's selection of his hair-style with his taste for food, for certain kinds of music, art, and reading—all of which are "fundamental in our constitutional scheme." "An epidemic of lice might conceivably authorize a shearing of locks," under the state's police powers, and other such crises could be imagined.

Noting that the federal courts are in "conflict and the decisions in disarray," and that the Supreme Court has denied certiorari both where the lower court has sustained the school board and also where it has overruled the school board, Douglas concludes that the "question tendered is of great personal concern to many and of unusual constitutional importance which we should resolve."[124] *Compare this with Justice Black's statement that the states should be left free "to perform their own constitutional duties."*

Finally, there is a kind of analogy between inmates in a prison and students who are compelled by the state to attend a school; the student haircut cases have been cited and distinguished by the courts in situations involving prisoners who also refuse to obey "grooming" rules. Thus, in *Brooks v. Wainwright*[125] where an inmate protested the rule that he "shave twice a week and receive periodic haircuts," the Court cited *Ferrell v. Dallas Independent School District* to support its argument that the prison regulation did not violate the inmate's "freedom of expression."[126] In *Blake v. Pryse,*[127] a prison inmate objected to regulation of his "hair, beard and/or moustache" which are, "as much a part of the petitioner as his arm or leg and therefore not subject to the prejudice and/or personal value judgments of the . . . prison officials.[128] To which the Court replied that the prison regulation was justified for "purposes of identification and hygiene." The Court distinguished *Westley v. Rossi,*[129] a school case, as being far different from a "situation involving a prisoner." In *Winsby v. Walsh,*[130] a 1971 California prison case, the district court held that

prison rules and regulations forbidding prisoners from wearing long hair and beards were reasonable especially in view of difficulty guards would have in identifying prisoners if they were permitted to have changing lengths of hair and beards in various styles and lengths.

The inmate held the "key" to his release from segregation from the other prisoners at any time he agreed to comply with the reasonable grooming rules, and hence the "fact that he was placed in segregation for period of ten months did not constitute cruel and unusual punishment."

In *Kientz v. Department of Corrections* (1973),[131] where a correctional officer at San Quentin State Prison was dismissed because he refused "to trim his sideburns to the middle of the ear" which his superiors said violated the rules that officers be of a "neat and clean" appearance, there being no written regulations at the Prison on the length of sideburns, the California Court of Appeal reversed a decision of the trial court, saying that "the standard of grooming was unconstitutionally vague and thus deprived" the employee of due process. The court cited high school hair regulation cases—*Finot, Myers,* and *Montalvo*—to show that the wearing of one's hair in a certain fashion is a form of expression protected by the First Amendment. A public agency that would require a waiver of such rights as a condition of public employment must demonstrate that the political restraints rationally relate to the enhancement of the public service, that the benefits the public gains by the restraints outweigh the resulting impairment of constitutional rights, and that no alternatives less subversive of constitutional rights are available.[132]

In sum, the order given the petitioner to cut his sideburns was based upon a standard that was defective in that it lacked the specificity required of governmental regulations which limit the exercise of constitutional rights.[133]

If the wearing of sideburns is a form of expression, per se, and as such is entitled to the protection of the Fourteenth Amendment, a waiver of such constitutional right may be exacted as a condition of public employment only where there is a "compelling" public interest justifying such waiver; on the other hand, if the right is protected only by the due process clauses of the Constitution, the regulation is presumed valid in the absence of a clear violation of the constitutional right; the burden is upon those who assail it to prove its invalidity; and the regulation need only be justified by some reasonable relationship between the legitimate concerns of the governmental agency or body promulgating the regulation and the objectives of the regulations.[134]

Disciplinary Actions by School Authorities

There is a wide range of disciplinary actions that school administrators and teachers may take when a pupil violates a school rule, and these include such "minimal" punishments as withholding school privileges, removal from the classroom, detention after school (if no hazard is incurred when the child returns for home at a later hour), writing a sentence repeatedly on the blackboard, sitting in an isolated part of the classroom, assignment of additional homework, a trip to the principal's office, and so forth. Courts generally uphold school authorities when they impose such "minimal" punishments, and it is doubtful if the misbehaving pupil would even have a case in most such instances.

However, other forms of disciplinary action, such as "suspension" from school, the use of "corporal punishment," etc. have been tested in recent court cases. *Exclusion* from school generally refers to a statutory requirement that a school district must deny admission of a child to a public school in the first instance, as for health reasons, a condition that affects the welfare of the other students, or age; *suspension* signifies dismissal from the school for a specific period of time (a day or several days) and usually by the principal, but also in some cases by a teacher;[135] while *expulsion* means permanent dismissal. It is not clear that a pupil can be permanently expelled from a public school; however, for good cause, a pupil can be removed permanently from a *regular* public school if the state places him in a special school.

Very often the court cases involving "suspension" have turned not upon the question whether the school has a regulation governing the student's misconduct nor upon the "reasonableness" of the regulation if one does exist, but rather on the legal issue whether the student had a right to a *"prior* hearing" and whether that right had been violated. This is called "due process."

Not only must the rules and regulations adopted by the school district for maintaining discipline be reasonable, but they must also be applied and enforced with *due process*. The Fourteenth Amendment declares: "nor shall any State deprive any person of life, liberty, or property, without due process of law." Stated positively, the reverse of this is that a state may deprive a person of his life, liberty, or property, it it is accomplished by due process of law. The question naturally arises as to what do we mean by "due process of law" when that term is applied to discipline cases in education.

There are *two types of due process* which must be carefully observed by school administrators when handling discipline cases: *procedural* due process, and *substantive* due process.

Procedural due process means that if an individual student (or his parents) is to be deprived of his rights (as cited above), a constitutionally approved procedure must be followed. There are three necessary factors if constitutional procedural due process is to exist; these are:

1. *Notice.* The individual must be given proper notice that he is about to be deprived of his rights;

2. *Hearing.* He must be given an opportunity to be heard by the school authorities.

3. *Fairness.* The hearing must be conducted fairly. An example of procedural due process in a school situation might be this: if a parent is to be punished for refusal to comply with the compulsory school attendance law, he must be given proper notice, afforded an opportunity to be heard, and the hearing must be fairly conducted. A leading case on procedural due process for students is *Dixon v. Alabama State Board of Education*, 294 F. 2d 150 (1961), wherein the Court said that the nature of the hearing would depend upon the facts and circumstances of each particular case and would involve a balancing of the interests of the school in preserving the educational atmosphere against the student's right to due process.

Substantive due process means that the state, if it is going to deprive a person of his right to life, liberty, or property, must have a *valid objective* and the means which is used must be reasonably calculated to achieve that objective. For example, the courts have consistently held that the state may require school age children to submit to vaccination before attending school. The state's objective is clear; it is to provide for the general health and well-being of school children. If the child is to remain in reasonably good health and in regular attendance at the school, he needs immunization from common diseases. This is a valid objective and vaccination is a means reasonably calculated to achieve it. Vaccination of school children, therefore, meets the substantive due process requirement of the law. The vaccination requirement has been uniformly upheld as constitutional. A recent case, *In Re Elwell*, 284 N.Y.S. 2d 924 (1967), upheld a New York law requiring school children to submit to immunization against poliomyelitis.[136]

As a practical matter, in most instances involving the "minimal" punishments referred to above, due process is not involved, although where a case is brought by a student a court may question whether the student's rights were infringed because of the lack of a "hearing."

A most favorable due process case for school students is *Mills v. Board of Education*,[137] which ordered a hearing prior to suspension "for any period in excess of two days." *Murray v. West Baton Rouge Parish School Board*[138] supports the educator's right to inflict "minimal punishments" by a summary suspension for "a few days."

"The Seventh and Eighth Circuits have upheld suspensions of 7 and 3 days (reduced from 5) respectively without prior hearings";[139] in one of these cases, the court approved an Illinois law requiring safeguards for suspensions in excess of seven days, while suspensions for less than that time "for reasonably proscribed conduct" were viewed as a "minor disciplinary penalty."[140] Expulsion from school, however, is an entirely different matter; thus, in *Givens v. Poe*,[141] the court said that due process requires a hearing prior to "expulsion or prolonged suspension from school." In *DeJesus v. Penberthy*,[142] the court voided an expulsion and granted leave to the plaintiff to reapply for admission to the school "unless the Board holds a new hearing within ten days."

Suspension must be for violations of school rules that "reasonably proscribe student conduct"; otherwise, courts will not support the actions of school authorities. Unlawful suspensions have been ordered expunged from school records.[143]

The New Jersey Commissioner of Education has held that schools may regulate the attendance of students at an off-campus "prom," and that *parents as well as the students* must abide by such regulations.[144] "Where pupils are under the charge of the principal, he has the authority to make rules and regulations covering their conduct," in this case the means of transportation to and from the "prom" (by bus) and the times of departure and return to the school. The fact that the parents of some students picked them up at the "prom" earlier than the scheduled departure time did not justify violation of the school regulation. The subsequent prevention of these students from participation in class activities was a proper disciplinary action.

Not only must parents abide by reasonable regulations established by the schools for the control of the conduct of their children; they may also be liable for acts of vandalism that result in the destruction of school property.[145] In Los Angeles, the schools superintendent has announced that "any identifiable parent who can be held liable" will be prosecuted by the school district in civil suits to recover the cost of windows broken and equipment burned or stolen by youngsters.[146] Although juvenile court records are "highly confidential," the presiding judge of the court has agreed to provide the necessary information to the school district or to any victim of juvenile vandalism "who wishes to file a civil suit."

In *Goetz v. Ansell*,[147] a high school student asserted his First Amendment right to sit quietly during the flag salute, while the school district offered him the alternatives of leaving the room or standing silently. The penalty for noncompliance was suspension. The court of appeals held that the school district's regulation violated *West Virginia State Board of Education v. Barnett*[148] and *Tinker v. Des Moines Independent Community School District*[149] and reasoned: standing is like saluting or uttering words, a gesture of acceptance, which "cannot be compelled over . . . deeply held conviction," while leaving the schoolroom may be viewed by some as a punishment; and the record in the case contains no evidence of school disruption or disorder or invasion of the rights of others.

Likewise, in a case involving a tenth-grade teacher, Susan Russo, the Second U.S. Circuit Court of Appeals held that a teacher need not join in reciting the "Pledge of Allegiance" to the flag, but she can stand silently not saying a word. The decision said that "patriotism that is forced is a false patriotism, just as loyalty that is coerced is the very antithesis of loyalty."[150] The court noted that since the U.S. Supreme Court has held that students cannot be forced to salute the flag, it would be unreasonable not to permit the same right to teachers.

A five-day suspension was involved in *Karp v. Becken*,[151] (1973), wherein the Ninth Circuit Court of Appeals overturned the district court's judgment, which was in favor of the school district, and held that

in absence of justification, public high school students could not properly be suspended for exercising free speech rights by bringing onto campus and attempting to distribute signs protesting refusal of the school to renew the teaching contract of an English instructor, notwithstanding that at the time of the attempted distribution the school officials were justified in taking the signs from the students because of reasonable anticipation or forecast of possible violence.

However, the court said that the student *could have been suspended* for violation of "an existing reasonable rule, such as going to the school parking lot during school hours to secure signs from his automobile."

A couple of days after the incident the school officials advised the student that he was suspended for five days, but offered to reduce this to three days if he would refrain from bringing similar signs on the campus; the student and his father refused to make such an agreement, whereupon the student was expelled for the full five days.

The appellate court reviewed the law and authorities on student rights and suspension, saying:

The difficulties inherent in "federal court supervision" of student disciplinary problems in the 23,390 public school systems of this country were anticipated by Supreme Court Justice Hugo Black in his dissenting opinion in the *Tinker case*.[152] "The reason for his concern is amply demonstrated in this case, which presents a conflict between asserted Constitutional rights and good-faith actions by school officials."[153] The *Tinker* decision established the standards by which actions of school authorities must be measured in handling disciplinary problems of this nature: public high school students have a right to freedom of speech that is not shed at the schoolhouse gate.[154] However, it is equally clear that the daily administration of "public schools is committed to school officials."[155] That responsibility carries with it the authority to prescribe and control conduct in the schools. When a conflict arises, the *Tinker* holding provides that students' rights to free speech may not be abridged in the absence of "FACTS WHICH

MIGHT REASONABLY HAVE LED SCHOOL AUTHORITIES TO FORECAST SUBSTANTIAL DISRUPTION OF OR MATERIAL INTERFERENCE WITH SCHOOL ACTIVITIES."[156]

Courts have thus recognized that the interests of the state in maintenance of its educational system is "a compelling one," which requires the balancing of the student's First Amendment rights with the state's effort to preserve and protect its educational process.

The *Tinker* rule is simply stated; application, however, is more difficult. Years ago, in a free speech case, Chief Justice Vinson noted "that neither Justice Holmes nor Justice Brandeis ever envisioned that a shorthand phrase should be crystalized into a rigid rule to be applied inflexibly without regard to the circumstances of each case." *Dennis v. United States*, 341 U.S. 494, 508 (1951). The shorthand phrase referred to in *Dennis* was "clear and present danger," but the remarks are equally appropriate to "substantial disruption or material interference"; federal courts should treat the *Tinker* rule as a flexible one dependent upon the totality of relevant facts in each case. See *Grayned v. City of Rockford*, 408 U.S. 104, 119 (1972).

The difficulty of application is even more pronounced because disruptive conduct was absent in *Tinker*; there were "no disturbances or disorders on the school premises. . . . " The *Tinker* court borrowed the phraseology of the rule from the Fifth Circuit decision in *Burnside v. Byars, supra*; but there, too, disruption or interference was absent, there being only a "mild curiosity." Consequently, the two cases which provided the rule give little assistance in its application to specific facts. However, the Fifth Circuit panel which decided *Burnside* also decided *Blackwell vs. Issaquena County Board of Education*. In *Blackwell*, they found more than a "mild curiosity"; in fact, "there was an unusual degree of commotion, boisterous conduct, a collision with the rights of others, an undermining of authority, and a lack of order, discipline and decorum." Evidently, such conduct resulted in substantial disruption, for the court upheld a regulation banning the wearing of buttons though the regulation was similar to the one struck down in *Burnside*.[157]

Thus, mild curiosity alone will not justify abridgement though Blackwellian disorder and disruption will.

The question presented by the case was whether incidents falling between the two extremes might also permit the imposition of restraints. For three reasons, the Court believed so.

First, the First Amendment does not require school officials to wait until disruption actually occurs before they may act. In fact, they have a duty to prevent the occurrence of disturbances.

Second, *Tinker* does not demand a certainty that disruption will occur, but rather the existence of facts that might reasonably lead school officials to forecast substantial disruption.

And finally, because of the state's interest in education, the level of disturbance required to justify official intervention is relatively lower in a public school than it might be on a street corner.

The actions of one claiming free speech abridgement on a school campus cannot be dissected from reality and observed in a vacuum.

The same false cry of "fire" may be permissible in an empty theater, but certainly not when there is a capacity crowd. *Schenck v. United States*, 249 U.S. 47, 52 (1919) (Holmes, J.). The striking of a match may have no effect in an open field, but be lethal in a closed room filled with gases.[158]

Similarly, in making a determination in this case, in addition to consideration of the acts of appellant, all other circumstances confronting the school administrators which might reasonably portend disruption must be evaluated.

The court in *Tinker* emphasized that there was no evidence documenting the school officials' forecast of disruption of the educational processes. In contrast, the record in this case reflects the following facts, justifying a "reasonable forecast" of *material interference* with the school's work:

1. On the morning involved, there was a newspaper article relating to the planned assembly walkout. The article indicated that the newspaper's source of information was a reporter's conversation with appellant.

2. The high school principal and other school officials testified that the school officials testified that the school athletes had threatened to stop the proposed demonstration.

3. The assembly was cancelled because school officials feared a walkout might provoke violence.

4. Later in the morning, newsmen appeared on the campus and set up their equipment. During this time, appellant and other students, during a free period, were milling around outside the building talking with these newsmen.

5. The vice-principal testified to his impression that there was a general atmosphere of excitement and expectation pervading the campus and classrooms. There was an intense feeling something was about to happen.

6. Some students actually walked out from class, notwithstanding the cancellation of the assembly.

7. About the time when the assembly walkout would have occurred, someone pulled the school fire alarm, which, had it not been previously disconnected by the vice-principal, would have emptied every room in the entire school.

8. Approximately fifty students gathered in the area of the multipurpose room and talked among themselves and with news media personnel.

9. Excited by the situation, twenty to thirty of the junior high students who share facilities with the high school and who were eating at the high school cafeteria during their lunch period, interrupted their lunch and ran into the area of the multipurpose room to watch the group of students and news people gathered there. The junior high students ran about the group excitedly and, as a result, their supervisors determined their lunch period should be shortened and they were returned to their classrooms earlier than usual.

10. Appellant went to the school parking lot and took the signs from his car to the area where the students had congregated near the multipurpose room and proceeded to distribute them.

In view of these facts, the sole question is whether this evidence is substantial enough to support the school officials' forecast of a reasonable likelihood of substantial disruption. The temptation to be a "Monday morning quarterback" should be resisted—focus should be upon whether the apprehension of the school officials was unreasonable under the circumstances. The officials in *Tinker* anticipated a level of disruption which did not justify curtailment of free speech. The officials in this case testified, and the trier of fact apparently believed, that they feared the provocation of an incident, including possible violence, and that they took the signs from the appellant in an effort to prevent such an incident. Considering all the facts, we do not find that such an anticipation, or forecast, was unreasonable.[159]

However a determination that the school officials were justified in taking the signs from appellant (and thus curtailing his exercise of claimed First Amendment rights) does not terminate the case.

The second question is whether the school officials properly suspended him from school for five days. The district court found that the suspension resulted from "his activities in connection with the planned 'walkout,' the demonstration, and, principally, because of his conduct in bringing the signs on campus and attempting to distribute them." That the primary reason for suspension was the sign activity is further demonstrated by the fact that the school officials would have shortened the suspension to three days if he had agreed to refrain from bringing similar signs onto the campus.

The sign activity in this case constituted the exercise of *pure speech* rather than conduct. As such, it came within the protective umbrella of the First Amendment. School officials may curtail the exercise of First Amendment rights when they can "reasonably forecast material interference of substantial disruption." However, for discipline resulting from the use of *pure speech* to pass muster under the First Amendment, the school officials have the burden to show justification for their action. Here they failed to do so. Absent justification, such as violation of a statute or school rule, they cannot discipline a student for exercising those rights. The balancing necessary to enable school officials to maintain discipline and order allows curtailment but not necessarily punishment. Consequently, appellant could not be suspended for his activities with the signs.

What we have said does not mean that the school officials could not have suspended appellant for violating an existing reasonable rule. In fact, in securing the signs, he broke a regulation by going to the parking lot during school hours. However, this was not a basis of the suspension. We have only held that, under the circumstances of this case, appellant could not be suspended on the sole basis of his exercising pure free speech when no justification was demonstrated.[160]

Corporal Punishment

By the early law, a husband might administer to his wife (or child) "moderate correction" and restrain her conduct by "domestic chastisement."[161] The courts in this country once said it was not a criminal offense if he beat her with "a stick no thicker than his thumb."[162] Even before the present-day Women's Liberation Movement,[163] the courts had done away with such discipline for a wife; however, in the case of children the right of discipline remains, and under the legal doctrine of *in loco parentis*, courts have held that this power of the parent over the child, in some cases, is transfered to the school authorities.[164] The following instruments for inflicting bodily pain on children have sometimes been used: rubber hose, strap, bundle of sticks, wet towels (often knotted), rope, bones, hands, rulers, rolled newspapers, books, and even pins. A school cane was manufactured and sold in Europe for the "sole purpose of flogging students."[165] The general rule has been stated as follows:

A parent, or one standing in place of a parent [i.e., a teacher] may use reasonable force for the correction or punishment of a child. Military and naval officers, and the master of a ship, have similar disciplinary authority.[166]

A parent (or one who stands in the place of a parent) may use reasonable force, including corporal punishment, for discipline and control. A school teacher has the same authority.[167]

A parent, by sending his child to a school, delegates his right of discipline to the child's teachers.[168]

But this general rule is under attack in a number of states, including California. The California Education Code, Section 10,854, contains the following provisions:

The governing board of any school district shall adopt rules and regulations authorizing teachers, principals, and other certificated personnel to administer reasonable corporal or other punishment to pupils when such action is deemed an appropriate corrective measure.[169]

The language of the code is *mandatory* ("shall adopt rules and regulations"), yet the use of the disjunctive particle "or" to define what punishments may be administered ("reasonable corporal *or* other punishment") has led to some question about the use of corporal punishment in California public schools. Although local boards of education have voted to affirm the right of teachers to administer reasonable corporal punishment, a test case may be made in the courts.[170]

Pursuant to Section 10,854 of the California *Education Code*, one metropolitan school district in the state issued the following bulletin and "comment" on the use of corporal punishment to teachers and administrators, "for your information only."

Administrative Action

Corporal Punishment:

Reasonable corporal punishment as a form of disciplinary action may be used when such action is deemed an appropriate corrective measure. The following policies will be adhered to:

1. Corporal punishment shall be administered by, or under the direction of the principal, assistant principal, dean of boys or girls, student advisor, or other certificated person specifically designated by the principal. A witness who shall be an employee of the School District must be present when corporal punishment is administered.
2. Students shall not be punished in the presence of other students, nor by other students.
3. Punishment shall be administered by a light paddle or leather strap to the buttocks only. Slapping, hair pulling, shoving, and other similar techniques of punishment are not permitted.
4. School personnel shall keep the use of corporal punishment to a minimum.
5. A written report of all corporal punishments shall be sent immediately to the office of Child Welfare and Attendance by the principal.

EDUCATION CODE 10854

Comment:

This has been the usual policy followed at this school, but since this bulletin is so specific, it is clear that what is intended is that a parent must be notified before swats can be administered. Then too, the principal, assistant principal or student advisor must be a witness.

(This is for your information only.)

November, 1972

The Riverside Unified School District student handbook, *Regulations for School Behavior,*[171] sets forth the following clear statement of state law, board policy, and district administrative regulations on the use of corporal punishment:

CORPORAL PUNISHMENT

STATE LAW

Education Code - Section 1052
"The governing board of any school district shall prescribe rules not inconsistent with law or with the rules prescribed by the State Board of Education, for the government and discipline of the schools under its jurisdiction." (Amended by Stats. 1969, Ch. 1265.)

Education Code - Section 10854
"The governing board of any school district shall adopt rules and regulations authorizing teachers, principals and other certificated personnel to administer reasonable corporal [or other] punishment to pupils when such action is deemed an appropriate measure."

BOARD POLICY

1. Corporal punishment shall be defined as the application of a hand or paddle to the seat or posterior of the pupil.
2. The paddle used shall be of uniform measurements as prescribed in the administrative regulations.
3. Generally, corporal punishment is used when other corrective measures . . . have failed and when it is judged to be most effective in correcting pupils' misbehavior.
4. The responsibility to administer corporal punishment is vested in the principal, although he may delegate it to a vice-principal or to a teacher. When corporal punishment is administered, it must be witnessed by a member of the certificated staff.
5. Corporal punishment shall be *reasonable* in amount and administered without anger.
6. In each instance where corporal punishment is under consideration, the administrator shall attempt to ascertain that no health condition exists which could cause injury to the pupil.
7. After administration of corporal punishment, a Corporal Punishment Form shall be filed with the Supervisor of Attendance and Child Welfare.
8. Unless extenuating circumstances exist, the principal or his designee shall notify the parent(s) whenever corporal punishment is administered. When these circumstances exist, a written statement shall be attached to the corporal punishment form submitted to the Office of Child Welfare.

ADMINISTRATIVE REGULATIONS

1. The paddle used shall be within the following specifications:

Length	—15 to 24 inches	Thickness	—1/4 to 3/8 inches
Width	—not less than 3 inches	Material	—of hard wood

2. In all cases in which parental objection may have been incurred, the office of the Supervisor of Child Welfare and Attendance shall be notified by telephone that corporal punishment has been used. Information shall be given regarding reasons for and circumstances of the punishment. This will acquaint the office with facts of the case prior to receipt of the completed Corporal Punishment Form.

In *Glaser v. Marietta,*[172] the district court, while holding that corporal punishment is constitutionally permissible when the school system is empowered by the legislature to administer such punishment, ruled that *school authorities may not use corporal punishment if a child's parents notify the school that such discipline is prohibited.* A "spanking," which is a reasonable form of chastisement, reasonably used by the school district is not prohibited by the Fifth, Eighth, or Fourteenth Amendments to the Constitution, "as long as the disciplinary methods used are reasonable, properly administered so as not to cause harm, and legally authorized, the child has no constitutional grounds to object."[173] However, this does not decide the issue of the parents' right to raise children as they think proper:

"A state's interest in universal education, however highly we rank it, is not totally free from a balancing process when it impinges on other fundamental rights and interest, such as ... the traditional interest of parents with respect to the religious upbringing of their children,"

quoting from the United States Supreme Court decision in *Wisconsin v. Yoder,*[174] and from *Stanley v. Illinois*[175] to the effect that the "rights to conceive and to raise one's children have been deemed essential, basic civil rights of man, and rights far more precious than property rights." The "balancing" of rights and interests requires that the court examine the interest of the state and determine if it "presents the powerful countervailing interest required by *Stanley* to overrule the private rights of parents."

When balancing the respective interests of the parent and the school system, the court finds that the regulation [on use of corporal punishment] satisfies neither the "reasonably necessary" nor the "powerful countervailing interest" test, and therefore cannot prevail over the asserted claim of the basic parental right to raise one's children as thought proper.[176]

A leading case on the use of corporal punishment in the schools is *Ware v. Estes,*[177] decided in 1971, wherein the Dallas Independent School District's policy permitting reasonable corporal punishment under controlled conditions was held *not* to be "arbitrary, capricious, unreasonable, or wholly unrelated to the competency of the state in determining educational policy." The Dallas policy was adopted after a conference with Professor B.F. Skinner of Harvard, who indicated that *in some cases* corporal punishment will be helpful:

According to the testimony, it cannot be said that the Dallas Independent School District's policy on the use of corporal punishment bears no reasonable relation to some purpose within the competency of the state in its educational function. Dr. David Gil, an expert in education and social policy, testified that according to tests and studies he conducted there was a higher rate of delinquency among those children exposed to physical discipline than there was among children who were not physically chastised. It was his opinion that corporal punishment is always detrimental to a child's development. Dr. Robert Dane, an assistant professor of psychology at a nearby medical school, testified that there was evidence to show that corporal punishment makes it difficult for a child to develop; however, he also said that there was evidence to the effect that corporal punishment may be helpful to some children in the long run but not for the majority. Dr. Nolan Estes, Superintendent of the Dallas Independent School District, testified that the District's policy on corporal punishment was adopted after a conference with Professor B.F. Skinner of Harvard University, a recognized authority on child and educational psychology. Dr. Estes stated that the District's policy on corporal punishment reflects the philosophy of Dr. Skinner, i.e., in some cases corporal punishment will be helpful.[178]

While school district authorities are not compelled to use corporal punishment, they are certainly allowed to use it under Texas statutory law; moreover, corporal punishment, as authorized by Texas law and the policy of the Dallas Independent School District, does not amount to "cruel and unusual punishment."[179] When punishment of children is excessive or unreasonable it is no longer lawful and the teacher may be criminally and civilly liable.[180] "The law and policy do not sanction child abuse."[181]

The *Estes case* began with this general statement: "In this suit, the Court is called upon to resolve *another* conflict between the Constitution and the campus,"[182] and ended with the following precept and quotation from the *Epperson case*:[183]

In closing this opinion the Court feels compelled to utter a general precept in light of the many cases it has had to entertain in the recent past embodying allegations of constitutional violations by the local school district. The following quote will succinctly and accurately describe the Court's attitude with respect to these cases.

"Judicial interposition in the operation of the public school system of the Nation raises problems requiring care and restraint. . . . By and large, public education in our Nation is committed to the control of state and local authorities. Courts do not and cannot intervene in the resolution of conflicts which arise in the daily operation of school systems and which do not directly and sharply implicate basic constitutional values." *Epperson v. Arkansas,* 393 U.S. 97, 104 (1968). Plaintiff's complaint is hereby dismissed.[184]

The Supreme Court of the United States refused to review this case; consequently, the

Dallas public schools can keep the spanking rules they adopted after consultation with B.F. Skinner. . . . District Court Judge W.M. Taylor, in dismissing the case, found the claims that the Fourteenth Amendment was violated "insubstantial," and said he believed that corporal punishment had a reasonable relationship to an educational goal that outweighed any parental right. The Fifth Circuit Court upheld Taylor, and the Supreme Court agreed. Since it was not a formal decision, but only a refusal to review the case, the precedent is binding only in the Fifth Circuit and merely "persuasive" in the nine other federal circuits.[185]

Achievement Tests and Scholastic Aptitude Test Scores

Courts have questioned the use of achievement tests and scholastic aptitude tests in the schools. A number of cases have challenged the constitutionality of such tests when used for pupil placement purposes. This has occurred at a time when testing is assuming a more important role in education generally; for example, scores on achievement tests were the basis for making payments to "performance contractors" (not without some controversy, however),[186] and achievement tests results are the principal basis for making educational decisions about the effectiveness of innovative programs.[187] Scores on such tests are widely used for diagnostic purposes, for determining the effectiveness of school programs, but, a number of courts have said that such scores may *not* be used by school authorities for pupil assignment purposes where such assignment would result in racially segregated classes.

The use of tests and test scores came under a major attack in 1967,[188] when Judge Skelly Wright invalidated the "track system" then being used in the public school of Washington, D.C. Scores on aptitude tests were employed to assign pupils to the various "tracks." Judge Wright's opinion looked in detail at the use and misuse of tests, at the accuracy of test measurements, and at misjudgments and "under-education" resulting from using test scores for pupil placement purposes.[189] Concerning the "track system" and the use of tests, Wright by way of summary declared:

The track system as used in the district's public schools is a form of ability grouping in which students are divided in separate, self-contained curricula or tracks ranging from "basic" for the slow student to "honors" for the gifted.

The aptitude tests used to assign children to the various tracks are standardized primarily on white middle class children. Since these tests do not relate to the Negro and disadvantaged child, track assignment based on such tests relegates Negro and disadvantaged children to the lower tracks from which, because of the reduced curricula and the absence of adequate remedial and compensatory education, as well as continued inappropriate testing, the chance of escape is remote.

Education in the lower tracks is geared to . . . the "blue collar" student. Thus, such children, so stigmatized by inappropriate aptitude testing procedures, are denied equal opportunity to obtain the white collar education available to the white and more affluent children.[190]

Thus, the method by which pupils were assigned to tracks depended essentially upon the standardized aptitude tests, which tests, the court found, were relevant to white middle class pupils and produced inaccurate and misleading scores when given to lower class and Negro pupils,

rather than being classified according to their ability to learn, these [latter] students are in reality being classified according to their socio-economic or racial status, or—more precisely—according to environmental and psychological factors which have nothing to do with innate ability.

Consequently, the defendants were permanently enjoined from operating the "track system" in the District of Columbia.[191]

School administrators have been prohibited by courts from testing students' abilities for assignment purposes in recently desegregated schools. Courts in the South have held that assignment to classes on the basis of achievement test scores is not permissible, if its effect is to resegregate pupils. In *U.S. and Driver v. Tunica County School District*, a Mississippi district court issued a decree (July 1969) in a desegregation suit, "requiring assignment of students to schools on the basis of achievement-test scores."[192] However, in *Singleton v. Jackson*

Municipal Separate School District,[193] also decided in 1969, the circuit court, while declining to discuss "the validity *per se*" of desegregation plans based on achievement test scores, declared that "testing cannot be employed in any event until unitary school systems have been established."[194]

"Heterogeneous, racially integrated classes" were ordered by the court in *Moses v. Washington Parish School Board,*[195] which involved standardized ability and achievement tests administered to students in a recently desegregated school. Assignments of students were to eleven levels (instead of six grades) on the basis of their test scores, and within each level the students were grouped homogeneously into sections. Basis of the grouping was scores in reading, but not in mathematics and science. Negro students, subjected to such testing for the first time, the court said, "were put at a disadvantage by being tested in reading alone, in which they tended to score lower than in mathematics and science."[196] A fairly predictable racial pattern emerged: 82 percent of the white pupils scored high on the tests and were assigned to the top three sections in each level, while about 42 percent of the Negroes were placed in all-Negro classes. Nearly all students remained in the same level and section for the full school year; therefore, the system's lack of mobility tended to lock students, especially those in the bottom sections, into the same sections throughout grammar school." Such assignment policy based on test scores violates the Fourteenth Amendment, and the court ordered the students reassigned to "heterogeneous, racially integrated classes."

Lemon v. Bossier Parish School Board (1971)[197] held that a school district that operated as a unitary system for only one semester could not assign students to schools within the district on the basis of achievement test scores: "Formerly segregated school district must operate as a unitary system for several years before students may be assigned within the system on the basis of achievement test scores." Involved were students in grades 4-12, and the district court had approved the use of test scores as a basis for assigning pupils to schools and to classes. On appeal the circuit court, citing *Singleton,* reversed and said:

> In *Singleton* we made it clear that regardless of the innate validity of testing, it could not be used until a school district had been established as a unitary system. We think at a minimum this means that the district in question must have for several years operated as a unitary system.[198]

Outside the South, testing has been challenged in a number of cases; thus, a lawsuit filed in April 1972 charged that the achievement tests administered in Los Angeles city schools "discriminate against Mexican-American children because the examinations are based on the Anglo culture."[199] An injunction was sought against the Board of Education "limiting the use of achievement testing." The plaintiffs, students in the age range six to seventeen, charged that "the test fail to take into account that Mexican-American students are not proficient in English, come from a different culture, and are not provided with quality schools. Because of their different backgrounds, Mexican-American children generally do poorly on the tests and consequently "are placed in lower ability groupings, denying them equal education."

Intelligence Quotient (IQ) Scores

In December, 1971, a class action suit seeking to stop school districts from placing intelligence quotient (IQ) scores on pupils' records was brought by the California Rural Legal Assistance.[200] The superior court suit filed in Sacramento against the California State Board of Education charged that IQ scores entered on the students' records are relied upon by teachers and administrators to develop "low ability expectations" for Mexican-American children and are used "to teach, place, evaluate, and encourage them accordingly." The plaintiff further charged that IQ tests "have no validity as a measure of plaintiff's ability to learn."

A U.S. district court, in *P. v. Riles*,[201] found that a denial of equal protection to Black students was established when the school district failed to demonstrate that IQ test scores used for placing students in classes for the educable mentally retarded were rationally related to the purpose of segregating students according to their ability to learn in regular classes. The court granted a preliminary injunction as to future testing and ordered future evaluations; Black students who were currently enrolled in such classes, however, could be retained, and the school district was not required to take affirmative action to compensate those students who had been placed in such classes at some time in the past. However, the fact that Black students who were wrongfully placed in such classes were able to achieve their way out of such classes by means of yearly evaluations was no basis for concluding that they were not irreparably harmed, since placement in such classes was noted on the student's record permanently, his education was retarded in some degree, and he was exposed to humiliation by being separated into classes for the educable mentally retarded.

Low IQ scores, low achievement test scores, and language difficiencies were cited in *Serna v. Portales Municipal Schools*[202] to show that the plaintiffs, Spanish-surnamed students, were denied equal educational opportunity because the schools' educational programs were tailored for the middle-class Anglo children without regard to the "educational needs"[203] of Spanish-speaking children. The court discarded the arguments that the "special needs" of the children were not the result of "state action" and that financial considerations made expansion of bilingual-bicultural programs impossible.[204]

Legislation that abolishes mandatory group IQ testing by the state in California public schools was signed by the governor on August 18, 1972.[205] Assembly Bill No. 665 modifies the provisions of the state *Education Code* which control statewide testing of students and deletes provisions for scholastic aptitude tests in grades 6 and 12.[206] Furthermore, a pending bill in the California Legislature, Assembly Bill No. 368, provides for the addition of the following new Section 12,821.5 to the California *Education Code*:

No school district may administer in connection with the statewide testing program, or otherwise, any group standardized test, or any other test, which measures or attempts to measure the scholastic aptitude of a pupil or group of pupils in the district. Individual scores from any such test shall not be used by any school district or employee thereof.[207]

A similar bill, introduced in the California Legislature in 1972, was vetoed by the governor, who described it as "a direct challenge to the authority and competence of the State Board of Education and local school boards."[208]

The controversy over the use of IQ tests in California schools has led to the investigation of possible new ways of eliminating cultural bias and the language factor from such tests. The state senate has adopted, 27 to 1, a resolution, SCR-50, authorizing a pilot study of the basic intelligence of Spanish-speaking children using the electronic "Neural Efficiency Analyzer" developed by John Ertl, which is said not to be influenced by cultural or language factors.[209] A *Phi Delta Kappan* interview with the inventor discloses how the Ertl "Analyzer" works:[210]

Ertl: Basically, the test consists of applying electrodes—small silver discs—to the scalp with conductive jelly. There's no pain, of course, and nothing is put into or taken out of the brain. The electrical amplitude of the evoked response is very weak, less than 1/1,000,000 of a volt, and is usually drowned out in the brain's ongoing activity, which is from 5 to 20 times more powerful. The amplifier which enlarges these very minute signals so we can measure them is battery operated; there is no electrical hazard to the subject.

An interesting feature of the neural efficiency analyzer system is that the brain waves themselves control the moment at which the first light will be flashed. This is done by a closed-loop feedback system to ensure that each subject starts the test at the same point in brain-wave phase, avoiding inaccuracies. Exactly 100 flashes of light are delivered by the computer at random intervals, with an average time of one second between flashes. The brain waves are amplified and displayed simultaneously on a monitor oscilloscope. At the same time, the data are fed into the computer, which computes the average time between specific parameters of the evoked response. Thus the test is completed in about 100 seconds and two 3-digit numbers appear on the analyzer screen. Both of these numbers are entered on a table or nomogram, which first gives the neural efficiency score and then predicts what the subject would score on an IQ test if the test were valid.

At the moment, we can't get away from relating to the IQ test system, which has been established for 60 or 70 years. This IQ score is simply our best estimate of what the subject would score on an ideal IQ test. Analyzer test-retest scores over a short period of time are very accurate; over a longer period they are less accurate, but they are still much better than test-retest scores on an IQ test. In my experience with several thousand children's IQ tests, there were differences of as much as 40 points for the same child tested with three different tests, and the tests were given days, not years, apart. I found such discrepancies for perhaps 2 or 3% of the children taking IQ tests.

Kappan: With what tests do you generally correlate your scores?

Ertl: Currently, the most popular IQ tests are the Wechsler Intelligence Scale for Children (WISC), the Primary Mental Abilities Test (PMA), and the Otis. We have used these three for our standardization sample.

Kappan: The SAT is pretty much a test of achievement, so you wouldn't use that, would you?

Ertl: I don't mind using *any* test, as long as final evaluation is based on which test can predict *future* achievement better. There has been no study on this yet. Unfortunately, it takes time.

Kappan: How long does it take to train a person to operate your machine and interpret the scores?

Ertl: It takes no time at all to interpret the scores, because the desired numbers appear on the machine. Machine operation consists of pushing one knob to start the test. This is the total mechanical manipulation required. Brief training, 20 to 25 minutes, is needed to recognize a good EEG, an EEG with the electrodes properly in contact with the head. The subject must not move about. He must be seated in a reasonably relaxed situation. A small monitor oscilloscope is part of the analyzer, to let you view the subject's brain-waves. The training manual provides graphic illustrations of artifacts such as excessive muscle tension or eye blinks or interference from the lights. All of these must be recognized and corrected. Correction is quite easy in most cases. The machine will simply not operate unless conditions are perfect for testing.

The Ertl machine has "triggered a storm of controversy" among scientists and educators, some of which is reported in the January 1973 issue of the *Phi Delta Kappan*;[211]

Whether the miniaturized equipment now used by Dr. Ertl will yield latency scores that have practical utility for educators remains to be seen. Until carefully designed experimental studies have been completed, latency scores of the type obtained by Dr. Ertl should be used only for research purposes.[212]

Reporting Pupil Progress:
Class and Course Grades

The use of the so-called "bell-shaped curve" in assigning course grades has been questioned as being unfair because it has a "strong tendency to collect a proportionately high percentage of black students at the low end of the curve."[213] The issue was raised at the Harvard Business School, where the older faculty members pointed out that overall student performance at the school based on past records shows over a time a standard statistical distribution (a "bell-shaped" curve) in final grades. "It was therefore concluded that a professor whose final grades did not reflect a bell-shaped curve was, to the extent of his deviation, contributing toward the erosion of traditional business school stand-ards." But Black students at Harvard Business School, partly because of years of racial discrimination and segregation in education, have lacked the necessary pregraduate school educational and work experiences for rapid assimilation into a business school. Consequently, a high percentage of minority students were asked to withdraw from the school because of poor academic performance.[214]

Reporting practices are changing to reflect new philosophies. Because they are a very visible and therefore vulnerable aspects of an educational plan, these practices must be defensible to educators and laymen alike.[215]

"K.C." v. Board of Education, (1973),[216] involved a junior high school student who challenged the school board's policy on grading after she was failed in an art class; the student contended that her grades of "A" and "F" should have been averaged, thus producing a passing grade. The school board maintained that grades of failure were not allowable when compiling student grade point averages for graduation. The grade assigned by the art teacher was made final. The board pointed out that a student who had a passing grade in a course could fail if he "gave up." On appeal, the New Jersey commissioner of education upheld the board's decision.

Tests and Teacher Employment and Promotion

The leading case on testing as it relates to employment generally is *Griggs v. Duke Power Company*,[217] decided in 1971, wherein the Supreme Court of the United States held that the Civil Rights Act of 1964 requires the elimination of "artificial, arbitrary, and unnecessary barriers to employment when the barriers operate invidiously to discriminate on the basis of racial or other impermissible classification."[218] The test required for employment and promotion—a high school diploma and satisfactory scores on two professionally prepared aptitude tests—must be shown to bear a "demonstrable relationship to successful performance of the jobs for which it is used." In this case, the high school diploma requirement and the general intelligence tests were both adopted "without meaningful study of their relationship to job-performance ability."[219] They were adopted to improve the "overall quality of the work force."

Congress, through the Civil Rights Act of 1964, placed the burden on the employer of showing that such tests have a manifest relationship to the employment in question; said the Court:

The facts of this case demonstrate the inadequacy of broad and general testing devices as well as the infirmity of using diplomas or degrees as fixed measures of capability. History is filled with examples of men and women who rendered highly effective performance without the conventional badges of accomplishment in terms of certificates, diplomas, or degrees. Diplomas and tests are useful servants, but Congress has mandated the common sense proposition that they are not to become masters of reality.[220]

Nothing in the Civil Rights Act of 1964 precludes the use of testing or measuring procedures—"obviously they are useful"—but such devices are not "controlling forces" unless they are "demonstrably a reasonable measure of job performance." Such tests, therefore, "must measure the person for the job and not the person in the abstract."

Thus, the stage was set for a series of court attacks on the constitutionality of school personnel practices as they related to initial employment of teachers and subsequent reemployment and promotion.[221] It has been noted that standardized tests "such as the National Teachers Examination and the Achievement sections of the Graduate Record examinations are seldom too helpful in selecting individuals for specific assignments because of their national standardization."[222] Recent court decisions challenging the use of such tests in school personnel work support this statement.

Teacher examinations have come under attack in a number of cases.

Armstead v. Starkville Municipal Separate School District 325 F. Supp. 560 (1971), 331 F. Supp. 567 (1971), 461 F. 2d 276 (1972).

Baker v. Columbus Municipal Separate School District, 329 F. Supp. 706. (1971), 462 F. 2d 1112 (1972).

Pickens v. Oklahoma Municipal Separate School District (D.C. N.D. Miss. Aug. 11, 1971).

Chance v. Board of Examiners, 458 F. 2d 1167 (1972).

Carter v. Morehouse Parish School Board, 441 F. 2d 380 (1971).

Contested in one or more of these decisions was the use of teacher scores on these examinations for employment or promotion purposes: the Graduate Record Examination, the National Teachers Examination, New York Competitive Supervisory Examination, and a sixth-grade achievement test (administered to an elementary school teacher whose score was described as "poor").

In *Armstead*, the National Teachers Association and the Mississippi Teachers Association joined with nine Negro teachers to enjoin the school district from enforcing a regulation "which required that both in-service teachers and new applicants for teaching positions achieve certain scores on the Graduate Record Examination (GRE) or hold a Master's degree as a condition for employment."[223] Discussing the GRE score requirement, the court observed that "no studies were conducted to test the validity or reliability of the scores as "instruments for selecting public school teachers"; and it was noted that no other state school system required its teachers to satisfy the requirements here in issue."[224] The court held this to be a "racially discriminatory testing policy" and said the school district must show an "overriding purpose" to justify the racial classification. The court found that the defendants had failed to meet this burden under the "job-related" concept announced in the *Duke Power case*.[225]

The school district was enjoined from utilizing the GRE in the selection of in-service teachers and applicants for new positions.

In *Baker*, the National Education Association and the Mississippi Teachers Association joined eight Negroes who challenged the school district's refusal to reemploy or hire Black teachers due to the requirement of a satisfactory test score (composite score of 1000) on the National Teachers Examination (NTE)[226] as a precondition to retention or employment. The NTE score requirement for employment had been adopted, the court found, "without investigating or studying the validity and reliability of the examination and the particular cut-off score as a means of selecting teachers for hiring and re-election." The court further found that "NTE examinations are not measures of classroom teaching performance" and that implementation of the score requirement would "continue to disqualify substantially more Black applicants for teaching positions . . . than white applicants for the next few years."

Since the school district failed to carry the "very heavy burden" of justifying the testing policy, the NTE cut-off score requirement was held to be an "unconstitutional racial classification," and apart from the discriminatory aspects, the court found the requirement to be an "arbitrary and unreasonable qualification for reemployment and employment as a teacher," in violation of the Fourteenth Amendment.

The Fifth U.S. Circuit Court of Appeals, however, went even further and applied the new equal protection standard to the *Baker case*, declaring that the requirement that applicants obtain a combined score of 1000 on the National Teacher Examination was subject to "strict scrutiny" where the policy resulted in the exclusion of proportionately more Black than white teachers from the profession, and that although the policy did not purport to classify on racial lines, yet the effect was the same as if it did; the court found no overriding purpose of the state to continue the policy independently of its racial effects. The court of appeals looks with disfavor on any test or school district policy that obviously disadvantages Black teachers, especially when this is due to past inferior educational opportunities suffered by them. The NTE was adopted as a condition of employment without any investigation or study of its validity or reliability or of the cut-off score as a means of selecting teachers. On the contrary, the court found that the NTE does not measure manual skills, teaching aptitude, attitudes, personal characteristics, or classroom teaching performance.[227]

Pickens, an action brought by parents of Negro students who charged that the refusal of the school district to rehire several Negro teachers deprived their children of the right to receive a desegregated education, also involved the use of NTE cut-off scores for purposes of reemployment. The court found "no evidence indicating either the purpose of the NTE nor a correlation between scores and teaching ability."[228] The NTE requirement established a racial classification, the use of which could be continued only if the school district could show an "absolute, overwhelming necessity" for it. The court said that since the defendants failed to show even a "rational connection" between the scores and teaching ability, the testing procedure was "arbitrary, unreasonable, and unconstitutional."[229]

Armstead, Baker, and *Pickens* were all southern cases, while *Chance* was an action in a federal court in New York by two New York City teachers, one Negro and one Puerto Rican, to enjoin the city's use of competitive examinations as prerequisites to obtaining supervisory positions in the public schools. The examinations, it was argued, violated the equal protection clause of the Fourteenth Amendment because they had "not been shown to measure the skill, ability, and fitness of applicants to perform the duties of the position for which the examinations are given."[230] The court confirmed the discriminatory effect of the testing requirement, but said that the further question of whether the test is "job-related" must be considered. Since the discrimination was on the basis of race, a "strong showing of ability measurement correlation" was necessary to justify use of the tests, and this had not been done. The court found in support of this that the chancellor of the school system had expressed doubts concerning the validity of the examination; major portions of the tests required simple memorization; and the oral examination left unanswered the question of "sub-conscious discrimination" against minorities.

Other tests, nonstandardized ones, have been struck down by the courts; thus, in *Carter v. Morehouse Parish School Board*, an elementary school teacher's poor score on a sixty-grade achievement test resulted in her dismissal on grounds of incompetency.[231] When the teacher sought a court order for reinstatement, the district judge interrupted the proceedings and stated *that this test score did not constitute a valid ground for her dismissal.* However, the court order, entered some three weeks later, said the teacher had been dismissed because of her race. On appeal, the circuit court said the trial judge committed a "reversible error" in refusing to hear the school district's evidence and in issuing a rule based on evidence which a party had not been allowed to rebut.[232]

In *Porcelli*, a school system suspended the established promotion list and promoted Negroes who were not on the list, this being done for the purpose of adding to the number of Negroes in administrative positions. This action was challenged by white principals and vice-principals, who sought to enjoin the school board; both the district court and the circuit court denied them relief, as also did the Supreme Court of the United States, which denied the plaintiff's petition for a writ of certiorari.[233]

"External tests," those administered by organizations other than the school the pupil attends, have also come under fire, and much criticism has been leveled at reliance on SAT scores, which have been called "the nail in the coffin of American intellectualism."[234] This "insult is probably not justified."[235] Moreover, it has been observed:

In all likelihood there is no legal remedy against SAT discrimination, but an argument can be made for one, at least in the case of state universities and colleges. State institutions have a constitutional duty not to impose racial barriers to admission. Any entrance requirement that discriminates according to race rather than ability is invalid as a violation of the equal protection clause of the Fourteenth Amendment.[236]

Thus, courts have enjoined college officials from imposing discriminatory requirements for college admission.

Meredith v. Fair[237] involved James Meredith's application for admission to the University of Mississippi and the school's requirements that all applicants must submit letters of recommendation from alumni. The court said the practice was discriminatory and therefore invalid:

We now hold that the requirement of recommendations, whether from alumni or from citizens generally, attesting to an applicant's good moral character or recommending an applicant for admission, is unconstitutional when, as this case demonstrates, the burden falls more heavily on the Negroes than on whites. This is not to say, of course, that good moral character is not a reasonable test for admission.[238]

Franklin v. Parker[239] struck down a requirement by the graduate school of Auburn University (a state school) that applicants must have completed their undergraduate work at an "accredited" school. Said the Court:

On its face, and standing alone, the requirement of Auburn University concerning graduation from an accredited institution as a prerequisite to being admitted to Graduate School is unobjectionable and a reasonable rule for a college or university to adopt. However, the effect of the rule on Harold A. Franklin—an Alabama Negro—and others in his class who may be similarly situated, is necessarily to preclude him from securing a postgraduate education at Auburn University solely because the state of Alabama discriminated against him in its undergraduate schools. Such racial discrimination on the part of the State of Alabama amounts to a clear denial of equal protection of the laws. This is true regardless of the good motives or purposes that Auburn University may have concerning the rule in question.[240]

While *Meredith* involved an overt attempt by the state university to discriminate against Negroes, in *Franklin* the school was acting in "good faith" in wishing to accept only adequately prepared graduate students, yet

such a rational condition fell only because of Alabama's previous policy of denying Negroes entrance to accredited colleges. *One could argue that there has been similar state action in every state that has not provided Negroes with educational opportunities equal to those of whites.*[241]

One school may have found a partial solution to the grading problem. The University of California at Santa Cruz, a pioneer in adopting the "pass/fail" grading system, has made an innovation in its marking system:

A Santa Cruz student will simply either pass a course or there will be no record whatever on his transcript that he ever took it. Thus, there is nothing to lose by failing—except the investment of his own and his instructor's time.[242]

The following are some conclusions about the legal implications of the use of tests in employment and in education:[243]

1. The field of educational testing presents new problems for the law, problems which are only now beginning to obtrude on the legal consciousness.

2. The assumption has been made that tests, despite their drawbacks, are an improvement over the conventional "subjective" techniques. This assumption is debatable.

3. The best of tests have a "validity coefficient of only .5."

4. In using tests, there are the very real problems of discrimination, technical difficulties in conducting adequate validation studies, and the practical and legal problems of differential scoring.

5. Advocates of testing point to the objectivity of tests as a check against the personal prejudices of teachers and other personnel.

6. Tests, however, introduce their own element of racial bias, and their results can provide a "smoke screen" for teachers who wish to discriminate.

7. It is too early to conclude that court regulation of tests cannot ensure fairness to all pupils or applicants. It is likewise too early to deny the possibility that the technical difficulties of testing will prove constitutionally overwhelming.

8. Testing techniques must be sufficiently refined to produce legally acceptable results. Otherwise court regulation in this area may ultimately give way to prohibition.

Degrees, Diplomas, and Admission and Graduation Requirements

At least a hundred "educational" institutions in California in 1958 were described as "diploma mills," that is, institutions which engaged in the sale of bogus degrees.[244] Legislation subsequently has made the granting and use of such degrees or diplomas illegal.[245] In 1973 the defendant in *People v. Sanchez*[246] was convicted of the use of a bogus degree for employment purposes; the state prosecuted him under Section 29,015 of the *Education Code* after he had told a prospective employer that he was a graduate of the University of California at Santa Barbara and later attempted to confirm that misrepresentation by handing the employer a diploma from the university, which proved to be a forgery. State law-enforcement agencies and regional accrediting associations attempt to control the granting and use of such illegal degrees and diplomas.[247]

A private institution in Colorado has been enjoined from issuing degrees, *Colorado Department of Education v. Colorado State Christian College of the Church of the Inner Power.*[248] The college provided degrees, bachelors through doctorates, for fifty weeks of correspondence study, had but one faculty member, and had issued some 400 to 500 degrees, which returned to the college earnings of $60,000 to $70,000. The court found that the college did not meet the definition of an institution of higher learning under the state statutes.

A law school's admissions policy was at issue in *DeFunis v. Odegaard,*[249] where a white applicant contended that he had been denied admission to the University of Washington Law School because of his race, while some thirty-eight students of minority races who were less academically qualified had been admitted to the school. The trial court found that DeFunis, the student, had been denied equal protection of the law,[250] and he was admitted to the school pending the outcome of his case, which was appealed by the University to the Washington State Supreme Court. The university defended its admissions policy on the grounds of a special need for minority race lawyers. The state supreme court held that a state law school's grant of admission preference to minority applicants over better qualified white applicants in order to produce a racially balanced student body, and to increase the number of minority attorneys in the state, does not violate the equal protection clause of the Fourteenth Amendment, nor Article I, Section 12 of the Washington State Constitution.[251] Said the court: *Brown v. Board of Education of Topeka* (1954) did not hold that all racial qualifications are per se unconstitutional; rather *invidious* racial classifications that stigmatize a racial group violate the Fourteenth Amendment. "The preferential minority admissions policy administered by the law school is clearly not a form of invidious discrimination since the goal of this policy is not to separate the races, but to bring them together." Supreme Court decisions since *Brown* make it clear that under some circumstances a "racial criterion" may or must be used by public educational institutions to bring about racial balance.

What "standard of review" is appropriate? When a classification is based on race, the state bears a heavy burden of showing that the classification is necessary to accomplish a "compelling state interest." The state has an overriding interest in promoting integration in public education; the educational interest of the state in producing a racially balanced student body is compelling.

Dissent: The goal of enabling students of certain minority races to enter the law school so that there will be a greater representation of practicing lawyers of those races in the legal profession is a laudable purpose. This cannot be accomplished, however, by a clear and willful discrimination against students of other races, as the admissions committee of the law school has done in this case.[252]

Following a number of complaints about the unfairness to minority groups of the process used for admission to the bar in California, the State Bar Board of Governors has created a "Commission to Study the Bar Examination Process," which will look into the following questions:[253]

1. Are there factors attributable to "cultural bias" which are not related to a person's effectiveness as a lawyer but which adversely affect that person's ability to do satisfactory work in law school or on the bar examination?
2. If there are such factors, what can be done to neutralize them consistent with insuring both a sound legal education and a bar examination process which adequately protect the *public interest* in having properly qualified lawyers.

The membership of the commission has been drawn from a broad spectrum of educational, racial, and ethnic backgrounds.

A lawsuit that raises unique questions about the quality of education and the legal liability of school districts and schoolteachers for failing to instill in their students so basic a skill as reading ability has been filed against the San Francisco Unified School District.[254] Peter N. Doe (a fictitious name assumed to spare the litigant public stigma and humiliation) graduated from the public schools of San Francisco with a B-minus average and received a high school diploma, yet he could hardly read at the fifth-grade level. When his mother discovered his plight, despite assurances by school authorities that her son was attaining the proper reading level, she decided to sue the San Francisco school district for $1 million, which her attorney says may be scaled down to around $5000 and recovery of the costs of private tutoring.

From a white, middle-class family background, Peter had no physical problems or disciplinary problems while in school, and he had a normal attendance record. Now working with a private tutor, within six months his reading ability is alleged to have jumped two years, which "establishes his ability to learn." The suit contends that Peter N. Doe graduated "unqualified for employment other than the most demeaning, unskilled, low-paid manual labor" and that under California law the school district was required to ensure that he met certain minimum requirements before receiving a high school diploma. The case "derives its legal basis from questions of negligence, misrepresentation, and several statutory claims."

Several opposing views of the possible outcome and propriety of this lawsuit are:

National attention attracted by the suit has "led to a lot of different strategies being developed in other states, including class action suits and challenges to teacher certification and other procedures of state educational systems."[255]

Teachers should not take lightly suits by "individual consumers who have already bought products and are not happy about it."[256]

Such "malpractice" suits attempt to make "scapegoats" out of teachers and school boards. "Teachers have little voice in financing, equipping, or organizing schools. *There is no constitutional right of literacy*, and the child himself might be guilty to contributory negligence."[257]

"With the age of accountability, teachers can no longer blame parents, the environment, or the socioeconomic status of the family for nonteaching."[258]

Elsewhere in this book is reference to insurance available to schoolteachers from private companies that insure against legal liability for "malpractice."[259]

Peter N. Doe's suit was filed in 1972 but as of July 1973 had not been served on the San Francisco school district, yet the district has "voluntarily said it will set goals for students and possibly would not issue diplomas if a student is unable to read at the proper level."[260] The issue raised by this lawsuit, however, is broader than just "reading ability," and a court decision, if it is favorable to the plaintiff, could involve all of the courses in the school curriculum.[261]

Some school districts have been investigating new guidelines for graduation from high school which would provide local school flexibility, while setting minimum standards of attainment for academic and career-oriented skills.[262] Also discussed is "career education," whereby every student is required to graduate from high school with a "saleable skill" even though he may be college bound. One innovation in this area is the "furlough plan," an experimental project approved by the board of education for the Los Angeles city schools whereby up to 980 high school seniors in the district may annually leave their schools for a year-long furlough to work or study; the three-year program is aimed at persuading potential "dropouts" to obtain high school credits outside the regular curriculum and return later and graduate upon completing the necessary basic academic subjects.

Education furloughs will be granted students who have been identified by the school district staff as potential dropouts. The evaluation will be based on sporadic attendance, low academic achievement, discipline problems, lack of motivation, and special economic needs.[263]

The project, if it is successful, could lead to major modifications in school compulsory-attendance laws.

Extracurricular Activities

The Jefferson County "Decree" ordered that no student should be segregated or discriminated against on account of race or color in extracurricular activities and provided expressly that

a student attending school for the first time on a desegregated basis may not be subject to any disqualification or waiting period for participation in activities and programs, including athletics which might otherwise apply because he is a transfer or newly assigned student except that such transferees shall be subject to long-standing, non-racially based rules of city, county, or state athletic associations dealing with the eligibility of or transfer students for athletic contests.[264]

This provision has been repeated in a number of subsequent district court opinions.[265]

The question was raised in 1970 when a white student was denied the right to play football because the rule of a state high school association made a transfer student ineligible for athletic teams until he had attended the new school for an entire year. The rule was upheld in *Paschal v. Perdue.*[266] The student, a member of a Florida public school football team in 1969, transferred to a private school in 1970 because of his "deteriorating academic performance." Because of the rule, he was rendered ineligible to participate in the sport. (The public school authorities had refused to execute a "waiver" that would make him eligible to play for the private school, and the state association approved that decision.) The boy sought injunctive relief under the Civil Rights Act of 1964; said the court: "While the Civil Rights Act of 1964 was enacted historically to correct abuses in the treatment of Blacks, it applies as well to equal protection of whites." And the court added: "although there is no federal constitutional right to play football, there is a federally enforceable right under the equal protection clause not to be denied eligibility by state action, to play football solely because of the color of the player's skin."[267] The action of the state association's officers in refusing a waiver was "state action" for constitutional purposes. However, the refusal in this case was *not motivated by racial considerations*, but rather was based on a long-standing rule adopted for the legitimate purpose of preventing interschool raids on athletic teams and of aiding in the maintenance of discipline by coaches:

The requirement of a waiver is designed to prevent "raids" upon athletic teams. Its objective is also to assure the effectiveness of discipline in preventing an athlete from summarily quitting a team when he dislikes an order of the coach or a requirement regarding training.[268]

Since the plaintiffs failed to carry "their burden" of proving that the boy was denied any rights because of race or color, the petition for the injunction was denied, and the case was dismissed.

Courts have held that a high school student does not have an absolute right to participate in interscholastic athletics,[269] that actions of state high school athletic associations are judicially reviewable,[270] and that the imposition of the one-year residency requirement for participation in interschool sports does not deny a student his fundamental right to an education.[271] In this latter case, *Sturrup v. Mahan,*[272] the court said that the student was exercising a fundamental right by moving into Indiana, and that therefore withholding the privilege of participating in athletics penalized his free exercise of this right and could be justified only by a "compelling state interest." The prevention of recruiting of athletes and "school-jumping" to maintain amateur standing of high school athletes was a "compelling state interest" that justified the one-year residency rule.

The courts are divided over whether school officials can regulate the hair of athletes. Thus, a hair-length rule established by the basketball coach at Emporia

High School in Kansas, which required that "hair will be neat and trim at all times and will be no longer than that of the members of the coaching staff," was struck down by the district court as being "vague, arbitrary, and essentially capricious" and prescribing an "impermissible standard."[273]

On the other hand, in *Neuhause v. Torrey*[274] a district court held that the following regulation applicable to athletes only had a rational and reasonable basis, was not arbitrary or capricious, and did not violate the Fourteenth Amendment rights of athletes:

Each athlete will be well groomed, neat in appearance . . . clean shaven. The hair will be out of the eyes, trimmed above the ears, and above the collar in the back. Willful violation of these rules will lead to suspension from all athletic competition during the season when the violation occurred.

The court noted that the regulation applied only to male athletes, not to the whole student body at the school, that this case invades the sensitive, delicate, and demanding role of athlete and coach, that athletic programs provide unique forms for the development of discipline not found in other school programs, that long hair could adversely affect performance, especially sprinters, but also swimmers and wrestlers, and that coaches had testified that enforcement of such regulations is a means of building team morale, discipline, and spirit.

In these parlous, troubled times when discipline in certain quarters appears to be an ugly word, it should not be considered unreasonable nor regarded as an impingement of constitutional prerogatives to require [athletes] . . . to bring themselves within the spirit, purpose and intendments of the questioned rule.

The following are some dress and grooming "guidelines" adopted by one high school for athletes:[275]

1. The professional leadership will determine appropriate day-of-game and uniform dress criteria.

2. Safety and performance criteria for each sport will be determined by the respective coaches.

3. Hair regulations will be made by students and coaches, each person having one vote, for each of the sports. A two-thirds majority vote will establish hair regulations, but if such a vote can't be reached, the coach will make a decision.

4. A student may appeal safety and performance disputes to a review board of five students and five coaches with the burden of proof resting with the student. Decision of the review board is final.

The doctrine of "separate but equal" apparently never has been applied to boys and girls who participate in school sports; the athletic programs at most schools have been very "separate and unequal" and tended to discriminate against the girls both by expulsion of them from participation on certain school teams and also in the amounts of money made available for support of the "dual" athletic programs. State legislatures, educational associations, and the courts are just beginning to take notice of this kind of discrimination between the sexes in school athletics.

The concept of sexual equality will be carried into the funding of athletic programs, if the Illinois Education Association is heeded. After active floor debate ... the IEA adopted a resolution accepting non-discrimination between the sexes and calling for equal funding.[276]

According to the resolution, equality in athletics covers equal "allotted time for use of gym and equipment and payment for qualified coaches for both boys and girls."

Two bills have been introduced into the California Senate[277] to end sex discrimination in the budgeting of high school and state college athletic programs; these bills call for efforts by school officials to provide "equal athletic facilities and programs for women students as for men." While the programs could be different for boys and girls, no longer would a school be able to spend, say, $40,000 on its boys' football program, but only $1000 on the girls' interscholastic gymnastic program. Not only equality in the amount of money expended, but equality in the basis of the funding of the programs would also be required:

In some cases the girls' program is financed by bake sales and hot-dog sales at football games, while the men's program is funded generously out of the school's general budget. If sales are poor, then the women's program suffers.[278]

One argument for equalizing expenditures on boys' and girls' athletic programs is that parents pay taxes on an equal basis, regardless of their child's sex, yet the income from those taxes is not being "distributed on an equal basis in public financed athletic programs, but in a manner which is overwhelmingly favorable to parents of males."

Some documented cases of such discrimination in school athletic programs have already been announced:[279]

1. At a high school in Davis, California, the boys' tennis team was permitted to practice on six new courts, while the girls' team was required to play on older courts described as "not really even suited for roller skating."

2. Los Altos High School is said to have spent $12,200 on men's athletic programs, but only $2800 on such programs for women.

3. At the above-mentioned school, boys were provided free uniforms, including "warming-up suits," while girls received uniforms bought using funds raised from "bake sales" and other such activities of the girls' athletic league.

4. Boys' teams often have more privileges than girls' teams when the two share the same facilities; thus, at one school the girls were evicted from the

swimming pool one hour before the boys' swim meet so that the boys could warm up; yet the girls were allowed only five minutes to warm up before the beginning of their meet.

The Illinois High School Associations' "bylaws" prohibiting girls from participating in boys' athletic programs was upheld by a U.S. district court judge in a case involving two girl swimmers who charged a violation of their Fourteenth Amendment rights.[280] The judge said that the question before him was whether there was a "rational basis" for the bylaws; he found that high school interscholastic sports are "properly a part of a school's overall education-al program" since they promote an interest in athletics and thereby encourage students to participate in activities that benefit them "physically and mentally." In weighing the "rationality" of the bylaws, the judge took judicial notice that "at the pinnacle of all sporting contests, the Olympia Games, the men's times in each event are consistently better than those of the women."[281] Furthermore, in this particular case the boys' times in state swimming championships were better than those of either of the girls who complained about the bylaws. "Finally, plaintiffs' claim that the physical and psychological differences between male and female athletes are 'unfounded assumptions' is refuted by expert testimony presented and received in a case that the 'plaintiffs' themselves cite in their favor." All of these facts, said the judge, lend substantial credence to the fears expressed by women coaches and athletes in the affidavits that unrestricted athletic competition between the sexes would consistently lead to male domination of interscholastic sports and actually result in a decrease in female participation in such events. Such opinions, added the judge, have a rational basis in fact and are a constitutionally sufficient reason for prohibiting athletic interscholastic competition between boys and girls.

Two high school girls, both otherwise fully qualified other than for their sex, wanted to participate in "non-contact" interscholastic sports, one in tennis and the other in skiing and cross-country running, but were denied permission because neither of their schools provided teams for females in these sports and because of the following regulation of the Minnesota State High School League, which barred girls from participating with boys in interscholastic athletics,

Girls shall be prohibited from participating in the boys' interscholastic athletic program either as a member of the boys' team or as a member of the girls' team playing the boys' team.
The girls' team shall not accept male members.[282]

Trial court in *Brenden v. Independent School District 742,*[283] said: "Brought to its base [the girls were discriminated against in athletics] solely on the basis of the fact of sex and sex alone," and the court held that the league rule was "arbitrary and unreasonable, in violation of the fourteenth amendment," and ordered that the girls be permitted to participate in the appropriate school teams with boys and enjoined the league from imposing any sanctions on any schools that engaged in games with the schools involved in this suit. On appeal, the Eighth U.S. Circuit Court of Appeals affirmed the trial court decision.[284] The court said this decision does not concern whether schools can satisfy their equal protection obligation by providing "separate but equal" athletic facilities for boys and girls, nor whether girls can participate with boys in "contact" sports. Although the Minnesota State High School League is a voluntary organization, both courts found "state action" in the fact that Minnesota law authorized public high schools to join the league. In evaluating a claim that "state action" violates the Constitution's equal protection clause, the appeals court said three criteria must be considered: the character of the classification in question; the individual interest affected by the classification; and the governmental interests asserted in support of the classification.[285] Courts, in recent years, have become sensitive to sex-based classifications.

There is no longer any doubt that sex-based classifications are subject to scrutiny under the Equal Protection Clause and will be struck down when they provide dissimilar treatment for men and women who are similarly situated with respect to the object of the classification.

Discrimination in high school interscholastic athletics "constitutes discrimination in education." Such sports are just as valuable for females as for males. The court then said:

A classification "must be reasonable, not arbitrary, and must rest upon some ground of difference having a *fair and substantial* relation to the object of the legislation, so that all persons in similar circumstances shall be treated alike."[286]

The Minnesota State High School League's rule barring girls from participating in boys' "non-contact" interscholastic sports failed to meet this test and therefore was arbitrary and unreasonable in violation of the equal protection clause of the Fourteenth Amendment.[287]

The court in the *Brenden case* referred to a 1969 experiment conducted by the New York State Department of Education which involved one hundred schools and which extended over a sixteen-months period in which the schools maintained athletic teams in which both males and females participated. Said the court: "The results of the experiment were overwhelmingly favorable to continuing mixed competition," and it quoted the following from a report on the experiment:

Should the practice of allowing girls to compete on boys' athletic teams be continued? Eighty percent of the principals, directors, women physical educators, coaches, and physicians involved in the experiment voted in favor of continuing the practice, either as an experiment or as legal policy. Slightly more than 90 percent of the boy team members, girl participants, parents, coaches, and opposing coaches also favored continuation of the practice.[288]

As a result of this experiment the state of New York amended its rules to allow females to compete with males. Girls may now participate on the same team with boys in interscholastic competition in the sports of: archery, badminton, bowling, fencing, golf, gymnastics, riflery, rowing (but only as coxswain), shuffleboard, skiing, swimming and diving, table tennis, tennis, and track and field. Participation is permissible, however, *provided*, that the school attended by the girl wishing to participate in the sport does not maintain a girls' team in that sport. In exceptional cases, the principal or chief executive officer may permit a girl to waive this last mentioned requirement.[289]

The district courts are divided on the question whether a rule like that of the Minnesota High School League is constitutional,[290] and no case on this subject has yet been taken to the Supreme Court of the United States for a decision; whereas that Court has refused to review student haircut cases and has thus left the country divided on that matter, it is possible that a case involving a "sex-based classification" in school athletics may eventually be offered to the Court. If so, a pronouncement such as the following can be expected in this area too:

There can be no doubt that our Nation has had a long and unfortunate history of sex discrimination. Traditionally, such discrimination was rationalized by an attitude of "romantic paternalism" which, in practical effect, put women not on a pedestal, but in a cage.[291]

Taxes on gate receipts, refunds to spectators because of the presidential "price freeze," and tickets to a Rose Bowl football game have been the subjects of lawsuits involving educational institutions. *Allen v. Regents of the University of Georgia*[292] involved the constitutionality of the federal "excise tax" on admissions tickets to athletic contests; the university argued that because the proceeds from such contests "were used to further the state's program of education," the federal "excise tax" collected on such tickets placed an "unconstitutional burden on the state in fulfilling its educational function." The university conceded that athletic events constituted a "business" that would ordinarily be taxable, but since the receipts were being used to further the educational purposes of the state, they should be free from such taxes.

The United States Supreme Court, however, decided to the contrary, and held that the federal "excise tax" does apply to "gate receipts" at athletic contests. *Only an Act of Congress could change this ruling*—and that is exactly what Georgians sought; for sixteen years they addressed Congress to exempt athletic contests from the tax. In 1958, Public Law-324 (March 31, 1954) resulted in a new U.S. Treasury regulation that provided for

exemption from tax for admission to athletic games and exhibitions, including wrestling and boxing matches between educational institutions, provided they are held during the regular athletic season for the particular activity involved, and provided that the proceeds inure exclusively to the benefit of the participating institutions. However, admissions to post-season games, such as bowl games, continue to be subject to tax. (*IRS Release*, April 1, 1954)

The University of Southern California, although victorious in the Rose Bowl, lost a scrimmage with the United States Supreme Court in February 1973 when the Court, 9-0, denied the University's petition for a writ of certiorari in the case of *University of Southern California v. Cost of Living Council;*[293] the justices voted unanimously to reject the University's claim that it need not refund 50 cents on each of the 140,000 tickets sold for games played during the 1971 "wage-price" freeze.[294] The university had sought reversal of a ruling by the Cost of Living Council and Emergency Appeals Court which ordered the refunds. Reserved seat tickets had been raised to $6.50 months before the economic controls began on August 15, 1971, but the council and the appeals court ruled that the "freeze" applied because the games were played after that date. Attornies for the university made these points in their argument: nonprofit institutions that raised ticket price to athletic events will be faced with an "overwhelming revenue loss"; the University is being punished for conduct which was legal at the time it was committed; punishment is being imposed without judicial trial; and the order of the council and the appeals court violated constitutional provisions against "ex post facto" laws and "bills of attainder." The Supreme Court, however, refused to comment on any of these arguments.

In *Weaver v. Pasadena Tournament of Roses,*[295] four plaintiffs who alleged that they brought suit on behalf of themselves and all others similarly situated, sued the Tournament of Roses for the recovery of a $100 penalty for wrongful exclusion from the Rose Bowl football game on New Year's Day, 1947. They alleged that the managers of the Tournament had publically advertised that 7500 tickets would go on sale on December 23, 1946 whereas in fact only 1500 tickets were sold to the public. The plaintiffs had stubs as evidence of their place in line entitling them to purchase two tickets each at the time the box office was closed and it was announced that there were no more available; the further fact was alleged that there were more tickets, but these were disposed of at private sale in disregard of the priority evidenced by the plaintiffs' stubs. The defendant demurred and the demurrer was sustained on appeal, the court holding that this was not a proper "class action."

The athletic programs at some high schools have been expanded to include "high risk" sports[296] such as scuba diving; this may give rise to a particular form of instructor's liability; "An instructor's liability doesn't end once a student completes a [scuba diving] course; he's open to a liability claim resulting from negligence in instruction for a number of years beyond the course."[297] Teacher insurance against claims giving rise to such liability is available from some private companies.

Other extracurricular cases include *Caldwell v. Craighead*[298] wherein a boy and his mother were dismissed from the same Tennessee high school, the boy for refusal to play the school song, "Dixie," in the "prep band" and the mother for her inability to perform satisfactorily her job as a teacher's aide. The Court on appeal upheld both dismissals: the boy had walked out of a band performance in violation of a clear and specific disciplinary regulation of which he had notice; and the mother's dismissal was not racially motivated but was simply because she had failed to perform her duties adequately.

One kind of "extracurricular activity" which bothers teachers and school administrators is teenage marriages, and some school districts accordingly have adopted special regulations to deal with married students, usually intended to minimize their contact with the other pupils, especially during school social activities. In support of this different treatment of married students, it is frequently argued that such students expect special consideration (and thus can be a disruptive influence), that they attend school irregularly,[299] and that they sometimes discuss matters of a "personal and intimate nature" while at school.[300] Although this approach to the problem is changing now,[301] courts in the past have upheld school regulations treating married pupils differently. In *Kissick v. Garland Independent School District* (1959),[302] a sixteen-year-old letterman on the school's football team was excluded from athletics when he married; the Texas school district had a policy restricting married students "wholly to classroom work" and excluding them from participating in athletics and other extracurricular activities, including holding a school office. The court saw nothing unreasonable or arbitrary in such a rule and, accordingly, upheld it.

However, school regulations that require the separation from the regular student body of pupils who marry, divorce, or become pregnant are under attack in some courts as violations of the student's constitutional rights. Thus, a divorcee, who was married at age fifteen, remained married for ten months, and then gave her child away for adoption has been ordered admitted to regular classes at her school. District Judge Allen B. Hannay ruled (1972) that the Houston, Texas school regulation excluding divorcees from classes violates the student's constitutional rights guaranteed by the equal protection clause of the Fourteenth Amendment.[303]

In *Ordway v. Hargraves*[304] (1971) the Massachusetts district court held that a pregnant, unmarried senior could not be excluded by the school authorities from attending regular classes at the high school. Miss Fay Ordway's baby was due in June near the time of her graduation, and the school officials, who had learned of the pregnancy only in January, proposed the following procedures for her relations with the school for the remainder of the year:

a) Fay will absent herself from school during regular school hours.
b) Fay will be allowed to make use of all school facilities such as library, guidance, administrative, teaching, etc., on any school day after the normal dismissal time of 2:16 P.M.
c) Fay will be allowed to attend all school functions such as games, dances, plays, etc.
d) Participation in senior activities such as class trip, reception, etc.
e) Seek extra help from her teachers during after school help sessions when needed.
f) Tutoring at no cost if necessary; such tutors to be approved by the administration.

g) Her name will remain on the second register for the remainder of the 1970-71 school year (to terminate on graduation day—tentatively scheduled for June 11, 1971).

h) Examinations will be taken periodically based upon mutual agreement between Fay and the respective teacher.[305]

The girl objected to this special, isolated treatment and retained counsel.

At the hearing, testimony was presented that the girl was in excellent health, that there were no medical reasons why she should not participate in all ordinary school activities except "violent calisthenics," and that

policies relating to allowing or forbidding pregnant girls to attend high school are now widely varying within the state and throughout the United States . . . both Boston and New York now allow attendance of unmarried pregnant students in their high schools.[306]

The school's principal was unable to state any "educational purpose" to be served by excluding the girl from regular classes, and he conceded that the pregnancy had not occasioned "any disruptive incident nor has it otherwise interfered with school activities." (Citing the *Tinker case*, where the Supreme Court limited school official's "curtailment of claimed rights to situations involving 'substantial' or 'material' interference with school activities.") However, the principal's testimony did imply that the policy of the school committee may have been based on a desire

not to appear to condone conduct on the part of unmarried students of a nature to cause pregnancy. The thrust of his testimony seems to be: the regional school has both junior and senior high school students in its student population; he finds the twelve-to-fourteen age group to be still flexible in their attitudes; they might be led to believe that the school authorities are condoning premarital relations if they were to allow girl students in plaintiff's situation to remain in school.[307]

The court saw no merit in this argument, however.

In summary, the court found no danger to the girl's health resulting from permitting her to attend classes during regular school hours and no likelihood that her presence would cause a disruption on the school campus, nor was any valid educational or other reason shown "to justify her segregation and to require her to receive a type of educational treatment which is not the equal of that given to all others in her class."[308] The burden of proof was placed on the school authorities. Said the court:

It would seem beyond argument that *the right to receive a public education is a basic personal right or liberty*. Consequently, the burden of justifying any school rule or regulation limiting or terminating that right is on the school authorities.[309]

The court found that the school district failed to carry that burden and ordered the girl readmitted to the high school "at 8 A.M., Monday, March 14, 1971."

The United States Supreme Court has made it clear that the right to marry is a fundamental right protected by the First, Ninth, and Fourteenth Amendments to the Constitution.[310] It is also well established that a student cannot be permanently expelled from the public schools because of his marital status without a factual showing of some misconduct or immorality, and without a clear and convincing demonstration that the welfare or discipline of the school would be harmfully affected by the presence of married students. Antimarriage school rules are constitutionally flawed because of their "sweeping, advance determination that every married student regardless of the circumstances" must be expelled from the schools.[311]

Where the government argued that the public school cases are inapposite to the control that must be maintained in the military academies and that the "no-marriage" rule of the Merchant Marine Academy is only a minor and temporary restraint, not a denial of the fundamental right to marry, the U.S. District Court in *O'Neill v. Dent* (1973),[312] held that such a rule violates the First and Fifth Amendment rights of cadets. The court said there are three equal protection tests that could conceivably be applied to the facts of this case:

1. The "strict scrutiny" test,[313]
2. The "substantial relation" test,[314] and
3. The "minimal scrutiny" test.[315]

In view of the fundamental nature of the right involved, the court elected to apply the first test, "strict scrutiny," and to require the government to demonstrate a "compelling necessity" for the regulation. The court concluded that the Academy failed to demonstrate the "clearest kind of imperative" for interference with the cadet's right to marry and failed even to satisfy the more lenient "substantial relation" test. "The irrebuttable presumption that all married cadets will perform poorer than single cadets cannot be accepted." Accordingly, the "no-marriage" rule violates the First and Fifth Amendments of the Constitution.

A girl who was refused initiation into the National Honor Society because of "alleged involvement with a male teacher"[316] complained to the New Jersey Commissioner of Education. In *Tiffany v. Board of Education*,[317] dated January 3, 1973, the commissioner upheld the girl's contention that the National Honor Society was an extracurricular activity under the sponsorship of the board and subject to their regulations; the board was ordered to answer the girl's plea. An appeal by the local board is pending.

Student Records

"Yet another area in which students' constitutional rights are ignored is the way pupil records are handled. At issue is chronic invasion of privacy."[318] Pupils and their parents generally have very little knowledge about what records a school keeps on a child and much less what sort of data has been placed in any particular file. With the development of "multilevel" information systems, which use computers for the transmittal and retrieval of data, the confidentiality of student records presents a potential legal problem for school districts. It has been observed:

Virtually all school systems maintain extensive pupil records containing, in addition to a pupil's attendance and achievement records, standardized test scores, personality data, information on family background and current status, health data, teacher and counselor observations, anecdotal records, and so on. Despite this fact, very few systems have clearly defined and systematically implemented policies regarding uses of information about pupils, the conditions under which such information is collected, and who may have access to it.[319]

Computerized multilevel information systems, which can have great value to school systems and for research purposes, bring into focus the problem of confidentiality and invasion of privacy and the need for guards against illegitimate access to such student data. While the flow of student data in such a system is to many interested and concerned parties,

files may be designated as public information and thus accessed to anyone, or files may be designated as proprietary information with ranges in the amount of access provided. Access to proprietary information is gained either by typing in a password or by using a terminal which the system has validated as accessible to given information.[320]

The problem for school districts involves both the collection *and* the dissemination of data in student files. The Russell Sage Foundation report quoted above recommends that "no information should be collected from students without the prior informed consent of the child and his parents" and that no information be given to anyone outside the school system without "written consent from the student's parents specifying records to be released, and to whom, and with a copy of the records to be released to the student's parents and/or student if desired by the parents," except under judicial process.[321] The report further recommends that files that contain possibly damaging information about a student should be periodically destroyed. The confidentiality of pupil records in California is governed by Section 10,751 of the *Education Code*, which prohibits any teacher, principal, employee, or governing board member of any public, private, or parochial school from permitting access to the written records concerning any pupil, except for certain designated persons or under judicial process.

Tests, questionnaires, surveys, or examinations that inquire about a student's personal beliefs or practices in sex, family life, morality, and religion (including questions about the student's parents' beliefs in these areas) are prohibited by law in California schools, unless the parent is notified in writing that such tests, etc. will be administered and gives written permission for such testing.[322]

The Student "Bill of Rights"

The California Federation of Teachers, in 1972, sponsored a conference on student rights that resulted in a publication entitled *The Rights of a Student as a Person,*[323] which proposed the idea of a new relationship between the student and his school. This publication, which declares that the right to an education is a "fundamental interest" and that a student is a person under the U.S. Constitution and entitled to protection of all the rights included therein, contained thirteen specific points:

1. The student has a right to a meaningful education which includes access to all points of view.

2. The student has freedom of speech and expression, including wearing of buttons, emblems, and other insignia.

3. The student has the right to form political and social organizations, to assemble, to petition, and to bring speakers to the campus. To achieve these ends, students have the right to assemble in suitable areas on the school grounds.

4. The student has the right to distribute printed or other material inside or outside of school during all times except in class areas while a class is in session.

5. Students must be informed in writing of their rights and responsibilities by the school administration, and of any amendments which may be adopted.

6. Students have the right to democratic representation in governing, administrative, and faculty bodies affecting students, curriculum, and students rights.

7. Students have the right to leave campus during nonacademic hours.

8. A student's person or property shall not be searched, seized, or violated until or unless probable cause has been established.

9. The students shall have the right to see their cumulative files, transcripts, and other student-related information; furthermore, the students must be informed of any information placed in their files and they must be afforded the opportunity to place a formal response in the file with respect to any data placed therein by any other person. No such information shall be divulged to anyone other than the student's parents or guardians (when the student is under eighteen years of age) without the student's consent.

10. Students have the right to free election of their peers in student government, and all students have the right to seek and hold office.

11. Students have the right to sanitary and safe conditions in school plants.

12. If a student feels his rights have been violated, he may request and receive a hearing before a school site appeals board.

13. Students who are eighteen shall have adult rights including, but not restricted to, the right to smoke in designated areas during free periods, the option of eliminating parent conferences, and the removal of the requirement for parent approval in any school-related matter.

Some of these student "rights" have been recognized by school districts as a result of the 1969 Supreme Court *Tinker* decision, while others are outside the scope of the requirements of that decision and would require legislative changes in state laws and codes affecting the schools.[324]

In another connection, although equally appropriately cited here, is the statement about school districts' handling of student records and the use of pressure, threats, and eventual lawsuits to change the system:

As with other rights of students under the Constitution, these recommendations are not likely to be widely implemented without persistent pressure on school authorities from students and parents, including but not limited to, the filing of law suits.[325]

Schoolteachers and administrators, whose actions are within the requirements of the law, must refuse to be intimidated by such pressure or threats. On the other hand, where school district authorities have adopted policies and practices that appear to violate students' rights—even students' "alleged rights"—these policies and practices should be reviewed and changed or sound constitutional arguments established for their continuance.

Conclusions

We're on the verge of the last and greatest frontier in civil and legal rights—the rights of children.[326]

Expanded rights for children raises the specter of students constantly litigating with their schools, but that is not quite true, because the legal rights that a child can claim are still relatively few. And where the schools are involved, the Supreme Court of the United States has said that these rights must be "applied in the light of the special characteristics of the school environment." Although students are persons under the Constitution and have a "full panoply of constitutional rights" flowing from the First, Fourth, Fifth, and Fourteenth Amendments, children's rights are not coextensive with the rights of adults. The challenge the courts face in these school cases involving student haircuts, pregnancy, testing and grading practices, record keeping and personal information dissemination, invasion of privacy, discrimination in interscholastic athletics, admission and graduation requirements, corporal punishment, etc. is to define the child's fundamental rights and interests in such a way that protects him against illegitimate abuse, but without undermining the efforts of school authorities in exercising the necessary control and discipline over the entire educational process. On the part of the courts, this involves a "balancing of the public interest" in education against the right of the child to be free from such abuse; on the part of the school authorities it involves, in part, forecasting student conduct that would interfere "materially and substantially" with the orderly operation and administration of the school. It is in the courtrooms and on the school campuses that these "balancing" and "forecasting" processes are taking place and where children's rights of the greatest value and number are still being worked out.

Today, many of the benefits of parental authority are missing in the home, which very often was broken by divorce or separation, and more and more children have "guardians," not their parents, to oversee their welfare. Under these circumstances, the school authorities acting *in loco parentis* must perform a very great public service which extends beyond the traditional bounds of public education. The danger lies to the public interest in developing educated good citizens if school administrators and schoolteachers ever become so circumscribed by court actions and threats of court actions that they abdicate that responsibility towards the child which historically and rightfully is theirs. Already some teachers in some school districts have taken the attitude that "it's hardly worth the candle" and leave the school premises at the end of the day almost as promptly as their students.

6

Conclusions, Applications, and Limitations

Wherever the law gives special rights to one, or imposes special burdens on another, it does so on the ground that certain special facts are true of those individuals. In all such cases, therefore, there is a twofold task. First to determine what are the facts to which the special consequences are attached; second, to ascertain the consequences.

Holmes, *The Common Law* (1881)

General Conclusions, Findings, and Reasoning

Based on the preceding analysis of court decisions that have affected the organization, administration, and programs of the public schools and on evidence collected from the social science and legal literature, the following principal findings of fact and conclusions of law emerge from this study.

There are three principal areas where constitutional law and education intersect: race, wealth, and individual rights. This is a fact; it has always been true, but only recently very widely recognized.

This fact has been obscured by another fact: the courts originally tended to ignore education; the federal courts viewed it as a state or local matter, while the state courts adopted a laissez faire attitude of "leaving education to the educators." Consequently, school policies and practices were generally reviewed only for *reasonableness*; unless they were shown to be "arbitrary, capricious, or unreasonable," courts would not question the educational wisdom of school rules.[1] This is also fact, documentable by thousands of state court decisions before 1950.[2]

It is a finding of this study that there developed, during this period (1850 to *circa* 1950), a broad body of statutory and decisional law at the state level which permitted and encouraged school policies and practices which did not meet minimum constitutional standards.[3]

It is a fact that federal court involvement in education came about primarily because of state statutes and educational policies that required separation of the races in the schools. It is a conclusion of law and a finding of this study that such statutes and educational policies violated the equal protection clause of the Fourteenth Amendment and were therefore unconstitutional, *Brown v. Board of Education of Topeka.*[4]

It is a true statement of fact, a valid conclusion of law, and a finding of this study that at least one state court has held that the right to an *equal educational opportunity*

149

1. is an inalienable right, within the Bill of Rights, the Fifth and Fourteenth Amendments of the United States Constitution;
2. is a fundamental right;
3. is a legal right;
4. is a species of property, equal to, if not greater than, other tangible property rights; it being the right to be a human being.[5]

However, this study finds not true, either by way of fact or conclusions of law, that the courts have yet identified the specific *constitutional right* to demand a public school education (*q.v.*, Ninth Amendment).[6]

It is a fact that broad powers have been exercised by the federal courts in the enforcement of the above-mentioned *right to an equal educational opportunity.* It is a finding of this study that these powers include: openings of public schools closed by the states to avoid desegregation; closings of public schools in the furtherance of integration; invalidation of contracts for the sale of public school buildings where such sale would contribute to school segregation; assignment of students and teachers to particular schools to achieve "racial balance"; and many other acts involving the courts in the organization, administration, and programs of the public schools, including, but not limited to, mandating "remedial education programs," busing students across school district lines, invalidation of school financing systems, and ordering taxation for the support of the schools.[7] It is a conclusion of law, however, that the equal protection clause of the Fourteenth Amendment empowers federal courts to thus actively intervene in a state function. This study further finds that some federal courts in some areas of public education have tended to become and do act as the "real" administrators of the schools, thereby challenging the Tenth Amendment's concept of education as one of the powers reserved as a state function.

It is a fact that education today is one of the important functions performed by state and local governments (*Brown v. Board of Education of Topeka,*[8] *Serrano v. Priest*[9]). However, it is a conclusion of law that the right to education in the public schools is a "fundamental interest" entitled to the stricter protection afforded by the New Equal Protection Standard. This study finds that originally in the states of California, Michigan, and *ab initio* New Jersey, education has been characterized by state courts as a "fundamental interest" and thus entitled to the stricter protection and review which is customarily afforded to a constitutional right.[10] However, the Supreme Court of the United States held in *San Antonio Independent School District v. Rodriguez* (36 L. Ed. 2d 16) that education is not a "fundamental interest" and not a federal matter since education is not among the rights afforded explicit protection under the federal Constitution.

It is a fact that students and teachers possess constitutionally protected rights of "freedom of expression" and other personal liberties under the First and Fourteenth Amendments, but it is a conclusion of law that, when an infringement of one of these rights or liberties is alleged, the burden of proof lies with the school district. This study finds that at least since 1969 the federal courts have placed this burden on the school districts.[11]

Additionally, there is proof in the literature and in court decisions to support the following statements, which are uncontradictable and hence are true facts:

1. Federal courts, at least since 1960, have adopted the practice of retaining jurisdiction over decided cases, thus extending their powers to act in the future if their orders are not carried out by school authorities.[12]

2. Whereas federal courts have countermanded state legislative acts designed to avoid desegregation of schools, only recently have they ordered legislatures to take affirmative action affecting the schools; on the other hand, such courts have frequently ordered school authorities to perform specific acts in and about the schools.[13]

The following are some conclusions of law that are accepted as true and that are incorporated as a part of the findings of this study:

1. Educational classifications based on *race* or *wealth* are inherently "suspect."[14]

2. Educational classifications based on *race* invidiously discriminate and therefore violate equal protection of the laws.[15]

3. A classification that touches on a "fundamental interest" is subject to the "compelling state purpose" test, regardless of the basis of the classification (see Chapter 4).

It is uncontrovertible and true and a finding of this study that in education, more than in any other field of human endeavor, "classification" is a widely used tool in our work. In schools, *classifying factors* such as IQ test scores, etc. are employed for the express purpose of categorizing people for *unequal* treatment. This study finds not true, however, that without classification the business of education could not proceed.[16]

It is a fact that school district power to suspend or to expel a student has been curtailed by recent decisions of some federal courts; however, it is a conclusion of law that the *right to receive a public school education is a basic personal right or liberty*. This study finds that the federal courts are not in agreement that education is a personal right or liberty protected under the due process clause of the Fifth and Fourteenth Amendments.[17]

However, it is a true fact that where the right to receive a public school education is treated as a *personal right or liberty*, the burden of justifying school rules or regulations that limit or terminate that right or liberty is placed on the school district.[18]

The following are some specific findings of this study all of which are true:

1. There is no right not to go to a school, except until after a certain age, or until after completion of a certain grade level.

2. There is no right to attend a public school, but there is a right to demand an "equal educational opportunity" from a public school.[19]

3. There is a right to choose a private education as against a public one.[20]

4. Pregnancy or marriage are not valid reasons for excluding a student from regular public school classes.[21]

5. Some courts hold that student grooming is a *personal right or liberty* protected under due process by the Fifth and Fourteenth Amendments. Such courts require that a "countervailing state interest" be either "self-evident" or "affirmatively shown" to justify school district intrusion upon this liberty.[22]

6. Student and teacher First and Fourteenth Amendment rights of "freedom of expression" include a "broad panoply" of methods of expression, including "nonverbal" messages.[23]

The following are, conclusions of law:

1. Education is (or is not) a "fundamental interest."[24]

2. School policies and practices which touch upon a "fundamental interest" are subject to *strict scrutiny* by the courts.

3. The burden of proof is on the state (i.e., schools) to show a "compelling state purpose" that necessitates continued use of school practices that touch upon a "fundamental interest."

4. School policies and practices must be *reasonable*, otherwise they will fail to meet even the "traditional" test.

5. Educational classifications based on *race* or *wealth* are suspect.

6. Educational classifications that discriminate on the basis of *race* are invidious and hence void.

It is a true fact, a conclusion of law, and a finding of this study that education in some schools in some parts of the country is now being conducted "under the control and supervision of the courts."[25]

Applications to Specific Areas of School Administration

The foregoing statements of fact, conclusions of law, and findings of this study can be shown to have direct relevance for the following areas of administrative studies in the field of education:

School Personnel Administration

School personnel policies and practices are especially vulnerable to attack under the new equal protection standard: they are, for the most part, state mandated;

they touch upon a "fundamental interest"; and, when challenged under the Fourteenth Amendment, they are subject to "strict scrutiny" by the courts. The school district must be prepared to bear the burden of establishing a "compelling state purpose" that necessitates the continued use of the challenged practices. This is true whether the practices are attacked because of their discriminatory effects or otherwise.

It goes without saying that personnel practices must be *reasonable*, otherwise they will fail even to meet the "traditional" test.

However, the traditional argument of "reasonableness" will not replace the need for the statement of a "compelling state purpose" when the courts examine with "strict scrutiny" such widely used personnel procedures as: "promotion lists" and "manning tables" for advancement of employees; job assignments based on required degrees and diplomas; the "patterned interview"; teacher evaluation procedures—tests and interviews that measure teacher "skills, attitudes, and knowledge" required for specific assignments; "cut-off" scores on employment and promotion examinations; differential salary schedules that classify on the basis of the job being done; teacher tenure and seniority systems; employee termination procedures; and compulsory retirement at a specific age. The school district's maintenance of a confidential "inventory of the skills, attitudes, and knowledge" of its teachers could be viewed as suspect, not only for its possible discriminatory effect but also for the lack of a clearly established or self-evident "compelling state purpose" that necessitates school district collecting and maintaining such information about its employees. And it might as well be anticipated now, because it can be reasonably and logically expected to follow under the California doctrine of *Serrano v. Priest*, that the state will eventually be required to establish the "compelling state purpose" that necessitates the requirement of the *teaching credential* itself.

Note also that testing and other employment practices that discriminate on the basis of race have already been enjoined by the Supreme Court of the United States on other grounds, i.e., "relation to job performance" (*Griggs v. Duke Power Company*).[26] This is true even in the absence of "discriminatory intent." Even though personnel tests and the requirement for degrees, diplomas, and credentials are shown to be "job related," it may still be necessary, when they are challenged under the new equal protection, for the school district to show a "compelling state purpose" that necessitates the continued use of such practices.

Supervision in Public Schools

Supervisors in California will soon discover that they have a powerful ally and some new tools to assist them in their work. The ally is the courts, which are likewise looking with "strict scrutiny" at the practices and procedures used in the instructional programs at the schools. The new tools are court "decrees" and "mandates" which order changes made in the schools.

The supervisor's role as the instructional leader becomes even more significant and meaningful in the period of "education under the supervision of the courts." He occupies the key position in effectuating court-ordered change in the instructional program. As the "man in the middle" with a "court order in his pocket," the supervisor has a new form of *persuasion* for getting things done, and promptly too. His position, however, is still a most difficult one.

Like personnel policies and practices described above, the procedures and techniques of supervision are not immune to "strict scrutiny" by the courts when they are challenged under the new equal protection. A "compelling state purpose" will be required to justify those procedures used by supervisors to evaluate the performance and effectiveness of teachers, the use of "rating indices," the assignment of "teacher aides" and paraprofessionals to some schools but not to others, the unequal distribution of professional specialists (librarians, health and guidance counsellors, etc.) throughout the district, equal opportunities for teacher development and growth, and so forth. For example, what "compelling state purpose" necessitates making a teacher's advancement on the salary schedule dependent upon her participation in the district in-service education program? Do we have sound evidence of the effectiveness of the particular in-service education program involved which would withstand "strict scrutiny" by the court? In staff utilization, the supervisor must begin to think in terms of the "compelling state purposes" that necessitate the various assignments of personnel and be prepared to defend his decisions under court scrutiny.

Supervisors who still use the old technique of "inspection and rating" for evaluation of teachers are especially vulnerable under the new equal protection, while those that employ the technique of "direction and guidance" will find their procedures easier to defend and more likely to withstand "strict scrutiny" when reviewed in court.

Governance of Public Schools

Far-reaching changes are occurring in the area of school governance, first in the South and now in the North, where school districts are under court orders to desegregate. Some of these changes are a result of lower federal court decisions that appear to be silently challenging the concept of education as a power reserved to the states under the Tenth Amendment. This is asserted as true and is shown by recent court of appeals decisions and district court decisions ordering busing across school district lines. Moreover, the revered concept of "local control" of the schools has already been expressly disallowed by a number of courts as not a valid argument (not a "compelling state purpose") for maintaining existing school financing systems. In *Serrano v. Priest*,[27] the California Supreme Court looked at "local control," which it assumed "arguendo" was a compelling interest of the state, and then concluded that it was an insufficient reason to justify the present fiscal scheme, noting however that no matter how a state finances its public schools, it can still leave the decision-making power to the local district. In the *Cahill case*,[28] however, the New Jersey superior court took a dim view of the value of "local control" and raised the question as to what extent such control is "real or mythical," described it in one sense as "illusory," and concluded that it is sometimes "control for the wealthy, not for the poor."

Local governance of the schools in some districts in the South has been critically circumscribed (if not virtually eliminated) where it has been used by the people to perpetuate discrimination based on race. So fundamental a matter as the right of a school district governing board to sell property has been placed under the necessity for prior court approval, as has the decision to build and where to locate new school buildings, the appointment of principals and other key school personnel, and so forth.

In the area of school governance, therefore, the requirements of the new equal protection encompass almost the whole of the state *Education Code* which itself can be expected in due course to come under the "strict scrutiny" of the courts when provisions of the *Code* are challenged under the new equal protection. The burden will be on the state to show a "compelling state purpose" that demonstrates the necessity for continuance of the challenged code-authorized practices. Other specific areas of governance particularly vulnerable to such strict review, certainly if they contribute to racial discrimination or school segregation, include: school-board decisions concerning student participation in the making of sensitive academic decisions; decisions about the merger of faculty and student governments; decisions affecting teacher unionization and collective bargaining with the school district; systems of teacher (and student) evaluation and accountability; the authorization of the use of "corporal punishment" in the schools; state-mandated school district boundary lines; and student and teacher assignments to specific schools within the district, and so forth.

School Finance

As shown in Chapter 4, the "compelling state interest" test was first applied to school financing systems in August 1971, when the Supreme Court of California announced in *Serrano v. Priest*[29] that education is a "fundamental interest," and that principle was quickly cited with approval and followed in courts across the country, e.g., Texas, Minnesota, and New Jersey; in *Robinson v. Cahill*, the New Jersey trial court went one step further and applied the principle to another aspect of school financing; "There is no compelling justification for making a taxpayer in one district pay at a higher rate than a taxpayer in another district, so long as the revenue serves a common state educational purpose."[30]

However, the Supreme Court of the United States two years later in *San*

Antonio Independent School District v. Rodriguez[31] refused to accept the "right-to-an-education" argument, saying that education is not one of the "rights" specified in the Constitution: "Education, of course, is not among the rights afforded explicit protection under our Federal Constitution. Nor do we find any basis for saying it is implicitly so protected." The Supreme Court, by thus rejecting the "federal-right-to-an-education" thesis, stemmed the tide of court cases that had spread across the country invalidating state school financing systems that used the local district property tax to support schools under the Fourteenth Amendment; however, the door was left open to court review of such systems on *state* constitutional grounds. Whereas, *ab initio*, the New Jersey trial court based its decision on state and federal constitutional provisions, the New Jersey appeals court relying on the state constitution found that the system of financing schools in that state failed to meet the requirement of providing a "thorough and efficient" system of education for all of the children in the state.[32]

Which leads to the next logical and natural questions: What constraints are there on this new judicial function of court supervision and control of the schools? Is there some "institutional limitation?" What constitutes violation of the concept of "judicial self-restraint?"

Limitations

We might perhaps begin by considering Cox's observation: "Once loosed, the idea of Equality is not easily cabined."[33] Gunther and Dowling, discussing future expansions of the new equal protection concept in general, suggest that there are "institutional limitations" that eventually will serve as restrictions on operation of such judicial power.[34] The fact is that a few court decisions involving the schools have already acknowledged the judge's awareness of such institutional limitations. Recall Judge Wright's regrets about his lack of "expertise" in this area and his announced willingness to have educational matters "resolved in the political arena by other branches of the government."[35] Also relevant is Judge James P. Coleman's observation, made in the midst of circuit court frustration over lack of school district compliance with the Supreme Court's order in the *Brown case*,[36] that it does no good to complain that the school people have had fifteen years in which to do something about segregation and yet have not done it. "As a matter of fact, most of the school districts now before us, if not all of them, have been *under the supervision of the federal courts for as much as five years*. I think it is quite clear what this proves."[37]

When the attorney general in *Robinson v. Cahill* (1972) expressed doubts about "the ability of the court to grapple with an issue as large and complex as the public school system," Judge Botter, who had just "grappled" in a thirty-four page opinion with the New Jersey school financing system, acknowledged that there was "merit" in this contention.[38]

Statements, some of which are cited elsewhere in this book,[39] have also been made by Supreme Court justices cautioning the Court about becoming a "super-school-board," especially the admonition by Mr. Justice Black, concurring in *Epperson v. Arkansas*:

However wise this Court may be or may become hereafter, it is doubtful that, sitting in Washington, it can successfully supervise and censor the curriculum of every public school in every hamlet and city in the United States. I doubt that our wisdom is so nearly infallible.[40]

Other such cautionary dicta could be cited to support the thesis that there are "institutional limitations" that constitute a point where a system so large and so complex as the public schools will cause court frustration—and hence restrict further court activity in the area.

There are suggestions in the literature of other limitations on the expansion of the equal protection concept generally. Thus, Sager observed: "Any move away from race as such ... stretches thin the fabric of judicial restraint." It would not be surprising "if the Court were *to assimilate a single area at a time into the new equal protection fold*, and were to do so rather cautiously."[41]

The role of the judiciary in education generally, and in the schools in particular, can be expected to change when state legislatures enact school laws that meet constitutionally required *minima*. Thus, as the developments "Note" on equal protection in the 1969 *Harvard Law Review*[42] observes, "The constitutional obligation to enforce the equal protection guarantee rests alike, after all, on the legislative as well as the judicial branch of the government." *As state legislatures move to make their school codes conform to the Constitution one would expect there to be less need for federal court concern with the management or operation of the schools.*[43]

Finally, as a "staple diet," it is conceivable that the courts will tire of educational issues and will reasonably and rationally conclude that there are more important problems for them to resolve, using Mr. Justice Black's words, than "the length of the hair of schoolboys."[44]

Notwithstanding anything previously said or written on the subject, the "state action" concept as applied to public education is not yet dead—and the Supreme Court in none of its school decisions to date has been willing to abandon it. "State action," then, appears to be a clear and present limitation, at this time, so far as the majority members of the Supreme Court of the United States are concerned,[45] but not for certain state courts.

Parting Word

"At last there emerges a rule or a principle," declares Mr. Justice Cardozo "which becomes a datum, a point of departure from which new lines will be run, from which new courses will be measured."[46] Such was the nature of the principle–education as a "fundamental interest"–which emerged in 1971 from the *Serrano* decision, and from which already new lines are being extended and new courses of action are being measured.

Cardozo cautioned, however, that there is a "tendency of a principle to expand to the limits of its logic,"[47] and Chief Justice Burger has said that "such expansion must always be contained by the historical frame of reference of the principle's purpose."[48] The broad language used by the Supreme Court of California in the *Serrano* decision makes it unmistakably clear that this new principle applies to all aspects of education discussed in this book, namely, the organization, administration, and programs of the public schools–and activities touching thereon. The Supreme Court of the United States and courts in other states disagree, however.

Notes

Notes

Chapter 1
Introduction

1. See James S. Coleman, "The Concept of Equality of Educational Opportunity," in *Equal Educational Opportunity*, (Cambridge, Mass.: Harvard University Press, 1970), pp. 9-24. Cf. Morris D. Forkosch, *Treatise on Labor Law*, Indianapolis, Indiana: The Bobbs-Merrill Company, 1965, pp. 135-152.

2. A remnant of this is found in today's law requiring work permits:

In order that children may be disciplined and trained in the habits of work and industry by their parents . . . nothing in this chapter shall require a permit to work to be issued to any minor or require a permit to employ to be issued to the parent or guardian when the work or intended work to be performed by the minor is for or under the control of his parent or guardian and is performed upon or in connection with the premises owned, operated, or controlled by the parent or guardian.

Manufacturing, mercantile, and similar nonagricultural enterprises are excepted. See *California Educational Code*, Sec. 12,782 (Stats. 1971, Ch. 1388).

3. From the beginning, public policy has dictated that the state assume a hands-off attitude towards private education, and this has endured, in large part, even until today. See *Pierce, Governor of Oregon v. Society of Sisters*, 268 U.S. 510 (1925). But see *Gonzales v. Fairfax-Brewster, Inc.*, 42 LAW WEEK 2077 (D.C., E. Va., July 27, 1973).

4. "The common schools are doorways opening into chambers of science, art, and the learned professions, as well as into fields of industrial and commercial activities. Opportunities for securing employment are often more or less dependent upon the rating which a youth, as a pupil of our public institutions, has received in his school work. These are rights and privileges that cannot be denied." *Piper v. Big Pine School District of Inyo County*, 193 Cal. 664, 673 (1924).

5. Coleman, p. 11.

6. "Education, like the postal service, has been socialized, or publicly financed and operated almost from its origin. The *type* of socialized education, not the question of its existence, is the only matter currently in dispute." *Rodriguez v. San Antonio Independent School District*, 337 F. Supp. 284 (1972).

7. See Chapter 2.

8. Coleman, p. 16. According to Coleman, the original meaning of the concept of "educational opportunity" included:

1. providing a *free* education up to a given level which constituted the principal entry point to the labor force;
2. providing *common curriculum* for all children, regardless of background;
3. partly by design and partly because of low population density, providing that children from diverse backgrounds attend the *same school;*
4. providing equality within a given *locality*, since local taxes provided the source of support for schools (p. 13).

9. Frederic Jesup Stimpson, *The Law of the Federal and State Constitutions of the United States, With an Historical Study of their Principles, A Chronological Table of English Social Legislation, and A Compartive Digest of the Constitutions of the Forty-Six States,* (Boston: Boston Book Company, 1908), p. 141.

10. See Chapter 3. For the extension of the "equality" concept into school finance, see Chapter 4, and into the area of student and teacher rights, Chapter 5.

11. In some States the Constitution declares that the people

have a right to education, which it is the duty of the State to guard and maintain, "without discrimination of race, color, caste, or sex." In others, that a general diffusion of knowledge and intelligence being essential to the preservation of the rights and liberties of the people, it shall be the duty of the Legislature to encourage the promotion of intellectual, scientific, moral, social, and agricultural improvement, "to cherish the interest of literature and the sciences," or "to encourage schools and the means of instruction." (Stimpson, p. 140.)

But not a word is said about *"equality* of educational opportunity."

12. The California Supreme Court has held that these provisions of the state constitution are "substantially equivalent" to the Fourteenth Amendment of the Federal Constitution. See *Serrano v. Priest*, 96 Cal. Rptr. 609 (1971).

13. Actually education serves not only the public interest, but individual interests, and social interests as well. See Roscoe Pound, *Outlines of Lectures on Jurisprudence*, (Cambridge, Mass.: Harvard University Press, 1943), pp. 96-97, and Chapter 4 of this book.

14. 347 U.S. 483 (1954).

15. Ibid., p. 493.

16. *Sullivan v. Houston Independent School District*, 333 F. Supp. 1149, 1172 (S.D. Tex. 1971).

17. *Williams v. Dade County School Board*, 441 F. 2d 299, 302 (5th Cir. 1971).

18. *Hosier v. Evans*, 302 F. Supp. 316, 319 (D. St. Croix 1970).

19. *Ordway v. Hargraves*, 332 F. Supp. 1155, 1158 (D. Mass. 1971).

20. *Chandler v. South Bend Community School Corporation*, N.D., Indiana, August 26, 1971, quoted in *Inequality in Education*, no. 12 (July 1972), p. 40.

21. *Crawford v. Board of Education of the City of Los Angeles*, Superior Court, State of California, Los Angeles County, "Minute Order" No. 822,854, February 11, 1970, p. 77. See excerpts from this decision reported in John C. Hogan, "The Role of the Courts in Certain Educational Policy Formation," *Policy Sciences*, vol. 1, no. 3 (Fall 1970), pp. 289-97.

22. 96 Cal. Rptr. 618.

23. 36 L. Ed. 2d 16-105 (1973).

24. Ibid., p. 44.

25. Violations of rights secured by the Constitution, whether they occur on a school campus or elsewhere are, of course, a federal matter in which courts may legitimately intervene.

26. 36 L. Ed. 2d 45.

Chapter 2
Changing Conceptions of the Role
of the Courts in Education

1. 269 F. Supp. 401-519 (1967), *aff'd sub. nom. Smuck v. Hobson*, 408 F. 2d 175 (D.C. Cir., 1969). Judge Wright, far from departing the educational scene as this quote might imply, is still actively engaged in the operation of the District of Columbia public schools. See *Hobson v. Hansen*, 327 F. Supp. 844 (D.C., D.C. 1971).

2. *Roberts v. The City of Boston*, 59 Mass. (5 Cushing) 198 (1849) was decided on the basis of state law. See discussion of the case in Chapter 3 below.

3. Four subdivisions of this stage have been noticed. See Harold L. Tyler, "The Legal Status of Pupil Placement in the Public Schools," in E.C. Bolmeier (ed.), *Legal Issues in Education, Abridged: Duke Doctoral Dissertations* (Charlottesville, Va.: The Michie Company, 1970), pp. 137-39.

4. A district court order dismissing a school integration case after a finding that the school district was desegregated and unitary was vacated by the court of appeals, which ordered the district court to reinstate the case and to retain jurisdiction for not less than three years, during which time the school district would be required to file semiannual reports with the court—and the dismissal of the case might even be further delayed after the three-year period. *Youngblood v. Board of Public Instruction of Bay County, Florida*, 448 F. 2d 770 (C.A. Fla. 1971). See *Calhoun v. Cook*, 451 F. 2d 583 (5th Cir. 1971).

5. 36 L. Ed. 2d 16-105 (1973).

6. Ibid., p. 44.

7. See further discussion, Chapter 3. See John C. Hogan, " 'Obtaining an Education' as a Right of the People," *3 NOLPE School Law Journal 15–26* (1973).

8. See "Note About the Estimate," Appendix B in John C. Hogan, *An*

Analysis of Selected Court Decisions Which Have Applied the Fourteenth Amendment to the Organization, Administration, and Programs of the Public Schools, 1950-1972, Ph.D. Dissertation, UCLA, 1972.

9. The increase after 1956 can be attributed, in large part, to attempts by courts to implement the mandate of *Brown v. Board of Education of Topeka* (1954) and the subsequent decisions concerned with the desegregation of southern school districts.

10. A significant decrease in court activity affecting education occurred during 1936-46, probably related to the decline in school enrollments during World War II. (But the number of federal cases actually had a modest increase during this period.)

11. *State, ex rel. Clark v. Haworth*, 122 Ind. 462 (1899).

12. *McQueen v. Port Huron City Commission*, 194 Mich. 328, p. 336 (1916).

13. *Brown v. Board of Education of Topeka*, 347 U.S. 483 (1954).

14. *Cooper v. Aaron*, 358 U.S. 1 (1958).

15. *United States v. Butler* 297 U.S. 1 (1936). *Helvering v. Davis*, 310 U.S. 619 (1937).

16. Federal court cases involving the schools have arisen under four sections of the Constitution: Art. 1, Sec. 10 (obligation of contracts), *First Amendment* (religion, speech, press, assembly, petition), *Fifth Amendment* (due process) and *Fourteenth Amendment* (due process, and equal protection). Since about 1950, the courts have made greatest use of the First and Fourteenth Amendments in cases affecting the schools.

17. See Chapter 5.

18. *Barron v. Baltimore*, 7 Pet. 243 (1833).

19. *Gitlow v. New York*, 268 U.S. 652 (1925). See also *Fiske v. Kansas*, 274 U.S. 380 (1927), where a state law was invalidated on the grounds that it abridged freedom of speech contrary to the due process clause of the Fourteenth Amendment.

20. *Memorandum Decisions*, 425 F. 2d 1211, 1214 (1970). Italics added. Guy S. Kelley, Superintendent of Schools for Wilcox County, Alabama, who carries a .32 gun, received a sheaf of daily reports from his schools and said in an interview: "Might as well mail them direct to the Federal Court. They're the ones running my schools these days." (Quoted by James T. Wooten, "Integration Comes and Teacher Asks, 'Where are the Children?' " *New York Times*, March 30, 1972.)

21. See *Steel v. Board of Public Instruction of Leon County*, 448 F. 2d 767 (1971).

22. Cases are discussed in Chapters 3 and 4 below.

23. *Smith v. St. Tammany Parish School Board*, 448 F. 2d 414 (C.A. La., 1971).

24. *Moore v. Board of Education of Chidester School District No. 54*, 448 F. 2d 709 (C.A. 8th Cir., 1971).

25. *U.S. v. Perry County Board of Education*, 445 F. 2d 302 (C.A. Ala., 1971).

26. *Northcross v. Board of Education of Memphis City Schools*, 444 F. 2d 1179 (C.A. Tenn., 1971).

27. *Lemon v. Bossier Parish School Board*, 444 F. 2d 1400 (C.A. La., 1971).

28. *Hobson v. Hansen*, 327 F. Supp. 844 (D.C., D.C., 1971).

29. *Clark v. Board of Directors of Little Rock School District*, 328 F. Supp. 205 (D.C., Ark., 1971). Italics added.

30. Northern cities already ordered to desegregate their schools include San Francisco, Los Angeles, Pontiac, Las Vegas, Indianapolis, and others. The first case involving *de facto* segregation to reach the Supreme Court of the United States was *Keyes v. School District No. 1, Denver*, 445 F. 2d 990 (10th Cir. 1971). See discussion of school desegregation outside of the South, Chapter 3; Betty E. Sinowitz, "School Integration and the Teacher," *Today's Education*, vol. 62, no. 5 (May 1973), pp. 31-33.

31. Estimated from figures on the federal judiciary found in *United States Government Organizational Manual, 1971/72*, (Washington, D.C.: Government Printing Office, 1971), pp. 45-53, and from figures on the state judiciary found in *The Book of the States, 1970-71* (Lexington, Ky.: The Council of State Government, 1970), table 2, p. 121.

32. There are approximately 300,000 lawyers in the United States.

33. But see *San Antonio Independent School District v. Rodriguez*, 36 L. Ed. 2d 16-105 (1973); Thomas A. Shannon, "Rodriguez: A Dream Shattered or a Call for Finance Reform?" *Phi Delta Kappan*, vol. 54, no. 9, (May 1973), pp. 587 ff.

34. 347 U.S. 483 (1954).

35. *State of Illinois ex rel. McCollum v. Board of Education of School District No. 71*, 333 U.S. 203, 237 (1948).

36. *Epperson v. Arkansas*, 393 U.S. 114 (1968).

37. 175 U.S. 528, 545 (1899).

38. See John C. Hogan, "The Role of the Courts in Certain Educational Policy Formation," *Policy Sciences* I (Fall 1970), pp. 289-97.

39. See Table No. 180, "Public Elementary and Secondary Schools—Segregation-Desegregation Status, 17 Southern States: 1955-1970." *Statistical Abstract of the United States, 1972*, Washington, D.C.: Government Printing Office, 1972, p. 118.

40. E.g., Pasadena, Inglewood, etc. school district desegregation decisions.

41. See California State Board of Education "Guidelines" on racial balance in the schools, and "Guidelines for Student Expression on Campus" designed to make state school policies conform to the *Tinker* decision. See discussion in Chapter 5.

42. E.g., *Alabama Civil Liberties Union v. Wallace*, 301 F. Supp. 969 (1971), attacking a state statute requiring daily reading of the Bible in the public schools

as a violation of the First Amendment. *Askew v. Hargrave*, 401 U.S. 476 (1970), brief *amicus curiae* by the Florida Educational Research Foundation.

43. See "Text of President's Statement," *New York Times*, March 17, 1972.

44. In a survey of public attitudes toward local government, a "substantial majority of 4,300 persons interviewed recently in 10 cities say their schools are very good or good enough." (K.J. Rabben, "Education Notebook: News Study Refutes Cherished Notions About Public Schools," *Santa Monica Evening Outlook*, January 1, 1971.)

45. George Gallup, "The Third Annual Survey of The Public's Attitudes Towards the Public Schools, 1971," *Phi Delta Kappan*, vol. 53, no. 1 (September 1971), p. 35. "There are definite differences of opinion between men in education and the general public on school questions. . . . The two groups simply see the same facts and problems through different lenses and with different funds of knowledge." (Ibid., p. 34.)

46. George Gallup, "Fourth Annual Gallup Poll of Public Attitudes Towards Education," *Phi Delta Kappan*, vol. 54, no. 1, (September 1972), p. 34.

47. See Charles E. Silberman, *Crisis in the Classroom: The Remaking of American Education* (New York: Random House, 1970); Ivan Illich, *Deschooling Society* (New York: Harper and Row, 1971).

Chapter 3
Race and Education

1. *Racial Isolation in the Public Schools*, A Report of the U.S. Commission on Civil Rights (Washington, D.C., U.S. Government Printing Office, vol. 1, 1967), p. 246.

2. See pp. 22 to 24 above.

3. Forkosch, *Constitutional Law* (Mineola, New York, The Foundation Press, Inc., 1969), p. 358.

4. *Strauder v. West Virginia*, 100 U.S. 303 (1880).

5. 16 Wall. 81 (1872). "If the judgments in . . . the school cases are not supportable on the basis of neutral constitutional principles, they deserve to be jettisoned. . . . The three post-Civil War Amendments were fashioned to one major end—an end to which we are only now making substantial strides—the full emancipation of the Negro." Pollock, "Racial Discrimination and Judicial Integrity: A Reply to Professor Wechsler," 108 *University of Pennsylvania Law Review* 31, (1959). See Wechsler, "Towards Neutral Principles of Constitutional Law," 72 *Harvard Law Review* 1-35 (1959).

6. 100 U.S. 303 (1880).

7. Forkosch, p. 513.

8. See Bickel, "The Original Understanding and the Segregation Decision," 69 *Harvard Law Review* 1-65 (1955). Note, "Developments in the Law—Equal Protection," 82 *Harvard Law Review* 1068-69 (1969).

9. "Miscellaneous Orders," June 8, 1953, 345 U.S. 972-973 (1953).

10. 347 U.S. 483, p. 489 (1954).

11. 400 U.S. 112, pp. 152-229 (1970), p. 201. Concerned with voting rights.

12. Ibid., pp. 139-40. Italics added.

13. See Harlan's opinion in *Oregon v. Mitchell*, 400 U.S. 152-229 (1970) tracing the history of the Fourteenth Amendment with respect to voting rights. Cooley, in 1871, observed that "new provisions" for personal liberty came into being as a result of enactment of the Thirteenth and Fourteenth Amendments, but that "the most important clause in the fourteenth amendment is that part of section 1 which declares that all persons born or naturalized in the United States, and subject to the jurisdiction thereof, are citizens of the United States and of the State wherein they reside. . . . It may be doubtful whether the further provisions of the same section surround the citizen with any protections additional to those possessed under state constitutions." (Cooley, *Constitutional Limitations*, p. 294.) "This Amendment of the Constitution does not concentrate power in the general government for any purpose of police government within the states" (Ibid., p. 294, n. 1.)

14. The prohibitions of the Fourteenth Amendment have reference to state action exclusively. *Virginia v. Rives*, 100 U.S. 318 (1897). No agency of the state nor officers or agents by whom its powers are exercised may deny to any person within its jurisdiction equal protection of the law. *Ex parte Virginia*, 100 U.S. 347 (1879). However, a valid law may be wrongfully administered by officers of the state, but that is another kind of action.

15. See *United States v. Cruikshank*, 92 U.S. 542 (1875).

16. 109 U.S. 3 (1883).

17. Horowitz, "The Misleading Search for 'State Action' under the Fourteenth Amendment," 30 *Southern California Law Review* 209 (1957). See Hale, "Rights Under the Fourteenth and Fifteenth Amendment Against Injuries Inflicted by Private Individuals," 6 *Lawyers Guild Review* 627 (1947).

18. *Reitman v. Mulkey*, 387 U.S. 369 (1967).

19. *Burton v. Wilmington Parking Authority*, 365 U.S. 715 (1961).

20. *Marsh v. Alabama*, 326 U.S. 501 (1946).

21. 382 U.S. 296 (1966), pp. 321-22. Italics added.

22. Van Alstyne and Karst, "State Action," 14 *Stanford Law Review* 28 (1961).

23. *Gonzales v. Fairfax-Brewster, Inc.*, 42 Law Week 2077 (August 7, 1973).

24. Civil Rights Act of 1866, 42 U.S.C. Sec. 1981.

25. George S. Leonard, Southern Independent Schools Association attorney, *Los Angeles Times*, July 30, 1973.

26. Allison Brown, attorney for the plaintiffs. (Ibid.)

27. Leonard, op. cit.

28. Williams, "The Twilight of State Action," 41 *Texas Law Review* 348-490 (1963). While the equal protection clause protects individuals against state action, "the involvement of the State" need not be "either exclusive or direct."

(*United States v. Guest*, 383 U.S. 745, 755.) "In a variety of situations the Court has found state action of a nature sufficient to create rights under the Equal Protection Clause even though the participation of the State was peripheral, or its action was only one of several co-operative forces leading to the constitutional violation." (Ibid., at 755-56.)

29. See *Keyes v. School District No. 1, Denver, Colorado*, 37 L. Ed. 2d 548-595 (1973).

30. 59 Mass. Rpts. (5 Cushing) 198 (1849), p. 205.

31. 59 Mass. Rpts. 207.

32. Harold W. Horowitz and Kenneth L. Karst, *Law, Lawyers and Social Change* (Indianapolis: The Bobbs-Merrill Company, 1969), p. 120. See discussion of *The New Equal Protection Standard* in John C. Hogan, " 'Obtaining an Education' As A Right of the People," 3 *NOLPE School Law Journal* 15 (1973).

33. 59 Mass. Rpts. 210.

34. 163 U.S. 537 (1896).

35. John C. Hogan, "The Role of the Courts in Certain Educational Policy Formation," *Policy Sciences*, I, (Fall 1970), p. 291, n. 11 lists the education race cases from *Plessy* to *Brown* and some of those decided after 1954.

36. 347 U.S. 483 (1954).

37. Ibid., p. 495. Some think

the time has come for a reevaluation of that landmark decision. That the Court's reliance upon controversial sociological and psychological data not only makes the decision itself questionable, but leaves the rationale of the case open to attack by proof of new and inconsistent theories. Bloomfield, "Equality of Educational Opportunity: Judicial Supervision of Public Education," 43 *Southern California Law Review* 276 (1970).

Recent research by David Armor presents evidence against school integration through busing. He cites evidence from several cities in which busing has taken place, showing no gains in achievement among black students, and he presents attitudinal data from one city showing that attitudes of whites and blacks toward one another became less positive after integration through busing. (David Armor, "The Evidence on Busing," *The Public Interest*, no. 28, Summer 1972.) Armor's research has been subject to criticism (see Thomas Pettigrew, et. al., "Busing, a Review of 'The Evidence'," and Armor's reply in *The Public Interest*, no. 30 (Winter 1973), and it is not clear just how the effects of integration through busing will turn out in the end. But the evidence is sufficiently ambiguous that statements like Bloomfield's can reasonably be made.

38. In *Gomperts v. Chase*, 30 L. Ed. 2d 30 (1971), Justice Douglas appears to revive the doctrine of "separate but equal" when he suggests that it still applies to segregated schools existing under *de facto* situations.

39. 175 U.S. 528 (1899).

40. 211 U.S. 45 (1908).

41. 275 U.S. 78 (1927).

42. Ibid., pp. 78-79.

43. 305 U.S. 337 (1938). Supreme Court of Missouri Reversed.

44. Ibid., pp. 349-51. Italics added. In *Missouri ex rel. Gaines v. Canada* (1938) and all the previous race cases, the word *negro* was printed in the official reports of the Supreme Court with a lower case *n*, while in *Sipuel v. Board of Regents of the University of Oklahoma* (1948) and all subsequent race cases the word was printed *Negro*.

45. 339 U.S. 629 (1950).

46. Ibid., pp. 633-34.

47. Ibid., p. 635.

48. 339 U.S. 637 (1950).

49. Ibid., p. 642.

50. 342 U.S. 350 (1951).

51. See John H. Sherry, *The Law of Innkeepers—for Hotels, Motels, Restaurants, and Clubs*. (Ithaca, New York: Cornell University Press, 1972), pp. 44-65.

52. "All marriages of white persons with negroes, Mongolians, members of the Malay race, or mulattoes are illegal and void." (*California Civil Code*, 1949 edition, Sec. 60.)

53. 32 C. 2d 711 (1948).

54. 374 U.S. 483 (1954). Italics added.

55. Justice Douglas in *Gomperts v. Chase*, 30 L. Ed. 2d 30 (1971).

56. 402 U.S. 1 (1971).

57. Ibid., pp. 22-23.

58. Ibid., p. 15.

59. 30 L. Ed. 2d 19 (1971).

60. Ibid., pp. 20-21.

61. Holmes' reference to the "clavical in the cat"—that reminant of the law of former times which "tells of the existence of some earlier creature to which a collar-bone was useful." (Holmes, *The Common Law*, p. 35.)

62. See pp. 113-18 below.

63. 59 Cal. 2d 876 (1963).

64. Ibid., p. 881.

65. Ibid., p. 610. Italics added. See *San Francisco Unified School District v. Johnson*, 3 C. 3d 937 (1971). See 1971 "Statutes, Racial or Ethnic Balance," Ch. 1765, *West's California Legislative Service*, No. 10 (1971).

66. The majority of cases reject the asserted affirmative duty to remedy *de facto* segregation; notable decisions are those of the Second Circuit (*Offermann v. Nitkowski* [2d Cir. 1967] 378 F.2d 22, 24 [dictim]); Sixth Circuit (*Deal v. Cincinnati Board of Education* [6th Cir. 1966] 369 F.2d 55, 61-62); Seventh Circuit (*Bell v. School City of Gary* [7th Cir. 1963] 324 F.2d 209, 212); and the Tenth Circuit (*Board of Education of Oklahoma City Public School v. Dowell*

[10th Cir. 1967] 375 F.2d 158, 166 [dictum] ; *Downs v. Board of Education of Kansas City* [10th Cir. 1964] 336 F.2d 988, 998).

Federal district courts, however, have asserted this affirmative duty in the District of Columbia (*Hobson v. Hansen* [D.C. 1967] 269 F. Supp. 401, 506-508); Massachusetts (*Barksdale v. Springfield School Committee* [D. Mass. 1965] 237 F. Supp. 543, 546-47); Michigan (*Davis v. School District of City of Pontiac, Inc.* [E.D. Mich 1970] 309 F. Supp. 734, 744); and New York (*Blocker v. Board of Education of Manhasset* [E.D.N.Y. 1964] 226 F. Supp. 208, 226-29: *Branche v. Board of Education of Town of Hempstead* [E.D.N.Y. 1962] 204 F. Supp. 150, 153-54).

67. 404 U.S. 1221 (1971). Opinion in chambers.

68. Ibid., p. 1228, quoting from *Swann*, p. 24. Italics added by Chief Justice Burger.

69. Ibid., pp. 1229-30.

70. Ibid., p. 1230.

71. Owen M. Fiss, "Racial Imbalance in the Public Schools: The Constitutional Concepts," 78 *Harvard Law Review* 573 (1965).

72. "Text of President's Statement," *New York Times*, March 16, 1972.

73. 338 F. Supp. 67 (1972). See "Civil Rights—Judicial Consolidation of Public School Districts to Achieve Racial Balance, 25 *Vanderbilt Law Review* 893-909 (1972).

74. *Bradley v. School Board of City of Richmond, Virginia*, 462 F 2d 1058, 1060 (1972).

75. Ibid., p. 1069.

We think it fair to say that the only educational reason offered by the numerous school experts in support of consolidation was the egalitarian concept that it is good for children of diverse economic, racial and social background to associate together more than would be possible within the Richmond school district. The experts thought that the optimum size school district was one having a school population of from 20,000 to 50,000 pupils. When a district is too small, specialized programs tend to be eliminated, and when a school district is too large, it tends to become unwieldy and cumbersome and to lose parent participation. Thus the consensus was that the three separate school districts were about the right size, and the consolidated district much larger than desirable for educational and administrative purposes." (Ibid., p. 1068.)

76. 41 *The United States Law Week* 4685 (May 21, 1973).

77. *Bradley v. Milliken*, 345 F. Supp. 914 (1972).

78. See *Washington Post*, December 9, 1972; and *Education Daily*, December 11, 1972, pp. 1-2.

79. Ibid.

80. Ibid.

81. Ibid.

82. *New York Times*, June 13, 1973. See T.A. Smedley, "The Last Two

Years in School Desegregation," *Race Relations Reporter*, vol. 9, no. 4 (May 1973), pp. 14-18, a condensation of an article from the *Vanderbilt Law Review*, (April 1973). Four members of the Supreme Court—Justices Burger, Rehnquist, Blackmun, and Stewart—have already indicated their unwillingness (the Richmond tie) to carry the desegregation effort across school district boundaries. Justice Powell, a former Virginia school board member who disqualified himself in the Richmond case, can be expected to participate when the Detroit appeal is heard, and his vote could be the vote that breaks the tie, leading either to a five to four decision in favor of the metropolitan districts or vice versa. Justice Stewart, who voted for "strict construction" in the *Rodriguez case* on school finance and who is reported to have joined the Nixon appointees in the Richmond tie, would not be expected to change his position.

83. 474 F. 2d 81 (1973), affirming 332 F. Supp. 655 (1971). See also 466 F. 2d 573 (1972). Case filed May 31, 1968.

84. 332 F. Supp. 656-57. On June 11, the district court rejected a "stabilization plan" submitted by the school board, and thus set the stage for a trial to begin in the suit to determine whether the nineteen suburban school districts should be involved in efforts to desegregate the schools of Indianapolis. *New York Times*, June 13, 1973.

85. 292 N.E. 2d 338 (1973). See *School Committee of Springfield v. Board of Education*, 287 N.E. 2d 438 (1972).

86. 292 N.E. 2d 341, note 5.

87. Ibid., p. 342, note 8, italics added.

88. 326 F. Supp. 1235 (1971), aff'd 404 U.S. 1072 (1972).

89. Ibid., pp. 1239-43.

90. 345 F. Supp. 795 (1972).

91. Ibid., p. 797.

92. 491 P. 2d 1234 (1971).

93. 350 F. Supp. 149 (1972).

94. *New York Times*, June 1, 1972; ibid., April 8, 1973.

95. *New York Times*, June 8, 1972. A three-judge panel later issued a stay pending outcome of the Supreme Court review of the Richmond, Virginia case. *Race Relations Reporter*, vol. 4, no. 3, February 19, 1973, p. 6.

96. 188 F. Supp. 401 (1959), (hereinafter known as *Calhoun v. Latimer*).

97. Ibid., 404.

98. 377 U.S. 263 (1964).

99. 443 F. 2d 1174 (1971).

100., See 332 F. Supp. 804-10 (1971).

101. 188 F. Supp. 809.

102. 451 F. 2d 583 (1971).

103. See note 75 above.

104. 469 F. 2d 1068 (1972).

105. Ibid., p. 1067.

106. Reginald Stuart, "Atlanta Splits on School Plan," *Race Relations Reporter*, vol. 4, no. 3 (February 19, 1973), pp. 6-7.

107. *Race Relations Reporter*, vol. 4, no. 9 (May 1973), p. 4.

108. Lonnie King, President, Atlanta Chapter, NAACP, ibid.

109. Said to be the NAACP/ACLU position, ibid., p. 5.

110. Benjamin Mays, Atlanta School Board President, ibid. See "Atlanta is No Longer a Shining Example," *Los Angeles Times*, July 29, 1973.

111. 41 LAW WEEK 5002-5-25 (June 19, 1971). See also discussion of "Northern Segregation," 42 LAW WEEK 3054 (July 10, 1973).

112. See 303 F. Supp. 279 (1969), 303 F. Supp. 289 (1969), 313 F. Supp. 61 (1970), and 313 F. Supp. 90 (1970).

113. 163 U.S. 537 (1896).

114. 445 F. 2d 990 (1971).

115. See 41 LAW WEEK 5002. Justices Douglas, Stewart, Marshall, and Blackmun joined Brennan.

116. Chief Justice Burger concurred in the result without a written opinion; Justice White took no part in the decision of the case; Justice Powell concurred in part and dissented in part; Justice Douglas filed a separate opinion; and Justice Rehnquist wrote a dissenting opinion.

117. See Linda Mathews, "Supreme Court—Nixon's Stamp Clearly Visible," *Los Angeles Times*, July 1, 1973.

118. "Hispanos," persons of Spanish, Mexican, or Cuban heritage, and in the Southwest more commonly referred to as "Chicanos" or "Mexican-Americans." 41 LAW WEEK 5003, note 6.

119. Ibid., p. 5004.

120. See pp. 51-52.

121. 41 LAW WEEK 5002.

122. Ibid., pp. 5005-6. Italics added.

123. Ibid.

124. II Wigmore, *Evidence* 200 (3d ed., 1940).

125. *Nye & Nissen v. United States*, 336 U.S. 613, 618 (1949).

126. 41 LAW WEEK 5007. See for example, cases cited in II Wigmore, *supra*, at 301-2.

127. 41 LAW WEEK 5007.

128. Ibid., p. 5008.

129. See discussion of shift of the "Burden of Proof" in school finance cases, pp. 63-64 below.

130. 41 LAW WEEK 5008.

131. Ibid., p. 5009.

132. Joining the majority in the opinion of the Court, but also expressing his agreement with Justice Powell that the *de jure/de facto* distinction should be abolished in school cases, was Justice Douglas who said:

The school board is a state agency and the lines it draws, the locations it selected for school sites, the allocation it makes of students, and the budgets it prepares are state action for Fourteenth Amendment purposes. . . .

I think it is time to state that there is no constitutional difference between *de jure* and *de facto* segregation, for each is the product of state action or policies.

Douglas further observed that while the individual has the right to seek such companions as he desires, the State, however, is "barred from creating by one device or another ghettos that determine the school one is compelled to attend." (41 LAW WEEK 2021.)

133. 41 LAW WEEK 5009-10. Italics added.

134. Ibid., p. 5010.

135. Ibid. Italics added.

136. Ibid., p. 5011.

137. Ibid., p. 5012.

138. Ibid., p. 5014.

139. Ibid., p. 5015.

140. 36 L. Ed. 2d 16-105 (1973). See also Chapter 4.

141. Ibid., p. 44.

142. 347 U.S. 488, 493-95 (1954).

143. 349 U.S. 294 (1955).

144. See A. Bickel, *The Supreme Court and the Idea of Progress* (New York: Harper and Row, 1970), pp. 126-30.

145. 391 U.S. 430 (1968).

146. Ibid., p. 438

147. 402 U.S. 1 (1972).

148. 41 LAW WEEK 5011 (1973).

149. Ibid., p. 5012. See Justice Douglas' comments at note 132 above.

150. Ibid., p. 5011.

151. Ibid., p. 5012.

152. Ibid.

153. Ibid.

154. Ibid., p. 5013.

155. Ibid., p. 5014.

156. Ibid., p. 5015.

157. Ibid., p. 5016.

158. Ibid., pp. 5016-17.

159. Ibid., p. 5017.

160. Ibid.

161. Ibid.

162. Ibid., pp. 5017-18.

163. Ibid., p. 5018.

164. Ibid.
165. Ibid.
166. 268 U.S. 510 (1925).
167. 262 U.S. 390 (1923).
168. 381 U.S. 479 (1965).
169. 41 LAW WEEK 5019.
170. Ibid.
171. Ibid.
172. Ibid. Italics added.
173. Ibid., p. 5020.
174. Ibid.
175. Ibid.
176. Ibid. `
177. Ibid.
178. Ibid., pp. 5020-21.
179. Ibid., p. 5021. A federal judge in Texas, who says he is opposed to busing "for the sole purpose of mixing bodies," has suggested that the Dallas Independent School District might satisfy the legal requirement to eliminate segregation in the elementary grades by means of television and the transfer of classes, on occasion, by busing. Judge William M. Taylor, in *Tasby v. Estes*, says this would enable different ethnic groups (in this case, white and Mexican-American children) to "communicate" during school hours, and would be cheaper, faster, and safer than cross-town busing; noting that Texas judges before him have faced recalcitrant school boards, e.g., Judge Woodrow Seals of Corpus Christi who confronted one that "stood like a balky steer in the road and refused to do anything," Taylor said:

I am opposed to and do not believe in massive cross-town busing of students for the sole purpose of mixing bodies. I doubt there is a Federal Judge anywhere that would advocate that type of integration as distinguished from desegregation. There are many, many other tools at the command of the School Board and I would direct its attention to part of one of the plans suggested by TEDTAC which proposed the use of television in the elementary grades and the transfer of classes on occasion by bus during school hours in order to enable the different ethnic groups to communicate. How better could lines of communication be established than by saying "I saw you on T.V. yesterday," and, besides that, television is much cheaper than busing and a lot faster and safer. This is in no sense a Court order but is merely something that the Board might consider. *Tasby v. Estes*, 342 F. Supp. 945, 948-49 (1971).

180. Ibid., p. 5021.
181. See further discussion of this subject in John C. Hogan, *An Analysis of Selected Court Decisions which have Applied The Fourteenth Amendment to the Organization, Administration, Programs of the Public Schools, 1950-1972*, UCLA, Ph.D. Dissertation, 1972, pp. 58-59. See also Hogan, " 'Obtaining an

Education' as a Right of the People," *NOLPE School Law Journal* (Spring 1973).

182. 347 U.S. 493.
183. 349 U.S. 298.
184. 41 LAW WEEK 5012.
185. Ibid.
186. Ibid., p. 5022.
187. Ibid.
188. Ibid.
189. Ibid.
190. See Chapter 2, *passim*.
191. 41 LAW WEEK 5022.
192. Ibid.
193. See p. 9ff.
194. 41 LAW WEEK 5024.
195. Ibid.

The Court has taken a long leap in this area of constitutional law in equating the district-wide consequences of gerrymandering individual attendance zones in a district where separation of the races was never required by law with statutes or ordinances in other jurisdictions which did so require. It then adds to this potpourri a confusing enunciation of evidentiary rules in order to make it more likely that the trial court will on remand reach the result which the Court apparently wants it to reach. Since I believe neither of these steps is justified by prior decisions of this Court, I dissent. (Ibid., p. 5025.)

196. Ibid.
197. 41 LAW WEEK 5025.
198. 335 U.S. 211, 214 (1948).
199. 41 LAW WEEK 5004, note 9.
200. The landmark California Supreme Court decision on school desegregation is *Jackson v. Pasadena City School District*, 59 C. 2d 867 (1963) wherein the court said that school boards must "take steps, insofar as reasonably feasible, to alleviate racial imbalance in schools regardless of its cause." In *Spangler v. Pasadena City Board of Education*, 311 F. Supp. 501 (DC CD Cal. 1970), the U.S. District Court enjoined the Pasadena School Board from discriminating on the basis of race in the operation of its schools. The Superior Court in *Mary Ellen Crawford v. Board of Education of the City of Los Angeles*, No. 822, 854 decided February 11, 1970, ordered the Board to adopt a meaningful "Master Plan of integration," and that case is presently on appeal. "Racial imbalance" in the Oxnard elementary schools was ordered eliminated "root and branch" in *Soria v. Oxnard School District Board of Trustees*, 328 F. Supp. 155 (1971). See also *People ex rel. Lynch v. San Diego School District*, 19 C. A. 3d 252 (1971); *Brice v. Landis*, 314 F. Supp. 974 (1969); *Janel Johnson v. Inglewood Unified*

School District, Superior Court, County of Los Angeles, No. 948,036, July 22, 1970; *Gomperts v. Chase*, 30 L. Ed. 2d 30 (1971); *Johnson v. San Francisco Unified School District*, 399 F. Supp. 1315 (1971); and *San Francisco Unified School District v. Johnson*, 3 C. 3d 937 (1971). *Guey Heung Lee v. Johnson*, 30 L. Ed. 2d 19 (1971) was an action by Americans of Chinese ancestry for a stay of the district court's desegregation order. Supreme Court Justice Douglas denied the stay, saying: "The school children of San Francisco can be counted upon to lead the way to unity. . . . they deserve no less than wholehearted support of all their elders." Ibid., p. 21. In *Lau v. Nichols*, where the Chinese of San Francisco sought to have the school district provide remedial programs to compensate for the English language deficiencies of their children, the district court decision denying the relief requested was affirmed by the Ninth U.S. Circuit Court of Appeals which said: ". . . we find that the language deficiency suffered by appellants was not caused directly or indirectly by any State action. . . . the Equal Protection Clause extends no further than to provide them with the same facilities, textbooks, teachers, and curriculum as is provided to other children in the district." 472 F. 2d 916 (1973). The United States Supreme Court agreed to review this case. 42 LAW WEEK 3060 (July 17, 1973).

201. But see Chapter 5 below, which discusses "Individual Rights and Education" wherein courts have become involved in the administration and programs of the public schools, not so much because of race but because of violations by school authorities of student and teacher First Amendment rights.

202. See *Robinson v. Cahill*, 41 LAW WEEK 2552-2553 (April 17, 1973) wherein the Supreme Court of New Jersey, in a case challenging the state's system for financing public education, said: "This court hesitates to turn this case upon the equal protection clause of the state constitution. The equal protection clause may be unmanageable if it is called upon to supply categorical answers in the vast area of human needs. . . . The court will not pursue this equal protection issue in the limited context of public education." These words of caution are also applicable to the federal constitution.

203. 347 U.S. 483 (1954).

204. See *Bolling v. Sharpe*, 347 U.S. 497 (1954) wherein the Supreme Court said that "it would be unthinkable that the same Constitution would impose a lesser duty on the Federal Government" than on the states and where the Court used the Fifth Amendment's due process clause for desegregating the schools of the District of Columbia. The Court cautioned, however: "we do not imply" that the equal protection and the due process clauses "are always interchangeable phrases." (Ibid., p. 499.) See also Morris D. Forkosch, *Constitutional Law*, (New York: The Foundation Press, 1969), p. 337. See "Constitutional Provisions which have Implications for the Schools," Appendix E, pp. 398-400 in John C. Hogan, *An Analysis of Selected Court Decisions which have Applied the Fourteenth Amendment to the Organization, Administration, Programs of the Public Schools, 1950-1972*, UCLA Ph.D. Dissertation, 1972. Bolmeier says that

fourteen different excerpts from the Constitution have been identified which have in one way or another affected the development of education in the United States. Edward C. Bolmeier, *The School in the Legal Structure*, p. 6, citing *Federal Regulations to Education*, Part II: Basic Facts, Report of the National Advisory Committee on Education (Washington, D.C.: National Advisory Committee on Education, 1931), pp. 4-9.

205. 36 L. Ed. 2d 16-105 (1973). See John C. Hogan, " 'Obtaining an Education' as a Right of the People," 68 *The Brief* 249-58 (Summer 1973).

Chapter 4
Wealth and Education

1. *San Antonio Independent School District v. Rodriguez*, 36 L. Ed. 2d 16-105 (1973).

2. See *Rodriguez v. San Antonio Independent School District*, 337 F. Supp. 280 (1971). *Van Dusartz v. Hatfield*, 344 F. Supp. 870 (1971).

3. 36 L. Ed. 2d 43.

4. See John C. Hogan, *An Analysis of Selected Court Decisions Which Have Applied the Fourteenth Amendment to the Organization, Administration, and Programs of the Public Schools, 1950-1972*. UCLA, Ph.D. Thesis, 1972.

5. 36 L. Ed. 2d 41.

6. *Serrano v. Priest*, 96 Cal. Rptr. 601 (1971).

7. *Milliken v. Green*, 203 N.W. 2d 457 (1972). Michigan Supreme Court has granted a rehearing in this case. 41 LAW WEEK 2424 (February 13, 1973).

8. *Robinson v. Cahill*, 287 A. 2d 187 (1972). But see *Robinson v. Cahill*, on appeal, 41 LAW WEEK 2552-53 (April 17, 1973). Holding with the New Jersey system on financing schools violates the state constitutional provision requiring the state to provide a "thorough and efficient" system of education of all school-age children, and wherein the Supreme Court of New Jersey declared:

This court hesitates to turn this case upon the equal protection clause of the state constitution. The equal protection clause may be unmanageable if it is called upon to supply categorical answers in the vast area of human needs. . . . *The court will not pursue this equal protection issue in the limited context of public education.* (Italics added.)

9. *Spano v. Board of Education of Lakeland Central School District*, 328 N.Y.S. 2d 229 (1972), *Jensen v. State Board of Tax Commissioners*, 41 LAW WEEK 2390 (January 1, 1973).

10. Pound, *Outlines of Lectures on Jurisprudence* (Cambridge, Mass.: Harvard University Press, 1943), p. 149.

11. Ibid., p. 96.

12. Cf. Merkel, *Juristische Encyklopädie* (2 ed.), Sec. 159, note, quoted in Pound, p. 149.

Power is that which a state may exercise over a right or interest, but always subject to constitutional limitations. Cf. Morris D. Forkosch, *Constitutional Law*, Mineola, New York: The Foundation Press, Inc., 1969, pp. 16 and 125.

13. III Jhering, *Geist des römischen Rechts*, Sec. 60, quoted in Pound, p. 149.

14. See Comment, "Ninth Amendment Vindication of Unenumerated Fundamental Rights," 42 *Temple Law Quarterly* 46 (1968); Kunter, "The Neglected Ninth Amendment: The 'Other Rights' Retained by the People," 51 *Marquette Law Review* 121 (1967); Redlick, "Are There 'Certain Rights . . . Retained by the People'?" 37 *New York University Law Review* 787 (1962); Bertelsman, "The Ninth Amendment and Due Process of Law—Towards a Viable Theory of Unenumerated Rights," 37 *University of Chicago Law Review* 777 (1968); Franklin, "The Relation of the Fifth, Ninth, and Fourteenth Amendments to the Third Constitution," 4 *Howard Law Journal* 170 (1958). Black, "The Unfinished Business of the Warren Court," 46 *Washington Law Review* 3 (1970); Franklin, "The Ninth Amendment as Civil Law Method and Its Implications for Republican Form of Government," 40 *Tulane Law Review* 487 (1966); B. Patterson, *The Fogotten Ninth Amendment* (1955). "The ninth amendment reserves to the people the *rights* not enumerated in the Constitution, whereas the tenth amendment reserves to the people and the states the *powers* not delegated to the United States. It is unlikely that Congress intended to be redundant in these two amendments"; 42 *Temple Law Quarterly* 46 (1968):

The only reported 'case' ever to discuss a claim based solely on the ninth amendment was *Ryan v. Tennessee*, 257 F. 2d 63 (6th Cir. 1958). However, the complaint failed to present a factual situation to the court or to state a controversy or issue between the parties, and contained as its only prayer for relief a request that the court make an abstract ruling concerning the construction and effect of the ninth amendment. The court therefore did not have the opportunity to explain the proper application of the amendment. (Ibid., p. 46, no. 1.) "[I]t cannot be presumed that any clause in the Constitution is intended to be without effect." In interpreting the Constitution, "real effect should be given to all the words it used." *Myers v. United States*, 272 U.S. 52, 151 (1926).

15. 403 U.S. 233-34 (1971).

16. *Griswold v. Connecticut*, 281 U.S. 492 (1965).

17. *Shapiro v. Thompson*, 394 U.S. 662 (1969). Italics added.

18. Cf. *Const. 1879*, as last amended November 3, 1970, Art. IX, Sec. 5, which is substantially the equivalent.

19. Ibid., Sec. 1, which is substantially the equivalent.

20. Ibid., Sec. 2, which is substantially the equivalent.

21. *Const. 1849*, Art. IX, Secs. 3, 2.

22. See *Roberts v. City of Boston*, 59 Mass. Repts (5 Cushing) 198 (1849) construing similar language in the Massachusetts Constitution not to create any new substantive rights.

23. See *Const. 1879*, as last amended November 3, 1970, Art. I, Sec. 1, which is substantially the equivalent. See discussion of education as a fundamental right, William W. Wells, "Drug Control of School Children: The Child's Right to Choose," 46 *Southern California Law Review* 602-604 (1973).

24. "The present writer reads the cases decided by the Supreme Court as in no way justifying the decisions in the *Serrano* and *Rodriguez* cases, and predicts that when the latter reaches the Court, it will be reversed." Jo Desha Lucas, "Serrano and Rodriguez—an Overextension of Equal Protection," 2 *NOLPE School Law Journal* 41 (Fall 1972).

25. Where a judgment of a state court rests on two grounds, one involving a federal question and the other not, the Supreme Court of the United States will not take jurisdiction. *Minnesota v. National Tea Company*, 309 U.S. 554 (1940). See also *Department of Mental Hygiene v. Kirchner*, 43 Cal. Rptr. 329 (1965).

26. 96 Cal. Rptr. 609 (1971). California Constitution, Article I, Section 11. "*Uniform General Laws.* All laws of a general nature shall have uniform operation." Section 21. "*Privileges and Immunities.* No special privileges or immunities shall ever be granted which may not be altered, revoked, or repealed by the Legislature; nor shall any citizen, or class of citizens, be granted privileges or immunities which, upon the same terms, shall not be granted to all citizens."

27. Assembly Constitutional Amendment No. 37, Assemblyman Alex P. Garcia, April 2, 1973. Italics added by the amendment.

28. Hershel Shanks, "Equal Education and the Law," *The American Scholar*, 39 (Spring 1970), 255-69; Coons, Clune, and Sugarman, "Educational Opportunity: A Workable Constitutional Test for State Financial Structures," 57 *California Law Review* 305-421 (1969).

29. 96 California Reporter 601-626 (1971). Remanded to the trial court with directions to overrule the demurs and to allow the defendants a reasonable time within which to answer (in other words, to proceed with a trial, which is now in progress in Los Angeles). It is not yet clear just what will be the effects of Senate Bill No. 90, approved by the governor, December 18, 1972, on the outcome of this case.

30. Ibid., p. 604. Italics added.

31. Ibid., p. 618.

32. *Stuart v. School District No. 1 of Village of Kalamazoo*, 30 Michigan 69 (1874).

33. *Brown v. Board of Education of Topeka*, 347 U.S. 483 (1954).

34. Forkosch, *Constitutional Law*, p. 519 (1969). Whereas *classification* is said to be the "jugular vein" of equal protection, it may also be analogized that *classification* is the "life-blood" of education. When we assign class grades, when we administer achievement tests and IQ tests, and when we separate pupils into special groups and classes for the express purpose of different treatment, we are classifying. Some have supposed that without classification the business of education could not proceed.

35. *Martin v. City of Struthers*, 319 U.S. 141, 154 (1943).

36. For a discussion of "reasonable," "forbidden," and "suspect" classifications, see Tussman and tenBroeck, "The Equal Protection of the Laws," 37 *California Law Review*, 341-81 (1949).

37. *F.S. Royster Co. v. Virginia*, 253 U.S. 412, 415 (1920). See note, "Developments in the Law—Equal Protection," 82 *Harvard Law Review* 1065-1192 (1969).

38. *Pugsley v. Sellmeyer*, 158 Ark. 247-55 (1923).

39. See Mr. Justice Harlan dissenting in *Shapiro v. Thompson*, 394 U.S. 618, 655 (1969). For a discussion of the "rational basis" test and of the "compelling state interest" test, see Wells, pp. 607-11.

40. *Westbrook v. Mihaly*, 2 Cal. 3d 765, 784-85 (1970).

41. Gunther and Dowling, *Constitutional Law*, p. 983 (1970).

42. *Private Wealth and Public Education*, p. 339. Italics added.

43. *San Antonio Independent School District v. Rodriguez*, 36 L. Ed. 2d 16-105 (1973). "Should an adverse decision come from the Supreme Court, State courts would nevertheless remain free to issue '*Serrano*-type' decisions based upon State constitutional grounds. Thus, there is little reason to believe that these cases will not leave their impact on American education." (Lawyers' Committee for Civil Rights Under Law, "Intrastate School Finance Court Cases," September 11, 1972.)

44. Federal court involvement in public school finance, however, can be traced to *Pawlet v. Clark*, 9 Cranch (13 U.S.) 292-338 (1815).

45. Lawyers' Committee for Civil Rights Under Law, Newsletter of April 14, 1972, p. 2, "The Status of Litigation." The chart entitled "Law Suits Challenging State School Finance Systems," *Education Daily*, March 8, 1972, pp. 5-8, summarized these court actions as of that date.

46. *Contra*, see n. 9.

47. 244 F. Supp. 256 (E.D., La. 1965). But see Coons, et al., p. 307, which says that "the original complaint" attacking the Michigan system was filed in the State Court in 1968, namely, *Board of Education v. Michigan*, General Civil No. 103,342 (Cir. Ct. Mich., Wayne County, *filed* Feb. 2, 1968).

48. 293 F. Supp. 327 (N.D., Ill. 1968), aff'd. *sub. nom.* in *McInnis v. Ogilvie*, 394 U.S. 322 (1969).

49. 310 F. Supp. 572 (W.D., Va. 1969), aff'd. *per curiam* 397 U.S. 44 (1970).

50. 413 F. 2d 320 (5th Cir. Fla. 1969), on remand *Hargrave v. Kirk*, 313 F. Supp. 944 (D.C., Fla. 1970), vacated and remanded *Askew v. Hargrave*, 401 U.S. 476 (1971). See also *Hargrave v. McKinney*, 302 F. Supp. 1381 (D.C., Fla. 1969).

51. Purver, "Validity of Basing Public School Financing System on Local Property Taxes," 41 ALR 3d 1220-30 (1972). Coons, *et al.*, *Private Wealth and Public Education*, pp. 306-15, and passim. Shanks, pp. 259-69. See also other works cited in the bibliography.

52. *Askew v. Hargrave*, 401 U.S. 476, 479 (1971).

53. 293 F. Supp. 332.

54. *Hargrave v. Kirk*, 313 F. Supp. 948.

55. 244 F. Supp. 256.

56. 293 F. Supp. 329.

57. Cf. Cubberly, *School Funds and Their Apportionment* (1905), Chapter 13, "Distribution with Reference to Effort and Need," p. 199ff.

58. 293 F. Supp. 329, no. 4.

59. 310 F. Supp. 574.

60. 10 Cal. App. 3d 1110 (1970).

61. 96 *Cal. Rptr.* 601-626 (1971).

The Serrano decision has been discussed and analyzed elsewhere in a number of convenient places: Arthur E. Wise, "The California Doctrine," *Saturday Review*, pp. 78-83, November 20, 1971; Jay D. Scribner (ed.), *California Supreme Court Decision (Serrano v. Priest): Implications for Equality of Educational Opportunity*, U.C.L.A. Extension Division, 1971; Jonathan M. Purver, "Annotation: Validity of Basing Public School Financing Systems on Local Property Taxes," 41 ALR 3d 1220-30 (1972).

62. 96 *Cal. Rptr.* 601, 604 (1971).

63. Cubberly, as long ago as 1905, had pointed to such inequalities in California school financing. See *School Funds and Their Apportionment*, pp. 50-51, especially table 13. See State of California, *Report of the Governor's Commission on Educational Reform* (Sacramento, 1971), pp. 3-4.

64. Ibid., pp. 611-12. See Cubberly, p. 250, conclusion no. 3: "That while it may be possible to maintain schools entirely or almost entirely by local taxation, the doing so involves very slight efforts on the part of some communities, and very excessive burdens for other communities, and that progress under such a plan is slow and difficult."

65. 96 Cal. Rptr. 615.

66. Ibid., pp. 615-18.

67. 374 U.S. 483 (1954).

68. Ibid., p. 493.

69. 193 Cal. 664 (1924).

70. 96 Cal. Rptr. 618.

71. Ibid., pp. 618-19.

72. Ibid., pp. 621-22. Citations omitted. See Horowitz and Neitring, "Equal Protection Aspects of Inequalities in Public Education and Public Assistance Programs From Place to Place Within a State," 15 *U.C.L.A. Law Review* 787 (1968).

73. 96 Cal. Rptr. 623. The court issued a subsequent "modification of opinion," which declared: "We emphasize that our decision is not a final judgment on the merits."

74. Shanks, writing before the *Serrano* decision, suggests the future:

And what is beyond a victory in the McInnis kind of situation? The next question is whether the state has an affirmative obligation to provide an equal education to its children, even though the inequality does not result from lines drawn on the basis of wealth—as it does in the McInnis-like situation. What if, for example, it costs more to educate properly a ghetto child than a suburban child? Is the ghetto child entitled to demand as a constitutional right that he be given the same education as the suburban child, even though it may cost more to educate him than the suburban child? And what of the blind child? Or the deaf child? Can they make the same demand? And what of the case where the inequality results not from differences in the tax base—as in a McInnis case—but from the fact that there are greater demands on local taxes in the city with its need for greater welfare expenditures and police protection? Can a city plead poverty because it must spend its money on other things besides schools? Perhaps the safest course is to note only that these are the kinds of legal questions that are opened by the thrust of current litigation. What will be the ultimate course of this constitutional development cannot be foretold." (Shanks, "Equal Education and the Law," *American Scholar*, 39 [Spring 1970], p. 269.) ©1970 by the United Chapters of Phi Beta Kappa. Reprinted by permission of the publishers.

75. See *Robinson v. Cahill*, 287 A. 2d 214 (1972).

76. 334 F. Supp. 870 (D.C. Minn. 1971).

77. 328 N.Y.S. 2d 229 (1972).

78. 287 A. 2d 187-221 (1972).

79. 337 F. Supp. 280 (W.D. Texas 1971).

80. 334 F. Supp. 870 (D.C. Minn. 1971).

81. Ibid., p. 872. Italics added.

82. Ibid., p. 876. See S.M. Barro, "Alternatives in California School Finance," Rand R-663-RC/CC, May 1971.

83. 328 N.Y.S. 2d 229 (1972).

84. Ibid., p. 231.

85. Ibid., p. 234.

86. 287 A. 2d 187 (1972).

87. Ibid., pp. 214, 217.

88. Ibid., p. 189. Italics added.

89. Ibid., p. 200. Italics added.

90. See Chapter 2.

91. 287 A. 2d 211.

92. 41 LAW WEEK 2552-53 (April 17, 1973).

93. 337 F. Supp. 282-83.

94. Ibid., p. 284.

95. Ibid., p. 285.

96. 36 L. Ed. 2d 16-105 (1973).

97. See p. 9ff.

98. 203 N.W. 2d 457 (1972).

99. Ibid., p. 469.

100. Ibid., p. 472.

101. Ibid., pp. 474-76.

102. 42 LAW WEEK 2327 (December 25, 1973).

103. See Horowitz and Karst, *Law, Lawyers, and Social Change* (1969), Chapter 3, "Implementation of *Brown v. Board of Education* in the South," pp. 239-397.

104. 287 A. 2d 217.

105. 334 F. Supp. 877, n. 14.

106. In addition to the cases cited above in this chapter, see those concerned with equalization of financing by merger or consolidation of school districts, Chapter 3.

107. *Robinson v. Cahill*, 287 A. 2d 200.

108. See Chapter 2 above.

109. *Spano v. Board of Education of Lakeland Central School District #1*, 328 N.Y.S. 2d 235.

Chapter 5
Individual Rights and Education

1. Popular books on this subject available to students include: Jean Strouse, *Up Against the Law: The Legal Rights of People Under 21*, (New York: New American Library, 1970); Michael Nussbaum, *Student Legal Rights: What They Are and How to Protect Them*, (New York: Harper & Row, 1970); Soren Hansen, *The Little Red Schoolbook*, (New York: Pocket Books, 1971); Kathy Boudin, et al., *The Bust Book: What to do Until the Lawyer Comes*, (New York: Grove Press, 1970).

2. See Floyd G. Delon, *Substantive Legal Aspects of Teacher Discipline*, (Topeka, Kansas: National Organization on Legal Problems of Education, 1972).

3. See Chapter 2 above.

4. "Conflicts over regulations touching on appearance-expression and association date back at least to 1874. . . . See *In re Patricia Dalrymple*, No. 7594 (New York State Dept. of Educ., March 14, 1966) wherein the commissioner cited an unpublished 1874 decision of the New York State Superintendent of Public Instruction, which decided a dispute between school authorities and the mother of a nine-year-old girl who refused to arrange her daughter's hair in the prescribed manner. . . . See the regulations challenged in *Pugsley v. Sellmeyer*, 158 Ark. 247 (1923) (ban on talcum powder and transparent hosiery) and *Stromberg v. French*, 60 N.D. 750 (1931) (taps on heels of shoes prohibited). In the early part of the century, it was apparently in vogue for school administrators to prescribe uniforms for pupils to wear." Note, "Public Secondary Education: Judicial Protection of Student Individuality," 42 *Southern California Law Review* 128 and nn. 17, 18 (1969).

5. See discussion of *burden of proof* in Chapters 3 and 4.

6. See Gunther and Dowling, *Constitutional Law* (1970), pp. 1053-56 for a chronological account of the evolution of talk about the "preferred position" of First Amendment rights.

7. See p. 104ff.

8. See p. 141ff.

9. 158 Ark. 247 (1923).

10. Ibid., p. 248.

11. Ibid., pp. 251-52.

12. *Ruling Case Law*, "Schools," Sec. 24, p. 576 (1919). Italics added.

13. 158 Ark. 253.

14. See Justice Black's comment in *Karr v. Schmidt*, pp. 105-106.

15. *Ware v. Estes*, 328 F. Supp. 657 (1971).

16. 158 Ark. 243.

17. Ibid., p. 254. The rule was rescinded after "this appeal was perfected. The case is therefore moot." (Ibid.)

18. *The Reasonable Man:*

He is an ideal, a standard, the embodiment of all those qualities which we demand of the good citizen. . . . He is one who invariably looks where he is going, and is careful to examine the immediate foreground before he executes a leap or a bound; who neither star-gazes nor is lost in meditation when approaching trapdoors or the margin of a dock; . . . who never mounts a moving omnibus and does not alight from any car while the train is in motion . . . and will inform himself of the history and habits of a dog before administering a caress; . . . who never drives his ball until those in front of him have definitely vacated the putting-green which is his own objective; who never from one year's end to another makes an excessive demand upon his wife, his neighbors, his servants, his ox, or his ass; . . . who never swears, gambles or loses his temper; who uses nothing except in moderation, and even while he flogs his child is meditating only on the golden mean. (A.P. Herbert, *Misleading Cases in the Common Law* [1930], pp. 12-16.)

19. See *Neuhaus v. Federico*, 505 P. 2d 939 (Or. App. 1973): Generally, a school rule is presumed to be valid and the burden is on the challenging party, but when the question is whether the school board had authority to adopt the rule, the board must show that its regulation falls within a clearly defined grant of statutory authority.

20. Note, "Public Secondary Education: Judicial Protection of Student Individuality," 42 *Southern California Law Review* 126, 130 (1969).

21. 319 U.S. 624 (1943).

22. Ibid., p. 639.

23. See Gunther and Dowling, pp. 1051-56.

24. See Robert L. Ackerly, "Controlling Student Conduct in the Reasonable Exercise of Authority," *Education Digest*, April 1970. These issues and the court cases are discussed in Lawrence E. Vredovoe, *Discipline* (Dubuque, Iowa: Kendall/Hunt Publishing Co., 1971), pp. 105-113.

25. Justice Fortas maintained there had been no change: "It can hardly be argued that either students or teachers shed their constitutional rights to freedom of speech or expression at the schoolhouse gate. This has been the unmistakable holding of this Court for almost 50 years." (*Tinker*, p. 506.)

26. 393 U.S. 503 (1969). Justice Stewart concurred in the opinion, saying: "I cannot share the Court's uncritical assumption that, school discipline aside, the First Amendment rights of children are co-extensive with those of adults. Indeed, I had thought the Court decided otherwise just last Term in *Ginsberg v. New York*, 390 U.S. 629." And Justice White declared: "While I join the Court's opinion, I deem it appropriate to note . . . that the Court continues to recognize a distinction between communicating by words and communicating by acts or conduct which sufficiently impinges on some valid state interest."

27. The district court upheld the constitutionality of the school authorities' action on the ground that it was *reasonable* in order to prevent disturbance of school discipline. The court referred to but expressly declined to follow the Fifth Circuit's holding in a similar case that the wearing of symbols like the armbands cannot be prohibited unless it *"MATERIALLY AND SUBSTAN-TIALLY* interfere[s] with the requirements of appropriate discipline in the operation of the school." *Burnside v. Byars*, 363 F. 2d 744, 749 (1966). The court of appeals, *en banc*, was equally divided and accordingly affirmed without opinion.

28. "This has been the unmistakable holding of this Court for almost 50 years. See *Meyer v. Nebraska*, 262 U.S. 390 (1923), where the Court held that the Due Process Clause of the Fourteenth Amendment prevents States from forbidding the teaching of a foreign language to young students. Statutes to this effect, the Court held, unconstitutionally interfere with the liberty of teacher, student, and parent. . . . On the other hand, the Court has repeatedly emphasized the need for affirming the comprehensive authority of the States and of school officials, consistent with fundamental constitutional safeguards, to prescribe and control conduct in the schools." (393 U.S. 506.)

29. *Burnside v. Byars*, p. 749.

30. "The District Court concluded that the action of the school authorities was reasonable because it was based upon their fear of a disturbance from the wearing of the armbands. But, in our system, undifferentiated fear or apprehension of disturbance is not enough to overcome the right to freedom of expression. Any departure from absolute regimentation may cause trouble. Any variation from the majority's opinion may inspire fear. Any word spoken, in class, in the lunchroom, or on the campus, that deviates from the views of another person may start an argument or cause a disturbance. But our Constitution says we must take this risk . . . and our history says that it is this sort of hazardous freedom—this kind of openness—that is the basis of our national strength and of the independence and vigor of Americans who grow up and live in this relatively permissive, often disputatious, society."

31. 393 U.S. 511.

32. Ibid.

33. Referring to the constitutional test of "reasonableness," Justice Black declared:

There was at one time a line of cases holding "reasonableness" as the court saw it to be the test of a "due process" violation. [T]he Court today heavily relies [on one that] used this test of reasonableness, *Meyer v. Nebraska*, 262 U.S. 390 (1923). . . . This constitutional test of reasonableness prevailed in this Court for a season. It was this test that brought on President Franklin Roosevelt's well-known Court fight. His proposed legislation did not pass, but the fight left the "reasonableness" constitutional test dead on the battlefield. . . . If the majority of the Court today, by agreeing to the opinion of my Brother Fortas, is resurrecting that old reasonableness-due process test, I think the constitutional change should be plainly, unequivocally, and forthrightly stated for the benefit of the bench and bar. It will be a sad day for the country, I believe, when the present-day Court returns to the McReynolds due process concept. (Ibid.)

34. Ibid.

35. *Los Angeles Times*, October 16, 1971.

36. Senate Bill No. 890 (introduced April 12, 1971).

37. *California Education Code*, Sec. 10,611. Added by Stats. 1971, Ch. 947.

38. These "guidelines" are reprinted in full in John C. Hogan, *An Analysis of Selected Court Decisions which Have Applied the Fourteenth Amendment to the Organization, Administration, and Programs of the Public Schools, 1950-1972*. UCLA, Ph.D. Dissertation, pp. 201-203.

39. *Santa Monica Evening Outlook*, March 17, 1972.

40. *Los Angeles Times*, March 16, 1972.

41. *Santa Monica Evening Outlook*, March 17, 1972.

42. *Student Rights and Responsibilities*, Los Angeles City Schools, 1972, p. 10.

43. See Doug Smith, "Students Lose 1st Round Over 'Red Tide' Paper," *Los Angeles Times*, October 5, 1972. "Hamilton High School: Paper Distribution OK Prior to Court Hearing," *Santa Monica Evening Outlook*, November 23, 1972. Doug Smith, "Principal Loses Battle on 'Red Tide'," *Los Angeles Times*, November 30, 1972: "Superior Court Judge Robert Wanke, who recently ruled against the publisher's demand *to sell* the 'Red Tide' at University High School, has issued a temporary restraining order that forces the principal . . . of Hamilton to allow students *to pass it out free.*" (Italics added.)

44. 41 LAW WEEK 2664 (June 12, 1973).

45. 453 F. 2d 54 (4th Cir. 1971).

46. 41 LAW WEEK 2664, quoting *Quarterman,* op. cit.

47. Ibid.

48. Ibid.

49. Superior Court, County of Ventura, California, filed May 7, 1973. Temporary Restraining Order and Order to Show Cause, No. 55674, issued May 7, 1973.

50. Plaintiff's Complaint for Permanent Injunction and Temporary Restraining Order, p. 3, filed May 7, 1973.

51. *Oxnard Press-Courier*, May 18, 1973.

52. Where a teacher engaged in civil rights activism which "became a part and parcel of his activity in the classroom" and conducted organizational meetings in the classroom (with outside citizens) which interfered with classroom activity and "culminated in frustration in the classroom and on the school campus," the Court ruled that the school district had good cause to dismiss the teacher and that the termination was not made on the basis of race. *Cooley v. Board of Education of Forrest City School District*, 327 F. Supp. 454 (D.C.E.D., Ark. 1971). In *Ahern v. Board of Education of Grand Island School District*, the Court held that, if reasonable alternatives for expression of dissent are available, teachers are not constitutionally entitled to use their classrooms as forums for expression of their disagreement with school administrators on internal school affairs. 327 F. Supp. 1391 (1971).

53. 363 F. 2d 744 (5th Cir. 1966).

54. 363 F. 2d 749. Italics added.

55. Ibid. (5th Cir. 1966).

56. Ibid., p. 753. "School officials should be careful in their monitoring of student expression in circumstances in which such expression does not substantially interfere with the operation of the school." (Ibid., p. 754.)

57. Gunther and Dowling, *Constitutional Law, 1971 Supplement* (New York: The Foundation Press, 1971), p. 110. See Berkman, "Students in Court: Free Speech and the Functions of Schooling in America," *Harvard Educational Review*, 40 (November 1970), 567-93.

58. 305 F. Supp. 472 (1969).

59. "The absence of a specific regulation prohibiting signs is not a constitutional flaw." *Karp v. Becken*, 477 F. 2d 171, 173, note 1 (1st Cir. 1973), citing *Richard v. Thurston*, op cit.

60. The *Tinker case* held: "Where there is no finding and no showing that the exercise of the forbidden right would 'materially and substantially interfere with the requirements of appropriate discipline in the operation of the school,' the prohibition cannot be sustained." (393 U.S. at 509, 89 S. Ct. at 738.)

61. 323 F. Supp. 55 (1971).

62. Ibid., p. 58.

63. 328 F. Supp. 88 (1971).

64. Ibid.

65. *Gaillot v. Orleans Parish School Board* (Civil District Court for Orleans Parish, January 29, 1971), reported in *Race Relations Law Survey*, 3, no. 2 (July 1971), 51.

66. *Smith and U.S. v. St. Tammany Parish School Board* (5th Cir. June 1, 1971).

67. 42 LAW WEEK 2107 (August 28, 1973).

68. Ibid.

69. 327 F. Supp. 528 (D.C. E.D. Texas, 1971).

70. Ibid. See Lines, "Codes for High School Students," 8 *Inequality in Education* 24-35 (1971), especially on "Drafting a Code," where it is said: "The code should contain three basic sections—(1) students' rights, (2) rules of conduct and sanctions for violations, and (3) hearing procedures." (Ibid., p. 31.)

71. See "Constitutional Law—Schools and School Districts—Prohibition of Long Hair Absent Showing of Actual Disruption Violates High School Student's Constitutional Rights," 84 *Harvard Law Review* 1702-17 (1971). Goldstein, "Reflections on Developing Trends in the Law of Student Rights," 118 *University of Pennsylvania Law Review* 612, 613 (1970); Goldstein, "The Scope and Sources of School Board Authority to Regulate Student Conduct and Status: A Nonconstitutional Analysis, 117 *University of Pennsylvania Law Review* 373 (1969); Comment "Constitutional Law—A Student's Right to Govern His Personal Appearance," 17 *Journal of Public Law* 151-57 (1968).

72. Whereas in Illinois a high school student has a federal constitutional right to wear his hair as he pleases, regardless of whether any political, racial, or religious expression is intended, the school district has broader discretion in *regulating clothes which may be worn at school* than in regulating hair. See *Copeland v. Hawkins,* 352 F. Supp. 1022 (D.C. Ill. 1973).

73. See *Olff v. East Side Union High School District,* 30 L Ed 2d 736-738, *cert. denied,* Justice Douglas dissenting.

74. Ibid., p. 738.

75. "The preference for federal courts is partly attributable to the traditional reluctance of state courts, with respect to a variety of issues other than hair, to hold that school regulations are beyond the authority of the local school board. Generally the state's delegation of rule-making authority to the board is very broad, and most courts have refused to strike down any rule that is not plainly unrelated to the efficient management of the school. See, e.g., Pugsley v. Sellmeyer." (84 *Harvard Law Review* 1702, n. 2.)

76. 393 U.S. 503 (1969).

77. In Utah, where people of the Uintah-Ouray Indian Tribe protested suspension of seven students for long hair, the school district modified its dress code to allow long hair if it is "braided, tied, or wrapped in a neat and orderly fashion." Students could wear such hair so long as it affects their religious, cultural, or traditional background. *Los Angeles Times*, November 23, 1972. But see *New Rider v. Board of Education of Independent School No. 1,* 41 LAW WEEK 2664 (June 12, 1973) where the Tenth U.S. Circuit Court of Appeals considering a long-braided-hair case involving the Pawnee Indians, upheld the school authorities, saying: "the wearing of long hair is not akin to pure speech. . . . *The judiciary was not designed to operate and manage school systems.*" (Ibid. Italics added.)

78. Cf. 84 *Harvard Law Review* 1703-1704.

79. Ibid., p. 1704. "Strictly speaking, hair, while not equivalent to 'pure

speech,' is not 'conduct,' but rather a fixed visual object accompanying the actor whatever his conduct. If it conveys anything, if it 'speaks,' it is a symbol of a very special sort—an extension of the human body which represents an idea. In this sense it is somewhat like clothing and the lack thereof, distinguishable from other actions, such as public draft card burning, which more directly reflect an actor's point of view or personality." Ibid., p. 707.

80. 349 Mass. 704 (1965).

81. 392 F. 2d 697 (1967).

82. In *Braxton v. Board of Public Instruction*, 303 F. Supp. 958, 959 (M.C. Fla. 1969), the court upheld the right of a black teacher to wear a goatee, relying on the Fourteenth Amendment but adding that where the beard is worn as "an appropriate expression of his heritage, culture and racial pride as a black man" its wearer also enjoys the protection of First Amendment rights.

83. *Stevenson v. Board of Education of Wheeler County*, 426 F. 2d 1154 (5th Cir. 1970), *cert. denied*, 400 U.S. 957 (1970).

84. *Finot v. Pasadena City Board of Education*, 250 Cal. App. 2d 189 (1967). A "no-moustache" rule for teachers is an "arbitrary, unreasonable, and capricious" regulation, not shown to be justifiably related to the legitimate purposes of the school. *Ramsey v. Hopkins* (D.C., N.D., Ala. December 18, 1970).

85. *Akin v. Board of Education of the Riverside Unified School District*, 262 C.A. 2d 161 (1968).

86. Ibid., pp. 167-68. See also *Kientz v. Department of Corrections*, discussed *infra*.

87. 21 Cal. App. 3d 323 (1972).

88. 269 C.A. 2d 549 (1969).

89. Ibid., p. 559.

90. Ibid., p. 557.

91. Ibid., p. 558.

92. Ibid., p. 560.

93. 269 F. Supp. 524 (1967).

94. 305 F. Supp. 706 (1969).

95. Ibid., pp. 713-14.

96. *King v. Saddleback Junior College District*, 445 F. 2d 932, 940 (1971). Italics added.

97. 424 F. 2d 1281 (1970).

98. Ibid., pp. 1282-83, nn. 3, 4. See also John C. Hogan, *An Analysis of Selected Court Decisions which have Applied the Fourteenth Amendment to the Organization, Administration, and the Programs of the Public Schools, 1950-1972*, Ph.D. Dissertation, UCLA, 1972, table 7, pp. 229-32, where the cases are collected.

99. Ibid., p. 1283.

100. Ibid.

101. "We do not say that the governance of the length and style of one's hair

is necessarily so fundamental as those substantive rights already found implicit in the "liberty" assurance of the Due Process Clause, requiring a "compelling" showing by the state before it may be impaired." (Ibid., p. 1284.)

102. Ibid., p. 1285.

103. Ibid.

104. Ibid., p. 1286.

105. 269 F. Supp. 524 (1967).

106. Ibid., p. 528.

107. Ibid., p. 529. See discussion of the Ninth Amendment and education, Chapter 4. See also John C. Hogan, " 'Obtaining and Education' As a Right of the People," *The Brief*, vol. 68, no. 4, Summer 1973, pp. 249-258.

108. 307 F. Supp. 485 (D.C. Iowa 1970).

The Court well knows that the field of female coiffure is one of shifting sand trodden only by the most resolute of men. The Court thus undertakes this journey with some trepidation. Since time immemorial attempts to impose standards of appearance upon the fairer sex have been fraught with peril. Arbiters of hirsute fashion, perhaps understanding the chameleon nature of the subject matter, have approached the problem with more innovation than insight. Against this delicate social milieu and ever mindful of the equal protection clause, this Court undertakes to comb the tangled roots of this hairy issue." (Ibid., p. 486.)

109. Ibid.

110. Cf., however, *In re Patricia Dalrymple* (1874), cited in note 1.

111. Ibid., p. 487.

112. The following is a paraphrase of the Court's language, ibid., pp. 487-88.

113. See *Crews v. Clonics*, 303 F. Supp. 1370 (S.D. *Ind.* 1969).

114. *Griffin v. Tatum*, 300 F. Supp. 60 (M.D. Ala. 1969); *Breen v. Kahl*, 296 F. Supp. 702 (W.D. Wis. 1969); *Davis v. Firment*, 269 F. Supp. 524 (E.D. La. 1967), *aff'd* 408 F. 2d 1085 (5th Cir. 1969); *Ferrell v. Dallas Independent School District*, 392 F. 2d 697 (5th Cir. 1968); *Westley v. Rossi*, 305 F. Supp. 706 (U.S.D.C. Minn. 1969).

115. 307 F. Supp. 487. "Incidents of disruption that have been shown to result from long hair have been in the nature of harassment, use of obscene or derogatory language, fights, health and sanitation problems, physical dangers, obscene appearance, and distraction of other students. (Ibid.)

116. *Griffin v. Tatum, supra; Breen v. Kahl, supra; Richards v. Thurston*, 304 F. Supp. 449 (D. Mass. 1969); *Westley v. Rossi, supra.*

117. *Leonard v. School Committee of Attleboro*, 349 Mass. 704, 212 N.E. 2d 468, 14 A.L.R. 3d 1192 (1965); *Contreras v. Merced Union High School District, unreported* (E.D. Cal. Dec. 13, 1968).

118. 307 F. Supp. 488.

119. 307 F. Supp. 489.

There has undoubtedly been too much said if not written concerning long hair and unusual hair styles. Mankind's experience has demonstrated that in this area of fashion, fads constantly come and go as the pendulum unceasingly swings from extreme to extreme. Thus, no doubt the proper characterization of the current controversy over students' hair is that of the proverbial tempest in a teapot. (Ibid., p. 489.)

120. 401 U.S. 1201-1203 (1971). See *Karr v. Schmidt*, 460 F. 2d 609 (5th Cir. 1972), cert. denied 409 U.S. 989 (1972). By this time the "federal courts had invested the time necessary to decide at least twenty-two cases involving the length of student hair." *Karp v. Becken*, 477 F. 2d 171, 174, note 2 (9th Cir. 1973).

121. See *Oloff v. East Side Union High School District*, Memorandum Case, No. 71-498, 30 L Ed 2d 736-738 (1972).

122. 381 U.S. 479 (1965).

123. 30 L Ed 2d 737.

124. Ibid., p. 738. And the United States Supreme Court has again refused to hear appeals in student haircut cases. "The cases . . . stemmed from Colorado, Utah, New Mexico, and Oklahoma. . . . The Court has received a number of such appeals but has never agreed to consider them." *Santa Monica Evening Outlook*, March 27, 1972.

125. 428 F. 2d 655 (5th Cir. 1970).

126. Ibid., p. 654.

127. 315 F. Supp. 625 (1970).

128. Ibid., p. 625.

129. 305 F. Supp. 706 (D. Minn. 1969).

130. 321 F. Supp. 523 (D.C. Calif. 1971).

131. 33 C.A. 3d 346 (1973).

132. Cf. *Bagley v. Washington Township Hospital District*, 65 Cal. 2d 499 (1972).

133. 33 C.A. 3d 355.

134. See 33 C.A. 3d 352-53. Employer's grooming code requiring different hair lengths for male and female job applicants was held to violate Section 703, Civil Rights Act of 1964, 42 U.S.C. Sec. 2000 (3) 2 which provides in pertinent part that it "shall be an unlawful employment practice for an employer to fail or refuse to hire any individual . . . because of such individual's sex." See *Willingham v. Macon Telegraph Publishing Company* (5th Cir. 1973), 42 LAW WEEK 2060-61 (July 31, 1973).

135. In California, a teacher may suspend, for good cause, "any pupil from his or her class for the day of the suspension and the day following." Education Code, Sec. 10601. Prior to 1971, a teacher in California could suspend a pupil, for good cause, *from the school* "for not exceeding one school day, plus the remainder of the school day during which the suspension occurred." (Ibid.)

136. See Lawrence E. Vredevoe, *Discipline*, (Dubuque, Iowa: Kendall/Hunt, 1971), pp. 103-104.

137. 348 F. Supp. 866 (1972).

138. 472 F. 2d 483 (1973).

139. "Student Rights: Due Process of Law in School Discipline—Recent Decisions," *Inequality in Education* no. 14, (July 1973), p. 56.

140. *Lindwood v. Board of Education*, 463 F. 2d 736, 768 (7th Cir. 1972).

141. 346 F. Supp. 202 (W.D. N.C. 1972).

142. 344 F. Supp. 70 (D.C. Conn. 1972).

143. *Pervis v. LaMarque Independent School District*, 466 F. 2d 1054 (1972). *Dunn v. Tyler Independent School District*, 460 F. 2d 146-47 (1972).

144. *Rovere v. Board of Education of the Village of Ridgefield Park, et al., Bergen County* (Decision of the N.J. Commissioner of Education, 1973), reported in 14 *NOLPE School Law Reporter* 11-12 (June 1973).

145. See "Willful Damage of School Property; Liability of Parent," *California Education Code*, Sec. 10,606. See also parent liability for any "reward" paid pursuant to *Government Code*, Sec. 53,069.5.

146. See "Parents Warned of Liability for Vandalism Acts," *Los Angeles Times*, August 23, 1973.

147. (2d Cir. 1973), digested in 14 *Inequality in Education* 66 (July 1973).

148. 319 U.S. 624 (1943).

149. 393 U.S. 503 (1969).

150. *Phi Delta Kappan*, February 1973, p. 426.

151. 477 F. 2d 171 (1973).

152. See 393 U.S. 503, 515 (1969).

153. 477 F. 2d 174.

154. 393 U.S. at 506, 511.

155. Cf. *Epperson v. Arkansas*, 393 U.S. 97, 104 (1968).

156. 477 U.S. 174. See 393 U.S. 514.

157. 477 F. 2d 174.

158. Ibid., p. 175.

159. Ibid.

160. Ibid., p. 177.

161. Blackstone, I *Commentaries*, *444.

162. *State v. Rhodes*, 6. N.C. 453 (1868).

163. See Marilyn Patel, "Is Legal Protection Equal Protection?" *Case and Comment*, July-August 1973, pp. 3-6. See sources and cases collected in *Frontiero v. Richardson*, 36 L. Ed. 2d 583 (1973), *Reed v. Reed*, 404 U.S. 71 (1971), and *Sail'er Inn Inc. v. Kirby*, 5 Cal. 3d 1 (1971). "History discloses the fact that women have always been dependent upon men." *Muller v. Oregon*, 208 U.S. 412, 422 (1908). Classifications based upon sex, like classifications based upon race, alienage, and national origin, are inherently suspect and must therefore be subjected to close judicial scrutiny. *Frontiero,* op. cit., p. 589. See also *Frontiero v. Laird*, 341 F. Supp. 201 (1972).

164. The history of education is laced with examples of classroom instruction

based upon pupil fear of physical punishment in the schools. Formerly, the standard procedure for stimulating learning and discouraging misbehavior in school children was not only the milder forms of chastisement, but also the use of the "cane" beating, and in some cases, floggings as well. See Henry F. Jenks, *A Catalogue of the Boston Public Latin School Established in 1635* (Boston: The Boston Latin School Association, 1866), passim.

165. Lawrence E. Vredevoe, *Discipline* (Dubuque, Iowa: Kendall/Hunt Publishing Co., 1971), p. 42.

166. Prosser, *Torts*, p. 166 (1941).

167. Ibid., p. 167. See Annotation, "Teacher's Civil Liability for Administering Corporal Punishment to Pupil," 43 A.L.R. 2d 469 (1955). Teachers, administrators, and other school officials by the very nature of their public employment are sometimes placed in embarrassing situations which could lead to personal legal liability; it is possible to insure against this risk through private companies which provide insurance coverage, in addition to any coverage provided by the school district, for damages arising from act of the teacher or administrator in the pursuit of his employment "resulting from but not limited to negligence, carelessness, dangerous and defective conditions of property, malicious prosecution, false arrest or false imprisonment, slander, libel, or malpractice." *On-the-Job Liability Insurance for School Employees*, United Pacific Insurance Company, Tacoma, Washington, 1973.

168. *State v. Pendergass*, 19 N.C. 365 (1837). See "*In Loco Parentis*: A Survey of the Attitudes of Parents of Undergraduate Students," by Joseph R. Serra, Doctoral Dissertation, Indiana University, 1968, the conclusions of which include the following: "Of particular importance to student personnel administration is the dichotomy that exists between student and parental attitudes [towards *in loco parentis*] .... Because of the significance of the parental supporting role, institutions should tap this resource in research and planning for a social atmosphere supportive of the educational process."

169. See Note, "California Schoolteachers' Privilege to Inflict Corporal Punishment," 15 *Hastings Law Journal* 600-604 (1964).

170. The Los Angeles Board of Education faced a suit from the American Civil Liberties Union which charged that use of corporal punishment in the schools violates the state consitution because it "permits cruel punishment." *Los Angeles Times*, February 9, 1972. See Assembly Bill No. 673 by Sieroty: "No person employed or engaged in any school or educational institution, whether public or private, shall inflict, or cause to be inflicted, corporal punishment upon a pupil attending such school or institution." *Los Angeles Herald and Express*, April 2, 1972, p. A-12.

171. Riverside Unified School District, Riverside, California, 2nd Revision, approved by the Board of Education, December 1, 1969. See pp. 4-5. A resolution which asks the State Department of Education to conduct a survey of California public schools to determine the extent and nature of corporal

punishment being administered was passed 27 to 4 by the State Senate on August 29, 1973. See ACR-69, Gonzales. See also Frank Del Olmo, "Guadalupe School Area 'Feudal,' Panel Charges: U.S. Group Accuses Santa Barbara County District of Excessively Punishing Students," *Los Angeles Times*, April 14, 1973, quoting from a report of the California Advisory Committee to the U.S. Commission on Civil Rights.

172. 41 LAW WEEK 2276-77 (November 28, 1972).

173. Ibid., p. 2276.

174. 406 U.S. 205 (1972).

175. 405 U.S. 645 (1972).

176. 41 LAW WEEK 2277.

177. 328 F. Supp. 657 (1971). Background information about the plaintiffs in this case is discussed in Nat Hentoff, "Why Students Want Their Constitutional Rights," *Saturday Review*, May 22, 1971, reprinted by American Civil Liberties Union, pp. 4-5 of reprint.

178. Ibid., p. 659.

179. Blackstone, in his *Commentaries on the Laws of England*, classifies the following as a "cruel and unusual punishment" prohibited by law:

Parricide, the murder of one's parents had sometimes in history, among the Romans, been punished as follows: "After being scourged, the delinquents were sewed up in a leather sack with a live dog, a cock, a viper, and an ape, and so cast into the sea." (4 *Commentaries* *202.)

Punishments, Blackstone says, "are chiefly intended for the prevention of future crimes" (ibid., *16) and hence "the punishment ought rather to exceed than equal the injury." (Ibid., *14.) These punishments were not cruel and unusual, depending upon the gravity of the crime committed—to be hanged by the neck and then cut down alive, the head to be cut off and the body divided into four parts or to stand with both ears nailed to the pillory. Ibid., *92-93, 138.

180. See Annotation, "Criminal Liability for Excessive or Improper Punishment Inflicted on Child by Parent, Teacher, or One In Loco Parentis," 89 A.L.R. 2d 396 (1963). A boy was awarded $19,000 in damages ($500.00 compensatory damages and $18,500 punitive damages) for a spanking with a wooden paddle by a junior high school principal in Florida. Considerable force had been used, and not at issue was the principal's right to use corporal punishment, but the extent of the force. *Los Angeles Times*, February 18, 1972.

181. 328 F. Supp. 660.

182. Ibid., p. 657.

183. *Epperson v. Arkansas*, 393 U.S. 97 (1968).

184. 328 F. Supp. 660.

185. *Phi Delta Kappan*, January 1973, p. 360.

186. See *Case Studies in Educational Performance Contracting: Conclusions and Implications*, Vol. 1, Polly Carpenter and George R. Hall, Rand Report R-900/1-HEW, 1971, pp. 26-30.

187. P. Carpenter and M. Rapp, "Testing in Innovative Programs," Rand P-4778, March 1972, p. 1. A moratorium on standardized testing was one of the recommendations reported after the NEA Center for Human Relations held a national conference on tests as violations of civil and human rights. *Phi Delta Kappan*, May 1972, p. 602.

188. *Hobson v. Hansen*, 267 F. Supp. 401-519 (D.C., D.C. 1967).

189. See "Topical Outline of the Court's Decision in *Hobson v. Hansen*," table 4, p. 64 in John C. Hogan, *An Analysis of Selected Court Decisions which Have Applied the Fourteenth Amendment to the Organization, Administration, and Programs of the Public Schools*, 1950-1972. UCLA Ph.D. Dissertation, 1972.

190. Ibid. See Comment, "Equality of Educational Opportunity: Are 'Compensatory Programs' Constitutionally Required?" 42 *Southern California Law Review* (1969) 146-68.

191. In *Smuck v. Hobson*, 408 F. 2d 175 (D.C. Cir. 1969), the U.S. Court of Appeals for the District of Columbia allowed a group of parents "to appeal those provisions of the decree which curtail the freedom of the school board to exercise its discretion in deciding upon educational policy," and among other things, affirmed the abolition of the "track system." See also *Hobson v. Hansen*, 327 F. Supp. 844 (1971). See Horowitz and Karst, *Law Lawyers and Social Change*, pp. 505-506.

192. *Race Relations Law Survey*, no. 3 (May 1971), p. 6.

193. Fifth Circuit, December 1, 1969.

194. Ibid.

195. 303 F. Supp. 1340 (E.D. La. 1971). Ibid., 456 F. 2d 1371 (5th Cir. 1972).

196. But see "Achievement Tests—Median Scores: 1965," table 176, *Statistical Abstract of the United States, 1970* (Washington, D.C.: Government Printing Office, 1970), p. 120.

197. 444 F. 2d 1400 (1971).

198. *Race Relations Law Survey*, no. 3 (September 1971), p. 92.

199. *Santa Monica Evening Outlook*, April 21, 1972.

200. *Santa Monica Evening Outlook*, December 18, 1971.

201. 343 F. Supp. 1306 (D.C., Cal. 1972).

202. 351 F. Supp. 1279 (D.C., N.M. 1972).

203. See discussion of "educational needs" in Chapter 4.

204. Center for Law and Education, Harvard University, *Inequality in Education*, No. 14 (July 1973), pp. 49-50. "It is interesting that the court never suggests that the I.Q. tests be administered in Spanish." 14 *NOLPE School Law Reporter* 30 (June 1973). See *Lau v. Nichols*, 472 F. 2d 509 (1973), discussed in Chapter 3. See *Morales v. Shannon*, 41 LAW WEEK 2451 (W.D. Tex. 1973) which follows the reasoning in the *Lau case*.

205. *Los Angeles Times*, August 18, 1872.

206. See Assembly Bill No. 665, Leroy F. Greene, March 2, 1972.

207. Assembly Bill No. 368, Assemblymen Brown and Alatorre, February 14, 1973.

208. *Los Angeles Times*, August 18, 1972. A Bill prohibiting giving of I.Q. tests to children until they have resided in the United States for two years passed the Senate and was signed by the governor (*Herald and Examiner*, August 1, 1972).

209. See "Day in Sacramento," *Los Angeles Times*, September 1, 1973.

210. Kappan Interview, "Goodbye I.Q., Hello E.I. (Ertl Index)," *Phi Delta Kappan*, October 1972, pp. 89-94, 91.

211. "Ertl Machine Triggers Controversy," *Phi Delta Kappan* 54, No. 5, January 1973, p. 360.

212. Frederick B. Davis, Center for Research in Evaluation and Measure, University of Pennsylvania, "The Measurement of Mental Capability Through Evoked-Potential Recordings," (Ibid.)

213. Charles E. Johnson, "Grading Blacks at Harvard," *MBA, The Master in Business Administration*, vol. 7, no. 1 (January 1973), pp. 18-19.

214. "As many as 40% of the black students were not permitted to return at the end of their first year." (Ibid., p. 18.)

215. James B. VanHoven, "Reporting Pupil Progress: A Broad Rationale For New Practices," *Phi Delta Kappan* (February 1972), p. 365.

216. New Jersey Commissioner of Education Decision, June 20, 1973. See *NOLPE Notes*, August 1973, p. 2.

217. 401 U.S. 424 (1971). Concerning testing and employment generally, see William C. Byham and Morton E. Spitzer, *The Law and Personnel Training* (New York: The American Management Association, 1971).

218. 401 U.S. 424 (1971).

219. Ibid.

220. Ibid., p. 433. For a discussion of the use of tests in school personnel work to measure "skills, attitudes, and knowledge," see Fawcett, *School Personnel Administration* (New York, The Macmillan Company, 1964) pp. 25-45.

221. The use of "personality tests" for the screening and selection of employees has been criticized by Justice William O. Douglas (particularly the *MMPI* test), and he concludes that "Ideological data—like personality data—is treacherous when fed into a computer." (*Points of Rebellion* [New York: Vintage Books, 1970] , pp. 24-25.)

222. Fawcett, *School Personnel Administration*, p. 38.

223. *Race Relations Law Survey*, vol. 3, no. 5 (January 1972), p. 179.

224. Ibid.

225. 401 U.S. 424 (1971).

226. See "Court Ruling on N.T.E.," *Phi Delta Kappan*, September 1971, p. 73.

227. 462 F. 2d 1112.

197

228. *Race Relations Law Survey*, vol. 3, no. 5 (January 1972), p. 180.

229. Ibid.

230. Ibid., p. 181.

231. *Carter v. Morehouse Parish School Board*, 441 F. 2d 380 (1971).

232. Ibid., p. 380.

233. *Porcelli v. Titus*, 91 S. Ct. 1612 (1971).

234. Martin Gross, quoted in "Testing–S.A.T.'s Under Fire," *Time*, January 5, 1968.

235. Note, "Legal Implications of the Use of Standardized Ability Tests in Employment and Education," 68 *Columbia Law Review* 740 (1968).

236. Ibid., p. 741.

237. 305 F. 2d 343 (5th Cir. 1961).

238. Ibid., p. 351.

239. 223 F. Supp. 724 (1963).

240. Ibid., p. 726.

241. Note, "Legal Implications of the Use of Standardized Ability Tests in Employment and Education," 68 *Columbia Law Review* 743 (1968). Italics added.

242. *Santa Monica Evening Outlook*, March 17, 1972. For a survey of grading practices and current national trends, see Mousley, "Report Cards Across the Nation," *Phi Delta Kappan*, 53 no. 7 (March 1972), 436-37.

243. Based on Note, "Legal Implications of the Use of Standardized Ability Texts in Employment and Education," pp. 743-44.

244. Robert H. Reid, *American Degree Mills: A Study of Their Operations and of Existing and Potential Ways to Control Them*, American Council on Education, Washington, D.C., 1959, p. 3. See also John Norris, *Bogus Diplomas: Phototypes of Diplomas Bought for $455.00 in May 1880, by a Representative of the "Philadelphia Record," Who Had No Knowledge of Medicine and Had Never Seen the Inside of a Medical College* (Bound phototypes in the Office of Education Library, Washington, D.C.), cited in Reid, p. 12, note 2.

245. California Education Code, Secs. 29013-29015.

246. 33 C.A. 3d 413 (1973).

247. See Iver Peterson, "200 Degrees on Faculties Held Bogus," *New York Times*, September 21, 1972. "A woman psychologist, arrested earlier this week in connection with ordering without authorization a duplicate of the seal stamp used to verify transcripts at UCLA was free on bail today." (*Santa Monica Evening Outlook*, November 27, 1971.)

248. D.C., Jefferson County, Colorado, No. 09461, June 4, 1973, referred to in *NOLPE Notes*, August 1973, p. 4.

249. 40 LAW WEEK 2211. Washington Superior Court, September 22, 1971, case abstracted in *Race Relations Law Survey*, vol. 3, no. 5 (January 1972), p. 164. See Philip Hager, "Reverse Racism: Does It Exist?" *Los Angeles Times*, February 5, 1973.

250. 40 LAW WEEK 2211.

251. *De Funis v. Odegaard* (Wash. Sup. Ct. 1973), 41 LAW WEEK 2536 (April 10, 1973). Appeal pending before U.S. Supreme Court.

252. 41 LAW WEEK 2536. See *Grafton v. Brooklyn Law School*, 41 LAW WEEK 2663 (June 12, 1973), challenging dismissal of a law student as in violation of 42 U.S.C. 1983.

253. *REPORTS: The State Bar of California*, vol. 13, no. 6, (June 1973), p. 1. (Italics added.)

254. See "Student Can't Read, Sues Board for Million," *Los Angeles Herald-Examiner*, July 15, 1973.

255. Ms. Suzanne Martinez, Esq., San Francisco attorney representing the plaintiff. Ibid., p. A-17.

256. S.D. Sugarman, University of California law professor. Ibid.

257. Judge Haskell C. Freedman of Middlesex, Mass. Ibid.

258. Mrs. Charlesetta Alston, Director, San Francisco Adult Literacy Center. Ibid.

259. See note 167 above.

260. Ibid. In May 1972, Peter's family had filed a claim against the district "which the district denied."

261. See K.J. Rabben, "Many Public School Graduates Can't Write, Study Discloses," *Santa Monica Evening Outlook*, April 7, 1972. Andrew Burnes, "Especially if He's White, Affluent: Reading Ability Reflects Background," *Washington Post*, May 9, 1972. See "Jonny Can Read Some Things. First Assessment Results Reveal," National Assessment of Educational Process, vol. 5, no. 4 (June-July 1972).

262. See Stella Zadeh, "L.A. High Schools: New Graduation Guidelines Urged," *Santa Monica Evening Outlook*, January 16, 1973.

263. *Los Angeles Times*, September 7, 1973.

264. *United States v. Jefferson County Board of Education*, 372 F. 2d 836, 899 (1966).

265. E.g., *Graves v. Walton*, 300 F. Supp. 188, 199 (1968).

266. 320 F. Supp. 1274-77 (1970).

267. Ibid., pp. 1274-75.

268. Ibid., p. 1276.

269. *Haas v. South Bend Community School*, 289 N.E. 2d 495 (Ind. 1972).

270. Ibid., overruling *State ex rel. IHSAA Association v. Lawrence Circuit Court*, 240 Ind. 114, 162 N.E. 2d 250.

271. 290 N.E. 2d 64 (Ind. App. 1972).

272. Ibid.

273. *Los Angeles Herald-Examiner*, March 2, 1972. See *Myers v. Board of Education of Emporia*, U.S. District Court, 253, D.C. Lyon County, Kansas, No. 28074, February 27, 1973. *NOLPE Notes* May 1973, p. 4.

274. 310 F. Supp. 192 (1970).

275. See "Dress, Grooming Guidelines for B.H. High Athletes Altered," *Los Angeles Times*, July 6, 1972.

276. *Phi Delta Kappan*, May 1972, p. 601.

277. See "Budgeting of Programs: Bills Introduced to End School Discrimination in Athletics," *Santa Monica Evening Outlook*, May 12, 1973. See likewise SB-1228, which passed the California Senate 21 to 4 and was sent to the Assembly August 31, 1973.

278. *Santa Monica Evening Outlook*, May 12, 1973.

279. Ibid.

280. See *Phi Delta Kappan*, February 1973, pp. 427-28.

281. But see Dave Distel, "The Girl Who Beat the Russians: Little Mary Decker Suddenly Very Big in World of Track, *Los Angeles Times*, August 21, 1973, reporting a fifteen-year-old fast "enough to win in Russia and win in Italy and win in Senegal. Fast enough to cover 800 meters ahead of Olympic veterans such as Niyole Sabaite, Russia's silver medalist at Munich." In Sacramento, California a fourteen-year-old cross-country runner lost her bid to compete against boys when a U.S. District Court judge refused to order the C.I.F. to abandon its regulations banning girls from participating in boys' athletic events. (Pending the girl's appeal, the judge further refused to permit her to run against boys in three footraces.) *Los Angeles Times*, October 21, 1972.

282. *Minnesota State High School League Official Handbook*, 1971-1972, Athletic Rules for Girls, Article III, Sec. 5.

283. 342 F. Supp. 1224, 1234 (1972).

284. 477 F. 2d 1292 (1973).

285. Ibid., p. 1296.

286. Ibid., p. 1299.

287. Other cases involving school athletic rules and programs include:

Mitchell v. Louisiana High School Athletic Association, 430 F. 2d 1155 (5th Cir. 1970).

Louisiana High School Athletic Association v. St. Augustine High School, 396 F. 2d 224 (5th Cir. 1968).

Oklahoma High School Athletic Association v. Bray, 321 F. 2d 269 (10th Cir. 1963).

Reed v. The Nebraska School Activities Association, 341 F. Supp. 258 (D. Neb. 1972).

Bucha v. Illinois High School Athletic Association, 351 F. Supp. 69 (N.D. Ill. 1972).

Haas v. South Bend Community School Corporation, 289 N.E. 2d 495 (Ind. 1972).

Cynthis Morris v. Michigan Board of Education, 472 F. 2d 1207 (6th Cir. 1973).

See also Note, "Sex Discrimination in High School Athletics," 57 Minn. L. Rev. 339 (1972). Leo Kanowitz, *Women and the Law* (Albuquerque: University of New Mexico Press, 1969).

288. University of the State of New York, The State Department of Education, Division of Health, Physical Education and Recreation, *Report on Experiment: Girls on Boys Interscholastic Athletic Teams, March 1969-June 1970,* (February 1972), p. 4.

289. State of New York, Regulations of the Commissioner of Education, Sec. 135.4. A new Michigan statute permits girls to participate in certain named "noncontact" interscholastic sports, and even if the school does have a girls' team "the female shall be permitted to compete for a position on the boys' team." M.C.L.A. 340.379 (2), Public Act No. 138 (Mich. May 22, 1972). Groups such as the National Collegiate Athletic Association and the Big Eight Athletic Conference have eliminated provisions in their rules prohibiting females from competing in interscholastic activities with men.

290. See cases in Note, "Sex Discrimination in High School Athletics," 57 Minn. L. Rev. 339 (1972).

291. Justice Brennan in *Frontiero v. Richardson*, 36 L. Ed. 2d 583, 590 (1973). "The pedestal upon which women have been placed has all too often, upon closer inspection, been revealed as a cage." *Sail'er Inn, Inc. v. Kirby*, 5 Cal. 3d 1 (1971).

292. 304 U.S. 439 (1938).

293. 35 L. Ed. 2d 590 (1973).

294. *Los Angeles Times*, February 21, 1973.

295. 32 C. 2d 833 (1948).

296. See "Danger: A "Must"–Risk Sports–Skiing, Polo, Riding–are Essential and 'Appreciably Improve' Sex Life, Scientist Claim," *Los Angeles Times*, April 1, 1973.

297. *Business Insurance*, August 13, 1973, p. 45. See also note 167 above.

298. 432 F. 2d 213 (1970), *cert. denied*, 91 S. Ct. 1617 (1971).

299. A married teenager is exempt from the compulsory school attendance laws. "The marriage relationship, regardless of the age of the persons involved, creates conditions and imposes obligations upon the parties that are obviously inconsistent with compulsory school attendance." *State v. Priest*, 210 La. 389 (1946).

300. See Alexander, Corns, and McCann, *Public School Law: Cases and Materials* (St. Paul, Minn.: West Publishing Company, 1969) p. 570.

301. See *Davis v. Meek*, 344 F. Supp. 298 (D.C. Ohio 1972) where a rule excluding married high school seniors from extracurricular activities was held to be an improper invasion of marital privacy. See discussion of this case in Irving C. Evers, "School Law: Seven Decisions that May Affect You," *Nation's Schools*, vol. 91, no. 3 (March 1973), p. 37.

302. 330 S.W. 2d 708 (1959).

303. *Los Angeles Times*, 1972. A high school student in Boston who was suspended from school for two to five days has asked the U.S. District Court to rule that he has a constitutional right to kiss his girl friend and hold hands with her on campus. The boy was suspended by school authorities because he greeted the girl with "a light salutary kiss" before classes every day and held her hand "while passing in the corridor before school or between classes." See "Court to Rule on Constitutional Right to Kiss," *Los Angeles Herald-Examiner*, March 2, 1973.

304. 323 F. Supp. 1155 (D.C. Mass. 1971).

305. Ibid., p. 1156.

306. Ibid., p. 1157.

307. Ibid., p. 1158.

308. Ibid. Thus, the "separate but equal doctrine" (discussed above in Chapter 3), if it ever pertained to married or to pregnant students, was struck down in this area too.

309. Ibid. Italics added. See *Richards v. Thurston*, 424 F. 2d 1281, at 1286 (1 Cir. 1970): "In the absence of an inherent, self-evident justification on the face of the rule, we conclude that the burden was on the defendant."

310. *Skinner v. Oklahoma*, 316 U.S. 532 (1942). *Loving v. Virginia*, 388 U.S. 1 (1967). *Boddie v. Connecticut*, 401 U.S. 371 (1971). See 42 LAW WEEK 2108 (August 8, 1973).

311. *Board of Education of Harrodsburg v. Bentley*, 383 S.W. 2d 677 (Ky. 1964).

312. 42 LAW WEEK 2107-08 (August 28, 1973).

313. *Shapiro v. Thompson*, 394 U.S. 618 (1969).

314. *Reed v. Reed*, 404 U.S. 71 (1971).

315. *McGowan v. Maryland*, 366 U.S. 420 (1961).

316. *NOLPE Notes*, March 1973, p. 2.

317. Ibid.

318. Nat Hentoff, "Why Students Want Their Constitutional Rights," reprint from *Saturday Review*, May 22, 1971.

319. Russell Sage Foundation Report, *Guidelines for the Collection and Dissemination of Pupil Records*, quoted in Hentoff, p. 5.

320. James S. Coleman and Nancy L. Karweit, *Information Systems and Performance Measures in Schools*, (Englewood Cliffs: N.J., Educational Technology Publications, 1972) pp. 63-64. See also, Lance J. Hoffman, *Security and Privacy in Computer Systems* (New York: Melville Publishing Company, 1973), for materials on privacy and security in computer systems.

321. Hentoff, n. 320.

322. California Education Code, Sec. 10,901.

More than half the students at two San Francisco Bay area high schools have had sexual intercourse but few know about effective conception. . . . Miller's findings in a survey of sexual behavior and attitudes were published in the August issue of *California Medical Association. . . .* he studied 180 students in a mostly white middle class school and 154 students in a racially and ethnically mixed lower class school. He was given permission for the study on condition he did not disclose the schools. (*Herald-Examiner*, August 12, 1973.)

323. *Los Angeles Times*, June 25, 1972.

324. Most public school districts and private schools have handbooks which set forth the rules governing student conduct and are based upon the requirements of state codes and court interpretations of student rights under the Constitution. See especially *Student Rights and Responsibilities: A Handbook for Elementary Schools and Junior and Senior High Schools* (Los Angeles City Schools, Office of the Superintendent, 1972), which sets forth rules and cites sections of the state and federal constitutions, court decisions, administrative rules, etc. Cf. *Westlake School: Student Handbook, 1972-1973*, Los Angeles, California which contains the "Rules and Regulations" of a private school respecting uniforms which must be worn by students, absence/tardiness, lock and lockers, suspension and expulsion, etc.

325. Hentoff, p. 5.

326. "Children's Rights: The Latest Crusade," *Time*, December 25, 1972, p. 41.

Chapter 6
Conclusions, Applications, and Limitations

1. Pugsley v. Sellmeyer, 158 Ark. 247 (1923); 24 Ruling Case Law, Sec. 24; and Chapter 5 above.

2. See *American Digest*, "Schools and School Districts," Key Numbers 170-72.

3. See examples of such policies and practices discussed in Chapters 3, 4, and 5.

4. 347 U.S. 483 (1954); cf. 349 U.S. 294 (1955).

5. Cf. Judge Gittleson's opinion, *Crawford v. Board of Education of the City of Los Angeles*, "Minute Order" No. 822,854, February 11, 1970; excerpts from the decision are reported in John C. Hogan, "The Role of the Courts in Certain Educational Policy Formation," *Policy Sciences*, vol. 1, no. 3 (Fall 1970), pp. 289-97.

6. Discussed in Chapter 4 above.

7. See court decisions analyzed in Chapter 3 above.

8. Op. cit. note 4 supra.

9. 96 Cal. Rptr. 601 (1971).

10. See John C. Hogan, " 'Obtaining and Education' As A Right of the People," 3 *NOLPE School Law Journal* 15-26 (Spring, 1973).

11. *Tinker v. De Moines Independent Community School District*, 393 U.S. 503 (1969).

12. See Chapter 2.

13. See Chapters 2 and 4 above.

14. *Bolling v. Sharpe*, 347 U.S. 497 (1954). *Harper v. Virginia Board of Elections*, 383 U.S. 663 (1960).

15. *Brown v. Board of Education of Topeka*, 347 U.S. 483. Cf. *Yick Wo v. Hopkins*, 118 U.S. 356, 367 (1886).

16. See discussion of "classification," Chapter 4 and tests and measurement practices in Chapter 5 above. See *Notes*, 68 Columbia Law Review 734-44 (1968).

17. See Justice Douglas, dissenting, "Memorandum Cases," 30 L. Ed. 2d 738 (1972).

18. *Richards v. Thurston*, 424 F. 2d 1281 (1970).

19. *Roberts v. The City of Boston*, 59 Mass. Rpts. (5 Cushing) 198 (1849); *Brown v. Board of Education of Topeka*, 347 U.S. 483.

20. *Pierce, Governor of Oregon, v. Society of Sisters*, 268 U.S. 510 (1925). Cf. *State of Wisconsin v. Yoder*, 32 L. Ed. 2d 15 (1972) wherein children of the Amish faith were excused from attending any public school after they had completed the eighth grade.

21. *Hargraves v. Ordway*, 323 F. Supp. 1155 (D.C. Mass. 1971).

22. *Richards v. Thurston*, 424 F. 2d 1281 (1970).

23. *Tinker v. De Moines Independent Community School District*, op. cit. note 11 supra.

24. Cf. *Serrano v. Priest*, op. cit. note 9·supra; *Milliken v. Green*, 203 N.W. 2d 457 (1972). But see the Texas school taxation case, *San Antonio Independent School District v. Rodriguez*, 36 L. Ed. 2d 16 (1973).

25. See Chapter 2 above.

26. 401 U.S. 424 (1971).

27. 96 *California Reporter* 620 (1971).

28. 287 A. 2d 212 (1972).

29. 96 *California Reporter* 601 (1971).

30. 287 A. 2d 216 (1972).

31. 36 L. Ed. 2d 16 (1973).

32. See 41 LAW WEEK 2552-53 (April 17, 1973).

33. Cox, "Foreword: Constitutional Adjudication and the Promotion of Human Rights," 80 *Harvard Law Review* 91 (1966).

34. Gunther and Dowling, *Constitutional Law*, pp. 1048-49 (1970).

35. *Hobson v. Hansen*, 269 F. Supp. 401, 517 (1967).

36. 347 U.S. 483-96 (1964).

37. *Memorandum Decisions*, 425 F. 2d 1211 (1970). Italics added.

38. 287 A. 2d 200 (1972).

39. See Chapters 2 and 3.

40. 393 U.S. 114 (1968).

41. Sager, "Tight Little Islands: Exclusionary Zoning, Equal Protection, and the Indigent," 21 *Stanford Law Review* 767, 779 (1969). Italics added.

42. "Developments in the Law—Equal Protection," 82 *Harvard Law Review*, 1065, 1192 (1969).

43. Note, in this connection; the prompt action by the California legislature to amend the state's *Education Code* to conform to the constitutional requirements of "freedom of expression" for students and teachers. See Chapter 5 above.

44. *Karr v. Schmidt*, 401 U.S. 1201 (1971).

45. See *Keyes v. School District No. 1, Denver, Colorado*, 37 L. Ed. 2d 548 (1973), majority opinion by Justice Brennan, and opinions by Justices Douglas and Powell who would abolish the *de jure/de facto* distinction. See discussion in Chapter 4.

46. Cardozo, *The Nature of the Judicial Process* (New Haven, Conn: Yale University Press, 1941), p. 48.

47. Cardozo, p. 51.

48. *Walz v. Tax Commission*, 397 U.S. 664, 697 (1970). Recall Justice Harlan's reference to the "era of judicial constitutional revision" in which we are living and his "complete astonishment" at the position taken by Justice Douglas in *Oregon v. Mitchell*, namely, that Harlan's history of the Fourteenth Amendment "is irrelevant to the present problems." See *Oregon v. Mitchell*, 400 U.S. 139-141 (1970).

Bibliography

Bibliography

General Works (Books)

Black, Jr., Charles L., *Perspectives in Constitutional Law* (Englewood Cliffs, N.J.: Prentice-Hall, 1970).

Black's Law Dictionary (St. Paul, Minn.: West Publishing Company, 1968).

Blackstone, Sir William, *Commentaries on the Laws of England* 4 vols. (London, 1844).

Cardozo, Benjamin N., *The Nature of the Judicial Process* (New Haven, Conn.: Yale University Press, 1941).

Constitution of the United States of America: Analysis and Interpretation (Washington, D.C.: Government Printing Office, 1953).

Crosskey, William W., *Politics and the Constitution in the History of the United States* (Chicago, Ill.: The University of Chicago Press, 1953) 2 vols.

Cubberley, Ellwood P., *Public Education in the United States: A Study and Interpretation of American Educational History* (New York: Houghton Mifflin Company, 1934).

_____*Readings in Public Education in the United States: A Collection of Sources and Readings to Illustrate the History of Educational Practice and Progress in the United States* (Boston: Houghton Mifflin, 1934).

Davis, Noah K., *Elements of Deductive Logic* (New York: Harper and Brothers, Publishers, 1896).

Dunne, Gerald T., *Justice Joseph Story and the Rise of the Supreme Court* (New York: Simon and Schuster, 1970).

Emerson, Thomas I., *Toward a General Theory of the First Amendment* (New York: Vantage Books, 1966).

Fellman, David, *The Supreme Court and Education* (New York: Teachers College Press, 1969).

Flack, Horace E., *The Adoption of the Fourteenth Amendment* (Baltimore, Md.: The Johns Hopkins Press, 1908).

Forkosch, Morris D., *Constitutional Law* (Mineola, N.Y.: The Foundation Press, Inc., 1969).

Gunther, Gerald, and Noel T. Dowling, *Constitutional Law: Cases and Materials* (Mineola, N.Y.: The Foundation Press, Inc., 1970).

_____*Constitutional Law and Individual Rights in Constitutional Law: Cases and Materials*, 1972 Supplement (Mineola, N.Y.: The Foundation Press, Inc., 1972).

_____*Individual Rights in Constitutional Law: Cases and Materials* (Mineola, N.Y.: The Foundation Press, Inc., 1970).

Haiman, Franklyn S., *The First Freedoms: Speech, Press, Assembly* (New York: American Civil Liberties Union, n.d.).

Hand, Learned, *The Bill of Rights* (Cambridge, Mass.: Harvard University Press, 1960).

Hicks, Frederick C., *Materials and Methods of Legal Research* (Rochester, N.Y.: The Lawyers Co-operative Publishing Company, 1942).

Holmes, Jr., Oliver Wendell, *The Common Law* (Boston: Little, Brown and Company, 1948).

Horowitz, Harold W., and Kenneth L. Karst, *Law, Lawyers and Social Change: Cases and Materials on the Abolition of Slavery, Racial Segregation, and Inequality of Educational Opportunity* (Indianapolis: The Bobbs-Merrill Company, Inc., 1969).

Huckins, W.C., *Ethical and Legal Considerations in Guidance* (Boston: Houghton Mifflin Company, 1968).

LeBuffe, Francis P., and James V. Hayes, *Jurisprudence* (New York: Fordham University Press, 1938).

Levy, Leonard W. (Ed.), *Judicial Review and the Supreme Court* (New York: Harper and Row, Publishers, 1967).

Lieber, Francis, *Legal and Political Hermeneutics* (St. Louis: F.H. Thomas and Company, 1880).

Lockhart, William B., Yale Kamisar, and Jesse H. Choper, *The American Constitution: Cases—Comments—Questions.* Supplement, 1973 (St. Paul, Minn.: West Publishing Company, 1970).

Martin, David V., "Case Analysis Format for Teaching School Law" pp. 211-228 in *Frontiers of School Law* (Topeka, Kan.: National Organization on Legal Problems of Education, 1973).

Matzen, John M., *State Constitutional Provisions for Education: Fundamental Attitude of the American People Regarding Education as Revealed by State Constitutional Provisions, 1776-1929* (New York: Teachers College, Columbia University, 1931; Reprint, New York: AMS Press, 1972).

Mohler, J.D., and E.C. Bolmeier, *Law of Extracurricular Activities in Secondary Schools* (Cincinnati: The W.H. Anderson Company, 1968).

Morgan, Edmund M., *Basic Problems of Evidence* (Philadelphia: American Law Institute, 1954).

Nolte, M. Chester (Comp.), *Bibliography of School Law Dissertations, 1952-1968* (Eugene, Ore.: University of Oregon, 1969).

Olds, Glenn A., *Kent's Commentaries Updated* (Topeka, Kansas: National Organization on Legal Problems of Education, 1973).

Parkinson, C. Northcote, *Parkinson's Law* (New York: Ballantine Books, 1969).

Patterson, Bennett B., *The Forgotten Ninth Amendment* (Indianapolis: The Bobbs-Merrill Company, 1955).

Peter, Lawrence J., and Raymond Hull, *The Peter Principle* (New York: Bantam Books, 1969).

Pound, Roscoe, *Outlines of Lectures on Jurisprudence* (Cambridge, Mass.: Harvard University Press, 1943).

Practicing Law Institute, *Schools and the Supreme Court* (New York: Practicing Law Institute, 1972).

Prosser, William L., *Handbook of the Law of Torts* (St. Paul, Minn.: West Publishing Company, 1971).

Reid, Robert H., *American Degree Mills: A Study of Their Operations and of Existing and Potential Ways to Control Them* (Washington, D.C.: American Council on Education, 1959).

Roalfe, William R., *How to Find the Law* (St. Paul, Minn.: West Publishing Company, 1965).

Sample Pages Illustrating Organization of and Research Techniques in West's Key Number Digests, National Reporter System, U.S.C.A., and Other West Statutes, Corpus Juris Secundum, Words and Phrases: Designed for Classroom Use in All Courses on Legal Research, (St. Paul, Minn.: West Publishing Company, 1970).

Schwartz, Mortimer D., and John C. Hogan, *Joseph Story: A Collection of Writings By and About an Eminent American Jurist* (New York: Oceana Publications, Inc., 1959).

Schultz, Theodore W., *The Economic Value of Education* (New York: Columbia University Press, 1967).

Shubert, Glendon A., *Constitutional Politics: The Political Behavior of Supreme Court Justices and Constitutional Policies They Make* (New York: Holt, Rinehart, and Winston, Inc., 1960).

Spurlock, Clark, *Education and the Supreme Court* (Westport, Conn.: Greenwood Press, 1973; Reprint of 1955 edition).

State of California, *Report of the Governor's Commission on Educational Reform* (Sacramento: Governor's Commission on Educational Reform, 1971).

Stimson, Frederic Jesup, *The Law of the Federal and State Constitutions of the United States with an Historical Study of Their Principles, a Chronological Table of English Social Legislation, and a Comparative Digest of the Constitutions of the Forty-Six States* (Boston: The Boston Book Company, 1908).

von Humboldt, Wilhelm, *The Limits of State Action* (Cambridge, England: Cambridge University Press, 1969).

Ware, Martha L. (Ed.), *Law of Guidance and Counseling*, (NOLPE Legal Problems of Education Series No. 4, Cincinnati: The W.H. Anderson Company, 1964).

Wirt, Frederick, and Michael Kirst, *The Political Web of American Schools* (Boston: Little, Brown, and Company, 1972).

Witkowiak, Stanislau B., *Limitations Imposed Upon the Rights and Powers of Respective States Over Education by the United States Supreme Court* (Washington, D.C.: The Catholic University of America, 1942).

Zelermyer, William, *Legal Reasoning* (Englewood Cliffs, N.J.: Prentice-Hall, Inc., 1960).

210

General Works (Articles)

Amar, Wesley F., "A Survival Kit for the Inner City School Principal," *Clearing House*, May 1973, p. 545.

"Arguments Before the Court: Schools and Colleges—Public School Desegregation; Geographic Attendance Zones; Consolidation of School Districts," 41 *LAW WEEK* 3577 (May 1, 1973).

Bassett, William, "Reemergence of the 'State Action' Requirement in Race Relations Cases," 22 Catholic University Law Review 39 (1972).

"Compulsory Education in the United States: Big Brother Goes to School," 3 Seton Hall Law Review 349 (1972).

"Constitutional Law—State Action Doctrine Invoked as a Limitation Upon the Reach of the Fourteenth Amendment," 25 Vanderbilt Law Review 1237 (1972).

"Decline and Fall of the New Equal Protection: A Polemical Approach," 58 Vanderbilt Law Review 1489 (1972).

Duffy, Patrick S., "The First Amendment is Not For Sale," Phi Delta Kappan, September 1971, p. 55.

Evers, Irving C., "School Law: Seven Decisions that May Effect You," 91 Nation's Schools 35 (1973).

Hafter, Jermore C., et al., "Segregated Academies and State Action," 82 Yale Law Journal 1436 (1973).

Hazard, William R., "Collective Bargaining and School Governance," 5 South Western Law Review 83 (1973).

"*Hobson v. Hansen*: Judicial Supervision of the Color-Blind School Board," 81 Harvard Law Review 1511 (1968).

Hogan, John C., "Law, Society, and the Schools," chapter in NSSE Yearbook (forthcoming, 1974).

_____ "'Obtaining an Education' As A Right of the People," 3 NOLPE School Law Journal 15 (1973), reprinted in 68 The Brief, Phi Delta Phi Quarterly 249 (1973).

_____ "The Role of the Courts in Certain Educational Policy Formation," 1 Policy Sciences 289 (1970), reprinted in 64 The Brief, Phi Delta Phi Quarterly 190 (1970).

_____ "School Desegregation—North, South, East, West: Trends in Court Decision, 1849-1973," Phi Delta Kappan, September 1973, p. 58.

Horowitz, Harold W., "The Misleading Search for 'State Action' Under the Fourteenth Amendment," 30 Southern California Law Review 208 (1957).

Houle, P.P., "Compelling State Interest v. Mere Rational Classification: The Practitioner's Equal Protection Dilemma," 3 Urban Lawyer 375 (1971).

Kurland, P.B., "Supreme Court, Compulsory Education, and the First Amendment's Religion Clauses," 75 West Virginia Law Review 213 (1973).

Kutner, Luis, "The Neglected Ninth Amendment: The 'Other Rights' Retained by the People," 51 Marquette Law Review 121 (1967).

"Law and the School: Legal Problems in an Educational Setting," 22 Buffalo
Law Review 523 (1973).

Nedurian, Jr., Vram, "Guidelines–Cooperation Between School Officials and
Police Departments," 2 NOLPE School Law Journal 57 (1972).

"Ninth Amendment Vindication of Unenumerated Fundamental Rights," 42
Temple Law Quarterly 46 (1968).

"Prior Restrain in Public High Schools," 82 Yale Law Journal 1325 (1973).

"Problems in Legal Education, 1971 (A Survey)," 20 Cleveland State Law
Review 441 (1971).

"Review of Supreme Court's Work: Decisions on Schools and Colleges," 42
LAW WEEK 3077 (August 14, 1973).

"Role of Law in Educational Decision Making–A Symposium," 17 Villanova
Law Review 993 (1972).

Saario, Terry N., et al., "Sex Role Stereotyping in the Public Schools," 43
Harvard Educational Review 386 (1973).

"Sex Discrimination in High School Athletics," 57 Minnesota Law Review 339
(1972).

Shannon, Thomas A., "Has the Fourteenth Done It Again?" Phi Delta Kappan,
April 1972, p. 466.

_____ "The Denver Decision: Death Knell for De Facto Segregation?" Phi
Delta Kappan, September 1973, p. 6.

"State Action and Private Education," 11 Journal of Family Law 765 (1972).

"State High School Athletic Associations: When Will a Court Interfere?" 36
Missouri Law Review 400 (1971).

van Alstyne, William W., and Kenneth L. Karst, "State Action," 14 Stanford
Law Review 3 (1961).

Williams, Jerre S., "The Twilight of State Action," 41 Texas Law Review 348
(1963).

"*Wisconsin v. Yoder*: The Right to be Different–First Amendment Exemption
for Amish Under the Free Exercise Clause," 22 De Paul Law Review 539
(1973).

Student Discipline (Books)

Bailey, Stephen K., *Disruption in Urban Public Secondary Schools* (Washington,
D.C.: National Association of Secondary School Principals, 1970).

Boudin, Kathy, et al., *The Bust Book: What to do Till the Lawyer Comes* (New
York: Grove Press, 1970).

Butler, Henry E., et al., *Legal Aspects of Student Records* (Topeka, Kan.:
National Organization on Legal Problems of Education, 1972).

Damgaard, John A., *The Student and the Courts: Campus Profile* (New York:
Exposition Press, 1971).

Guidelines for the Collection, Maintenance, and Dissemination of Pupil Records:

Report of a Conference on the Ethical and Legal Aspects of School Record Keeping (New York: Russell Sage Foundation, 1970).

Guidelines for Student Rights and Responsibilities (The University of the State of New York, the State Education Department, n.d.).

Hansen, Soren, and Jesper Jensen with Wallace Roberts, *The Little Red School-Book* (New York: Pocket Books, 1971).

LaMorte, Michael W., Harold W. Gentry, and D. Young Parker, *Students' Legal Rights and Responsibilities* (Cincinnati: W.H. Anderson Company, 1971).

Levine, Alan, et al., *Rights of Students* (New York: American Civil Liberties Union Handbook Series, R.W. Baron, 1973).

Mills, Joseph L., *Legal Rights of College Students and Administrators: A Handbook* (Washington, D.C.: Lerner Law Book Publishing Company, Inc., 1971).

Norton, John, and Eldon D. Wedlock, *Student Rights and Responsibilities in South Carolina* (Columbia, S.C.: American Friends Service Committee and American Civil Liberties Union, n.d.).

Nussbaum, Michael, *Student Legal Rights: What They Are and How to Protect Them* (New York: Harper and Row, Publishers, 1970).

Nygaard, Joseph M., *The Counselor and Students' Legal Rights* (Boston: Houghton Mifflin Company, 1973).

O'Hara, William T., and John G. Hill, Jr., *The Student–The College–The Law* (New York: Teachers College Press, 1972).

Phay, Robert E., *Suspension and Expulsion of Public School Students* (Topeka, Kan.: National Organization on Legal Problems of Education, 1971).

Punke, Harold H., *Social Implications of Law Suits Over Hairstyles* (Danville, Ill.: The Interstate Printers and Publishers, 1973).

Ratliff, Richard C., *Constitutional Rights of College Students* (New York: Scarecrow Press, Inc., 1972).

Regulations for School Behavior (Riverside, Calif.: Riverside Unified School District, 1969).

Reitman, Alan, Judith Follman, and Edward T. Ladd, *Corporal Punishment in the Public Schools: The Use of Force in Controlling Student Behavior* (New York: American Civil Liberties Union, 1972).

Reutter, Jr., E. Edmund, *Legal Aspects of Control of Student Activities By Public School Authorities* (Topeka, Kan.: National Organization on Legal Problems of Education, 1970).

Schoolgirl Pregnancy: Old Problems and New Solutions (Washington, D.C.: National School Public Relations Association, 1972).

Strouse, Jean, *Up Against the Law: The Legal Rights of People Under 21* (New York: The New American Library, 1970).

Students Rights and Responsibilities (Los Angeles City Schools, Office of the Superintendent, 1972).

von Brock, Robert C., *A Survey of Court Decisions Affecting Student Dress and*

Appearance (Baton Rouge, La.: Bureau of Educational Materials and Research, L.S.U., 1972).

Young, D. Parker, *Briefs of Selected Court Cases Affecting Student Dissent and Discipline* (Athens, Ga.: University of Georgia, Institute of Higher Education, 1970).

Student Discipline (Articles)

Berkman, Richard L., "Students in Court: Free Speech and the Functions of Schooling in America," 40 Harvard Educational Review 567 (1970).

"Comment. Public Secondary Education: Judicial Protection of Student Individuality," 42 Southern California Law Review 126 (1969).

"Constitutional Law—Schools and School Districts—Prohibition of Long Hair Absent Showing of Actual Disruption Violates High School Student's Constitutional Rights," 84 Harvard Law Review 1702 (1971).

"Constitutional Law—The Equal Protection Clause and the Student's Right to Vote Where He Attends School," 50 North Carolina Law Review 1148 (1972).

"Constitutional Law—Married High School Students—Participation in Extracurricular Activities," 40 Tennessee Law Review 268 (1973).

"Drug Control of School Children: The Child's Right to Choose," 46 Southern California Law Review 585 (1973).

"Emerging Rights of High School Students: The Law Comes of Age," 23 University of Florida Law Review 549 (1971).

Forde, K.M., "Liability of Schools for Injuries to Students," 17 Trial Lawyer's Guide 1 (1973).

Goldstein, Stephen R., "The Scope and Source of School Board Authority to Regulate Student Conduct and Status: A Nonconstitutional Analysis," 117 University of Pennsylvania Law Review 377 (1969).

Hargis, David M., "The Birch Rod, Due Process, and the Disciplinarian," 26 Arkansas Law Review 365 (1972).

Hudgin, H.C., "Action Not as Heavy on Student Rights," *Nation's Schools*, March 1972, p. 46.

Knowles, L.W., "High School Marriage, and the Fourteenth Amendment," 11 Journal of Family Law 711 (1972).

Ladd, Edward T., "Regulating Student Behavior Without Ending Up in Court," Phi Delta Kappan, January 1973, p. 304.

Langenbach, Michael, and George A. Letchworth, "Disciplinary Techniques: Repertoires and Relationships," Paper presented at Annual Meeting, AERA, New York, 1971.

Levitin, J.E. "Individual Freedom, Discipline, and the Law: A Continuing Dilemma of our Educational System," 5 Lincoln Law Review 35 (1969).

Lines, Patricia M., "Codes for High School Students," 8 Inequality in Education 24 (1971).

"Marriage vs. Education: A Constitutional Conflict," 44 Mississippi Law Journal 248 (1973).

Pressman, Robert, "Due Process of Law in School Discipline: Recent Decisions," 14 Inequality in Education 55 (1973).

Runkel, R.R., "Public Schools and Personal Appearance: Some Theories," 7 Willamette Law Journal 419 (1971).

Starkey, John, "Discipline Suggestions," Phi Delta Kappan, January 1973, p. 351.

Stroud, K.M., "Sex Discrimination in High School Athletics," 6 Indiana Law Review 661 (1973).

"Student Rights and Responsibilities," Today's Education, January 1972, p. 50.

Thomas, Arthur E., "Community Power and Student Rights," 42 Harvard Educational Review 173 (1972).

"Wellsand v. Valparasio Community School Corporation: Equal Protection for the Married Football Player," 47 Indiana Law Journal (1972).

Wallington, P., "Corporal Punishment in Schools," Juridical Review, 1972, p. 124.

Teacher Rights and Responsibilities
(Books)

Allen, Ira M., The Teacher's Contractual Status as Revealed by an Analysis of American Court Decisions (New York: Teachers College, Columbia University, 1928; reprinted by AMS Press, 1972).

Anderson, Earl W., The Teacher's Contract and Other Legal Phases of Teacher Status (New York: Teachers College, Columbia University, 1927; reprinted by AMS Press, 1972).

Bolmeier, Edward C., Teachers' Legal Rights, Restraints, and Liabilities (Cincinnati: W.H. Anderson Company, 1971).

Delon, Floyd G., Substantive Legal Aspects of Teacher Discipline (Topeka, Kan.: National Organization on Legal Problems of Education, 1972).

Fischer, Louis and David Schimmel, The Civil Rights of Teachers (New York: Harper and Row, Publishers, 1973).

Garber, Lee O., and Eugene Benedetti, The Law and the Teacher in California (Danville, Ill.: The Interstate Printers and Publishers, Inc., 1967).

Gatti, Daniel, and Richard Gatti, Teacher and the Law (Englewood Cliffs, N.J.: Prentice-Hall, 1972).

Gottesman, Michael, Due Process for Nontenured Teachers from the Teachers' Viewpoint (Topeka, Kan.: National Organization on Legal Problems of Education, 1973).

Holmstedt, Raleigh W., *A Study of the Effects of the Teacher Tenure Law in New Jersey* (New York: Teachers College, Columbia University, 1932; reprinted by AMS Press, 1972).

Kallen, Laurence, *Teachers' Rights and Liabilities Under the Law* (New York: ARCO Publishing Company, 1971).

Kigin, Denis J., *Teacher Liability in School-Shop Accidents* (Ann Arbor, Mich: Prakken Publications, Inc., 1973).

Perry, Charles R., and Wesley A. Wildman, *The Impact of Negotiations in Public Education: The Evidence from the Schools* (Worthington, Ohio: Charles A. Jones Publishing Company, 1970).

Rubin, David, *Rights of Teachers* (New York: American Civil Liberties Union Handbook Series, Avon Books, 1972).

Shannon, Thomas A., *Due Process for Nontenured Teachers and The Board's Viewpoint* (Topeka, Kan.: National Organization on Legal Problems of Education, 1973).

Smith, Bardwell L., *The Tenure Debate* (San Francisco: Jossey-Bass, 1972).

Teacher Rights and Responsibilities
(Articles)

Carpenter, Charles H., "California Schoolteacher's Privilege to Inflict Corporal Punishment," 15 Hastings Law Journal 600 (1964).

"Court Strikes Down Grading System for Teachers," *Education Daily*, September 24, 1973, p. 3.

"Criminal Liability for Excessive or Improper Punishment Inflicted on Child by Parent, Teacher, or One In Loco Parentis," 89 A.L.R. 2d 396 (1963).

"Personal Liability of Public School Officers, or Teachers, or Other Employees for Negligence," 32 A.L.R. 2d 1163 (1953).

Gerbner, George, "Teacher Image and the Hidden Curriculum," 42 The American Scholar 66 (1973).

Jorgensen, Craig, "Negligence Liability of Schoolteachers in California," 15 Hastings Law Journal 567 (1964).

"Mandatory Maternity Leaves and the Equal Protection Clause," 61 Kentucky Law Journal 589 (1973).

"Mandatory Maternity Leave: Title VII and Equal Protection," 14 William and Mary Law Review 1026 (1973).

Seitz, Reynolds C., "Legal Responsibility Under Tort Law of School Personnel and School Districts as Regards Negligent Conduct Towards Pupils," 15 Hastings Law Journal 495 (1964).

"Some Miscellaneous Legal Problems—Defamation: Libel and Slander; Right of Privacy; Tort Liability of Teachers," chapter 14 in John C. Hogan and Saul Cohen, *An Author's Guide to Scholarly Publishing and the Law* (Englewood Cliffs, N.J.: Prentice-Hall, 1965).

"Teacher's Civil Liability for Administering Corporal Punishment to Pupil," 43 A.L.R. 2d (1955).

"Teacher Qualifications—Use of Minimum Score on Standardized Examination as Requirement for Hiring and Retention of Teachers when Examination not Reasonably Related to Purpose for which it was Ostensibly Designed is Impermissible as Violative of Equal Protection of the Laws Under the Fourteenth Amendment," 22 Buffalo Law Review 655 (1973).

"Validity of Standardized Employment Testing Under Title VII and the Equal Protection Clause," 37 Missouri Law Review 693 (1972).

School Financing (Books)

Berke, Joel, and Michael Kirst, *Federal Aid to Education: Who Benefits? Who Governs?* (Lexington, Mass.: D.C. Heath and Company, 1972).

Cohen, Michael, Betsy Levin, and Richard Beaver, *The Political Limits to School Reform* (Washington, D.C.: The Urban Institute, 1973).

Coons, John E., William H. Clune III, and Stephen D. Sugarman, *Private Wealth and Public Education* (Cambridge, Mass.: Harvard University Press, 1970).

Cubberly, Ellwood P., *School Funds and Their Apportionment*(New York: Teachers College, Columbia University, 1905).

Garber, Lee O., and Newton Edwards, *The Law Governing the Financing of Public Education* (Danville, Ill.: Interstate Printers and Publishers, 1962).

Issues in School Finance, Select Committee on Equal Educational Opportunity, United States Senate (Washington, D.C.: Government Printing Office, 1972).

Johns, Roe L., and Edgar L. Morphet, *The Economics and Financing of Education: A Systems Approach* (Englewood Cliffs, N.J.: Prentice-Hall, 1969).

Levin, Betsy, et al., *Paying for Public Schools: Issues in School Finance in California* (Washington, D.C.: The Urban Institute, n.d.).

Levin, Betsy, Thomas Muller, and William J. Scanlon, *Schools and Taxes in North Carolina* (Washington, D.C.: The Urban Institute, 1973).

Major School Finance Changes in 1973 (Denver, Co.: Education Commission for the States, 1973).

Marland, Sidney· J., *Issues in School Finance* (Washington, D.C.: Department of Health, Education, and Welfare, U.S. Office of Education, 1972).

Meltsner, Arnold, et al., *Political Feasibility of Reform in School Financing: The Case of California* (New York: Frederick Praeger Company, 1973).

Mort, P.R., W.C. Reusser, and J.W. Polley, *Public School Finance* (New York: McGraw-Hill Book Company, 1960).

Norton, John K. (Ed.), *Dimensions on School Finance* (Washington, D.C.: National Education Association, 1966).

Schools Without Property Taxes: Hope or Illusion? (Bloomington, Ind.: Phi Delta Kappa Educational Foundation, 1972).

Scribner, Jay D. (Ed.), *California Supreme Court Decision (Serrano v. Priest):* *Implications for Equality of Educational Opportunity*, Proceedings of a Conference (U.C.L.A. Extension Division, 1971).

Soper, Wayne W., *Legal Limitations on the Rights and Powers of School Boards with Respect to Taxation* (New York: Teachers College, Columbia University, 1929; reprinted by AMS Press, 1972).

Strayer, George D. and Robert M. Haig, *The Financing of Education in the State of New York* (New York: The Macmillan Company, 1923).

Wise, Arthur E., *Rich Schools, Poor Schools: The Promise of Equal Educational Opportunity* (Chicago: The University of Chicago Press, 1968).

Yakel, Ralph, *The Legal Control of the Administration of Public School Expenditures* (New York: Teachers College Columbia University, 1929; reprinted by AMS Press, 1972).

School Financing (Articles)

"Arguments For and Against the Property Tax System in Financing Education," 47 Tulane Law Review 147 (1972).

Barro, Stephen M., "Alternatives in California School Finance," The Rand Corporation, R-663-RC/CC, May 1971.

Beebe, J.W. "School Financing—*Serrano v. Priest*: The Death Knell to Ad Valorem School Financing," 44 Pennsylvania Bar Association Quarterly 474 (1973).

Coons, John E., William H. Clune III, and Stephen D. Sugarman, "Educational Opportunity: A Workable Constitutional Test for State Financial Structures," 57 California Law Review 305 (1969).

Coons, John E., "Financing Public Schools After 'Rodriguez,'" *Saturday Review/World*, October 9, 1973, p. 44.

Dunn, J.T., "Double Standard in Public Education—Part II. Wealth Discrimination," 10 American Business Law Journal 231 (1973).

"Equal Protection and the Financing of Public Education in Wyoming," 8 Land and Water Law Review 273 (1973).

Freeman, Roger A., "Should States Finance the Schools," *Wall Street Journal*, March 31, 1972.

Glickstein, H.A. and W.L. Want, "Inequality in School Financing: The Role of the Law," 25 Stanford Law Review 335 (1973).

Karst, Kenneth, "*Serrano v. Priest*: A State Court's Responsibilities and Opportunities in the Development of Federal Constitutional Law," 60 California Law Review 720 (1972).

Lindman, Erick L. "School Finance Policy of the Next Decade," chapter 7 in James E. Bruno (Ed.), *Emerging Issues in Education: Policy Issues for the Schools* (Lexington, Mass.: D.C. Heath Company, 1972).

Lucas, Jo Desha, "Serrano and Rodriguez—An Overextension of Equal Protection," 2 NOLPE School Law Journal 18 (1972).

Hogan, John C., " 'Obtaining an Education' As A Right of the People," 3 NOLPE School Law Journal 15 (1973).

Michelson, Stephen, "Public School Finance in a Post- *Serrano* World," 8 Harvard Civil Rights-Civil Liberties Law Review 550 (1973).

O'Brien, Jerrold, "*Serrano v. Priest* and the Central City: A Case for Equity?" 37 Albany Law Review 442 (1973).

Post, A.A., and R.W. Brandsma, "Legislature's Response to *Serrano v. Priest*," 2 Pacific Law Journal 28 (1973).

"Public Support for Schools: Waxing or Waning?" *Education U.S.A.*, September 17, 1973, p. 13.

"Serrano and Its Successors: The Challenge to State Educational Finance Systems," 18 San Diego Law Review 133 (1973).

"Serrano Symposium: The Death Knell to Ad Valorem School Financing," 5 Urban Lawyer 83 (1973).

"*Serrano v. Priest* and its Impact on New Mexico," 2 New Mexico Law Review 266 (1972).

"*Serrano v. Priest*: Equal Protection and Public School Finance," 8 California Western Law Review 547 (1972).

"*Serrano v. Priest*: Renaissance For School Financing Through the Equal Protection Clause," 21 American University Law Review 685 (1972).

"Six States Reform Finances," *Education Commission of the States Bulletin*, July 1973, p. 3.

"Statistical Analysis of the School Finance Decisions: On Winning Battles and Losing Wars," 81 Yale Law Journal 1303 (1972).

Vieira, N., "Unequal Educational Expenditures: Some Minority Views on *Serrano v. Priest*," 37 Missouri Law Review 617 (1972).

Williams, Joseph A., et al., "The Attack on State Educational Finance Programs—An Overview," 2 NOLPE School Law Journal 1 (1972).

Wise, Arthur E., "The California Doctrine," *Saturday Review*, November 20, 1971, p. 78.

Equality, and Educational Opportunity
(Books)

Coleman, James S., *Equality of Educational Opportunity* (Washington, D.C.: Government Printing Office, 1966).

Cordasco, Francesco, *The Equality of Educational Opportunity: A Bibliography of Selected References* (Totowa, N.J.: Rowman and Littlefield, 1973).

Equal Educational Opportunity (Cambridge, Mass.: Harvard University Press, 1969).

Evers, Irving C., *Legal Ramifications of the E.E.O.C.* (Topeka, Kan.: National Organization on Legal Problems of Education, 1973).

Gardner, John W., *Excellence: Can We Be Equal and Excellent Too?* (New York: Harper and Row, Publishers, 1961).

Guthrie, James W., George B. Kleindorfer, Henry M. Levin, and Robert T. Stout, *Schools and Inequality* (Cambridge, Mass.: M.I.T. Press, 1971).

Harris, R.J., *The Quest for Equality: The Constitution, Congress, and The Supreme Court* (Baton Rouge, La.: State University Press, 1960).

Hughes, John F., and Anne O. Hughes, *Equal Education: A New National Strategy* (Bloomington, Ind.: Indiana University Press, 1973).

Mosteller, Frederick, and Daniel P. Moynihan, *On Equality of Educational Opportunity: Papers Deriving From the Harvard University Faculty Seminar on The Coleman Report* (New York: Vintage Books, 1972).

Picker, Jane, *Women's Right in Education* (Topeka, Kan.: National Organization on Legal Problems of Education, 1973).

Selected Court Decisions Relating to Equal Educational Opportunity, Select Committee on Equal Educational Opportunity, United States Senate (Washington, D.C., Government Printing Office, 1972).

Equality, and Educational Opportunity
(Articles)

"And Whose Little Girl are You? (Or I'd Like to Run for President but My Husband Won't Move to Washington)," 2 University of San Fernando Law Review 63 (1972-73).

Campbell, E.Q., "Defining and Attaining Equal Educational Opportunity in a Pluralistic Society," 26 Vanderbilt Law Review 461 (1973).

Carter, R.L., "Evaluation of Past and Current Legal Approaches to Vindication of the Fourteenth Amendment's Guarantee of Equal Educational Opportunity," Washington University Law Quarterly 479 (1972).

Cohen, David K., "Defining Racial Equality in Education," 16 U.C.L.A. Law Review 42 (1967).

_____ "Racial Imbalance in the Pasadena Public Schools," 2 Law and Society Review 42 (1967).

Coleman, James S., "The Concept of Equal Educational Opportunity," 38 Harvard Educational Review 7 (1968).

_____ "Equality of Educational Opportunity: Reply to Bowles and Levin," 3 Journal of Human Resources 237 (1968).

"Comment. Equality of Educational Opportunity: Are 'Compensatory Programs' Constitutionally Required?" 42 Southern California Law Review 146 (1969).

Cox, Archibald, "Constitutional Adjudication and the Promotion of Human Rights: Foreword to the Supreme Court 1965 Term," 80 Harvard Law Review 91 (1966).

"Developments in the Law—Equal Protection," 82 Harvard Law Review 1065 (1969).

Dyer, Henry, "School Factors and Educational Opportunity," 38 Harvard Educational Review 38 (1968).

Getman, J.G., "Emerging Constitutional Principle of Sexual Equality," Supreme Court Review, p. 157 (1972).

"Equal Educational Opportunity: 38 Harvard Educational Review 1 (1968).

"Equal Educational Opportunity: A Case for the Children," 18 Catholic Lawyer 113 (1972).

"Equal Protection and School Finance," 26 Arkansas Law Review 508 (1973).

"Equal Protection in Transition: An Analysis and a Proposal," 41 Fordham Law Review 605 (1973).

"Equal Rights and Equal Protection: Who Has Management and Control," 46 Southern California Law Review 892 (1973).

"Equality and the Schools: Education as a Fundamental Interest," 21 American University Law Review 716 (1972).

Fiss, Owen M., "Racial Imbalance in Public Schools: The Constitutional Concepts," 78 Harvard Law Review 564 (1965).

"Fundamental Personal Rights: Another Approach to Equal Protection," 40 University of Chicago Law Review 807 (1973).

Green, Winifred, "Separate and Unequal Again," 14 Inequality in Education 14 (1973).

Hogan, John C., "Law, Society, and the Schools," chapter in NSSE Yearbook (forthcoming, 1974).

Horowitz, Harold W., and Diana L. Neitring, "Equal Protection Aspects of Inequalities in Public Education and Public Assistance Programs from Place to Place within a State," 15 U.C.L.A. Law Review 787 (1968).

Horowitz, Harold W., "Constitutional Aspects of Equality of Educational Opportunity," chapter 3 in James E. Bruno (Ed.), *Emerging Issues in Education: Policy Issues for the Schools* (Lexington, Mass.: D.C. Heath Company, 1972).

_____ "Unseparate But Unequal—The Emerging Fourteenth Amendment Issue in Public School Education," 13 U.C.L.A. Law Review 1147 (1966).

Jencks, Christopher, "The Coleman Report and the Conventional Wisdom," in F. Mosteller and D.P. Moynihan, *On Equality of Educational Opportunity* (New York: Vintage Books, 1972).

Kelman, Mark, "The Social Cost of Inequity," *Dissent* (Summer 1973, p. 291.

Kirp, David L., "The Poor, the School, and Equal Protection," 38 Harvard Educational Review 655 (1968).

Kurland, Philip B., "Equal Educational Opportunity: The Limits of Constitutional Jurisprudence Undefined," 35 University of Chicago Law Review 583 (1968).

"Legislative Purpose, Rationality, and Equal Protection," 82 Yale Law Journal 123 (1972).

Lieberman, Myron, "Equality of Educational Opportunity," 29 Harvard Educational Review 167 (1959).

"Linguistic Minorities and the Right to an Effective Education," 3 California Western International Law Journal 112 (1972).

McDaniel, Bobby R., "Equal Protection in the Streets," 25 Arkansas Law Review 487 (1972).

"Mandatory Maternity Leaves for Teachers—The Equal Protection Clause and Title VII of the Civil Rights Act of 1964," 51 North Carolina Law Review 768 (1973).

Sager, Lawrence G., "Tight Little Islands: Exclusionary Zoning, Equal Protection, and the Indigent," 21 Stanford Law Review 767 (1969).

Shanks, Hershel, "Equal Education and the Law," 39 American Scholar 255 (1970).

Smith, Marshall S., "Equality of Educational Opportunity: The Basic Findings Reconsidered," in F. Mosteller and D.P. Moynihan, *On Equality of Educational Opportunity* (New York: Vintage Books, 1972).

"Sovereign Immunity: Denial of Equal Protection," 52 Boston University Law Review 202 (1972).

"Symposium—Women and the Law," 5 Valparaiso University Law Review 203 (1971).

Tussman, Joseph, and Jacobus tenBroek, "The Equal Protection of the Laws," 37 California Law Review 341 (1949).

Wise, Arthur E., "Is Denial of Equal Educational Opportunity Constitutional?" 13 Administrator's Notebook 1 (1965).

Wright, Lawrence, "Potential Landmark: High Court to Hear Lau Case," 4 Race Relations Reporter 1 (1973).

Yudof, M.G., "Equal Educational Opportunity and the Courts," 51 Texas Law Review 411 (1973).

School Desegregation (Books)

Bickel, Alexander M., *The Busing Controversy* (Topeka, Kan.: National Organization on Legal Problems of Education, 1973).

Blaustein, Albert P., and Clarence C. Ferguson. *Desegregation and the Law* (New Brunswick, N.J.: Rutgers University Press, 1957).

Bork, Robert H., *Constitutionality of the President's Busing Proposals* (Washington, D.C.: American Enterprise Institute for Public Policy Research, 1972).

DeMont, Roger, Larry Hillman, and Gerald Mansergh (Editors), *Busing, Taxes, and Desegregation* (Danville, Ill.: Interstate Printers and Publishers, 1973).

Hooker, Clifford P., *Bradley v. Richmond* (Topeka, Kan.: National Organization on Legal Problems of Education, 1973).

Hudgins, Jr., H.C., with Marshall B. Gorodetzer, *Public School Desegregation: Legal Issues and Judicial Decisions* (Topeka, Kan.: National Organization on Legal Problems of Education, 1973).

Teele, James E., *Evaluating School Busing: Case Study of Boston's Operation Exodus* (New York: Praeger, Publishers, 1973).

U.S. Commission on Civil Rights, *Racial Isolation in the Public Schools* (Washington, D.C.: U.S. Government Printing Office, 1967).

Weinberg, Meyer, *Race and Place: A Legal History of the Neighborhood School* (Washington, D.C.: U.S. Government Printing Office, 1967).

Woodward, C. Vann, *The Strange Career of Jim Crow* (New York: Oxford University Press, 1966).

School Desegregation (Articles)

Armor, David J., "The Double Standard: A Reply," 30 The Public Interest 119 (1973).

_____ "The Evidence on Busing," 28 The Public Interest 90 (1972).

Bickel, Alexander M., "The Original Understanding and the Segregation Decision," 69 Harvard Law Review 1 (1955).

"Busing as a Judicial Remedy: A Socio-legal Reappraisal," 6 Indiana Law Review 710 (1973).

"Consolidation for Desegregation: The Unresolved Issue of The Inevitable Sequel," 82 Yale Law Journal 1681 (1973).

Cook, G., "School Desegregation: To Brown and Back Again—The Great Circle," 23 Baylor Law Review 398 (1971).

Daniels, Norman, "The Smart White Man's Burden," *Harper's Magazine*, October 1973, p. 24.

"De Facto School Segregation and the 'State Action' Requirement: A Suggested New Approach," 48 Indiana Law Journal 304 (1973).

Forkosch, Morris D., "The Desegregation Opinion Revisited: Legal or Sociological?" 21 Vanderbilt Law Review 47 (1967).

Fulkerson, D. Ray, Arnold Horelick, Lloyd S. Shapley, and Daniel M. Weiler, "A Transportation Program for Filling Idle Classrooms in Los Angeles," P-3405, The Rand Corporation, July 1965.

"Gallup Poll on Busing," *Newsweek*, March 13, 1972, p. 24.

Goodman, Frank I., "De Facto School Segregation: A Constitutional and Empirical Analysis," 60 California Law Review 275 (1972).

Green, Robert L., Eugenia Smith, and John H. Schweirzer, "Busing and the Multiracial Classroom." Phi Delta Kappan, May 1972, p. 543.

Harvey, James C., and Charles H. Holmes, "Busing and School Desegregation," Phi Delta Kappan, May 1972, p. 540.

Herbst, Robert L., "The Legal Struggle to Integrate Public Schools in the North," 407 American Academy of Political and Social Science Annals 43 (1973).

Hogan, John C., "School Desegregation—North, South, East, West: Trends in Court Decision, 1849-1973," Phi Delta Kappan, September 1973, p. 58.

_____ "The Role of the Courts in Certain Educational Policy Formation," 1 Policy Sciences 289 (1970). Reprinted in 65 The Brief, Phi Delta Phi Quarterly 190 (1970).

_____ "Law, Society, and the Schools," chapter in NSSE Yearbook (forthcoming, 1974).

Hooker, Clifford P., "The Richmond Decision—An Expansion of the White Majority Thesis," 2 NOLPE School Law Journal 42 (1972).

"Integration," Civil Rights Digest, Summer 1973, p. 2.

"Interpreting the Anti-Busing Provisions of the Education Amendments of 1972," 10 Harvard Journal on Legislation 256 (1973).

Kaplan, John, "Segregation Litigation and the Schools—Part II: The Great Northern Problem," 58 Northwestern Law Review 157 (1963).

Kiesling, H.J., "The Value to Society of Integrated Education and Compensatory Education," 61 Georgetown Law Journal 857 (1973).

Levine, Daniel U., "Integration in Metropolitan Schools: Issues and Prospects," Phi Delta Kappan, June 1973, p. 651.

Marty, Myron A., "Is Busing Necessary?" Christian Century, July 18-25, 1973, p. 751.

"Metropolitan Approach to Integration," 17 St. Louis Law Journal 279 (1972).

Mondale, Walter F., "Foreward or Reverse: Busing Perspective," The New Republic, March 4, 1972, p. 16.

"The New Segregation: Private School Systems," Urban Read-Out, August 31, 1973, p. 10.

Newsweek. Gallup Poll on Busing. March 13, 1972, p. 24.

"The Other Side of Senator Sam," Race Relations Reporter, September 17, 1973, p. 1.

"Perspective on Busing," 11 Inequality in Education 1 (1972).

Pettigrew, Thomas F., et al., Busing: A Review of "The Evidence," 30 The Public Interest 88 (1973).

Pollack, Louis H., "Racial Discrimination and Judicial Integrity: A Reply to Professor Wechsler," 108 University of Pennsylvania Law Review 1 (1959).

"Post-Brown Private White Schools—An Imperfect Dualism," 26 Vanderbilt Law Review 587 (1973).

Preyer, R., "Beyond Desegregation—What Ought to be Done?" 51 North Carolina Law Review 657 (1973).

Ragsdale, J.W., "Strategies for Metropolitan Stabilization," 41 University of Missouri at Kansas City Law Review 1 (1972).

St. John, N., "Desegregation and Minority Group Performance," 40 Review of Educational Research 111 (1970).

"School District Consolidation: A Method for Achieving School Desegregation," Urban Law Annual, p. 267 (1973).

"School Integration in the North," Urban Read-Out, August 15, 1973, p. 8.

"Segregation in the Metropolitan Context: The 'White Noose' Tightens," 58 Iowa Law Review 322 (1972).

"Segregation of Poor and Minority Children into Classes for The Mentally Retarded by Use of I.Q. Tests," 71 Michigan Law Review 1212 (1973).

Shannon, Thomas A., "The Denver Decision: Death Knell for De Facto Desegregation?" Phi Delta Kappan, September 1973, p. 6.

Silard, J., "Towards Nationwide School Desegregation: A 'Compelling State Test' of Racial Concentration in Public Education," 51 North Carolina Law Review 675 (1973).

Sinowitz, Betty E., "School Integration and the Teacher," *Today's Education*, May 1973, p. 31.

Smedley, T.A., "Developments in the Law of School Desegregation," 26 Vanderbilt Law Review 405 (1973).

_____ "The Last Two Years in School Desegregation," 4 Race Relations Reporter 12 (1973).

Stuart, Reginald, "Atlanta Splits on School Plan," *Race Relations Reporter*, February 19, 1973, p. 5.

_____ "Busing and the Media in Nashville," *New South*, Spring 1973, p. 79.

"Suit Claims U.S., Exxon, Memphis Conspire Against Busing," *Education Daily*, August 28, 1973, p. 3.

"Text of President's Statement on Educational Opportunity and Busing," *New York Times*, March 17, 1972.

Trabulus, Norman, "Braking the Law: Antibusing Legislation and the Constitution," *New York Review of Law and Social Change*, Spring 1973, p. 119.

Watters, Pat, "Atlanta's Questionable Compromise," *Christian Century*, August 29, 1973, p. 819.

Welsh, James, "A Long Range Look at School Desegregation," *Educational Researcher*, September 1973, p. 17.

Wilson, James Q., "On Pettigrew and Armor: An Afterword," 30 The Public Interest 132 (1973).

Assessment of Factors Believed to Effect Achievement in School and Legal Implications Thereof (Books)

Averch, Harvey A., Stephen J. Carroll, Theodore S. Donaldson, Herbert J. Kiesling, and John Pincus, *How Effective is Schooling? A Critical Review of Research* (Englewood Cliffs, N.J.: Educational Technology Publications, 1974).

Coleman, James S., *Equality of Educational Opportunity*, U.S. Department of Health, Education, and Welfare, Office of Education (Washington, D.C.: U.S. Government Printing Office, 1966; the "Coleman Report.").

_____ *Supplemental Appendix to the Survey of On Equality of Educational Opportunity: Section 9.10/Correlation Tables*, Office of Education/U.S.

Department of Health, Education, and Welfare (Washington, D.C.: U.S. Government Printing Office, 1966).

_____*Equality of Educational Opportunity*, U.S. Department of Health, Education, and Welfare, Office of Education (Washington D.C.: U.S. Government Printing Office, 1966; reprint of pages 1-33 of the "Coleman Report").

Davis, Frederick B., *The Measurement of Mental Capability Through Evoked-Potential Recordings* (Greenwich, Conn.: Educational Records Bureau, 1971).

Harvard Educational Review, *Equal Educational Opportunity* (Cambridge, Mass.: Harvard University Press, 1969). (Hereinafter cited as simply HER/EEO/HUP.)

Jencks, Christopher, Marshall Smith, Henry Acland, Mary Jo Bane, David Cohen, Herbert Gintis, Barbara Heyns, and Stephan Michelson, *Inequality: A Reassessment of the Effect of Family and Schooling in America* (New York: Basic Books, Inc., Publishers, 1972).

Assessment of Factors Believed to Effect Achievement in School and Legal Implications Thereof (Articles)

Armor, David J., "The Double Standard: A Reply," 30 The Public Interest 119 (1973).

_____ "The Evidence on Busing," 28 The Public Interest 90 (1972).

Bowles, Samuel, "Towards Equality of Educational Opportunity?" in Harvard Educational Review, *Equal Educational Opportunity* Mass.: Harvard University Press, 1969), p. 11. (Hereinafter cited simply as HER/EEO/HUP.)

Brown v. Board of Education of Topeka, 347 U.S. 483 (1954).

Brazziel, William F., "A Letter from the South," 39 Harvard Educational Review 200 (1969).

Cain, G., and H. Watts, "Problems in Making Inferences from the Coleman Report," 35 American Sociological Review 000 (1970).

Clark, Kenneth B., "Alternative Public School Systems," in HER/EEO/HUP, p. 73 (1969).

_____ "Social Policy, Power, and Social Science Research," 43 Harvard Educational Review 113 (1973).

Clune, III, William H., "Law and Economics in *Hobson v. Hansen*: An Introductory Note," 7 The Journal of Human Resources 275 (1972).

Cohen, David K., "Policy for the Public Schools: Compensation and Integration," in HER/EEO/HUP, p. 91 (1969).

Coleman, James S., "A Brief Summary of the Coleman Report," in HER/EEO/HUP, p. 253 (1969).

_____ "The Concept of Equality of Educational Opportunity," in HER/EEO/HUP, p. 9 (1969).

226

Coleman, James S., "Equality of Opportunity and Equality of Results," 43 Harvard Educational Review 129 (1973).

Cronbach, Lee J., "Heredity, Environment, and Educational Policy," 39 Harvard Educational Review 338 (1969).

Crow, James F., "Genetic Theories and Influences: Comments on the Value of Diversity," 39 Harvard Educational Review 153 (1969).

Day, Noel A., "The Case for All-Black Schools," in HER/EEO/HUP, p. 205 (1969).

"Directs Department of Education to Conduct Pilot Study, Utilizing the Nueral Efficiency Analyzer, in Two Prescribed Elementary School Districts which Maintain Programs for Educable Mentally Retarded Involving a Significant Overpopulation of Spanish-Surname Pupils, in Order to Locate Pupils Who Have Been Misplaced in Educable Mentally Retarded Programs," Senate Concurrent Resolution No. 50, California Legislature, May 16, 1973.

Duncan, Beverly, "Comments on Inequality," 43 Harvard Educational Review 122 (1973).

Dyer, Henry S., "School Factors and Equal Educational Opportunity," in HER/EEO/HUP, p. 41 (1969).

Edmonds, Ronald, et al., "A Black Response to Christopher Jenck's Inequality and Certain Other Issues," 43 Harvard Educational Review 76 (1973).

"Education, SES, I.Q., and Their Effects," *Contemporary Psychology*, September 1973, p. 401.

Elkind, David, "Piagetian and Psychometric Conceptions of Intelligence," 39 Harvard Educational Review 319 (1969).

"Environment, Heredity, and Intelligence," reprint Series No. 2 (Cambridge, Mass.: Harvard Educational Review, 1969).

Epps, Edgar G., "Race, Intelligence, and Learning: Some Consequences of the Misuse of Test Results," Paper delivered at the American Sociological Association Meeting, Washington, D.C., 1970.

Ertl, J., "Evoked Potentials, Neural Efficiency, and I.Q.," Washington, D.C.: International Symposium for Biocybernetics, February 8, 1968.

Eysenck, H.J., "I.Q., Social Class, and Educational Policy," *Change*, September 1973, p. 38.

Gage, N.L., "I.Q. Heritability, Race Differences, and Educational Research," Phi Delta Kappan, January 1972, p. 308.

Freeman, Roger A., "Should States Finance the Schools?" *Wall Street Journal*, March 31, 1972.

Gage, N.L., "Replies to Shockley, Page, and Jensen," Phi Delta Kappan, March 1972, p. 422.

"Goodbye I.Q., Hello EI (ERTL Index)," Phi Delta Kappan, October 1972, p. 89.

Grant, Gerald, "Shaping Social Policy: The Politics of the Coleman Report," *Teachers College Record*, September 1973, p. 17.

Hamilton, Charles V., "Race and Education: A Search for Legitimacy," in HER/EEO/HUP, p. 187 (1969).

Herrenstein, Richard, "I.Q.," *The Atlantic Monthly*, September 1971, p. 43.

Hunt, J. McV., "Has Compensatory Education Failed? Has It Been Attempted?" 19 Harvard Educational Review 278 (1969).

Jackson, Philip W., "After Apple-Picking," 43 Harvard Educational Review 51 (1973).

Jencks, Christopher, "Inequality in Retrospect," 43 Harvard Educational Review 138 (1973).

_____ "Is the Public School Obsolete?" 1 The Public Interest 18 (1966).

Jensen, Arthur R., "How Much Can We Boost I.Q. and Scholastic Achievement?" 39 Harvard Educational Review 1 (1969).

_____ "A Reply to Gage: The Causes of Twin Differences in I.Q.," Phi Delta Kappan, March 1972, p. 420.

_____ "Reducing the Heredity-Environment Uncertainty," 39 Harvard Educational Review 449 (1969).

Kagan, Jerome, "The I.Q. Puzzle: What Are We Missing?" 14 Inequality in Education 5 (1973).

_____ "Inadequate Evidence and Illogical Conclusions," 39 Harvard Educational Review 274 (1969).

_____ "What is Intelligence?" *Social Policy*, July/August 1973, p. 88.

Katz, Irwin, "Academic Motivation and Equal Education Opportunity," in HER/EEO/HUP, p. 60 (1969).

Kirp, David L., "The Poor, The Schools, and Equal Protection," in HER/EEO/HUP, p. 139 (1969).

Landsberger, Betty H., "Home Environment and School Performance: The North Carolina Experience," *Children Today*, September/October 1973, p. 10.

"Legal Implications of the Use of Standardized Ability Tests in Employment and Education," 68 Columbia Law Review 691 (1968).

"Legal Implications of Cultural Bias in the Intelligence Testing of Disadvantaged School Children," 61 Georgetown Law Journal 1027 (1973).

Lesser, Gerald, and Susan S. Stodolsky, "Equal Opportunity for Maximum Development," in HER/EEO/HUP, p. 126 (1969).

Michelson, Stephan, "For the Plaintiff—Equal School Resource Allocation," 7 The Journal of Human Resources 284 (1972).

_____ "The Further Responsibility of Intellectuals," 43 Harvard Educational Review 92 (1973).

Moynihan, Daniel P., "Sources of Resistance to the Coleman Report," in HER/EEO/HUP, p. 25 (1969).

O'Neill, Dave M., Burton Gray, and Stanley Horowitz, "For the Defendants—Educational Equality and Expenditure Equalization Orders," 7 The Journal of Human Resources 307 (1972).

Page, Ellis B., "Backtalk," Phi Delta Kappan, March 1972, p. 461.

"Perspectives on Inequality: A Reassessment of the Effect of Family and School in America," 43 Harvard Educational Review 37 (1973).

Pettigrew, Thomas F., et al., "Busing: A Review of 'The Evidence,' " 30 The Public Interest 88 (1973).

_____ "Race and Equal Educational Opportunity," in HER/EEO/HUP, p. 69 (1969).

"Prohibits School Districts from Administering Tests, or Using Individual Scores from Tests, which Measure or Attempt to Measure the Scholastic Aptitude of Pupils," Assembly Bill No. 368, California Legislature, Brown and Alatorre, February 14, 1973.

Punke, H.H., "Competence as a Basis of Student Assignment," 32 Alabama Lawyer 24 (1971).

Rivlin, Alice M., "Forensic Social Science," 43 Harvard Educational Review 61 (1973).

Rosenwaike, Ira, "Interethnic Comparisons of Educational Attainment: An Analysis Based on Census Data for the City of New York," 00 American Journal of Sociology 68 (1973).

Sanday, Peggy R., "An Alternative Interpretation of the Relationship Between Heredity, Race, Environment, and I.Q.," Phi Delta Kappan, December 1972, p. 250.

"Science, Heritability, and I.Q." (Cambridge, Mass.: Harvard Educational Review, 1969), reprint Series No. 1.

Sherrer, C.W., and Roland A. Roston, "Some Legal and Psychological Concerns about Personality Testing in the Public Schools," 30 Federal Bar Journal 111 (1971).

Shockley, William, "Dysgenics, Geneticity, Raceology: A Challenge to the Intellectual Responsibility of Educators," Phi Delta Kappan, January 1972, p. 297.

_____ "A Debate Challenge: Geneticity is 80% for White Identical Twins' I.Q.'s," Phi Delta Kappan, March 1972, p. 415.

Sievert, William A., "Human Rights v. Research Stirs Berkeley," *Chronicle of Higher Education*, September 24, 1973, p. 1.

"State Bar Names Commission to Study Bar Exam Process," Reports: The State Bar of California, June 1973, p. 1.

"Tests and Tracking: Bias in the Classroom," 14 Inequality in Education 1 (1973).

Thurow, Lester C., "Proving the Absence of Positive Associations," 43 Harvard Educational Review 106 (1973).

Vodicka, Bruce, "Intelligence Testing Beyond Griggs v. Duke Power Company," 49 Chicago-Kent Law Review 82 (1972).

Wilson, James Q., "On Pettigrew and Armor: An Afterword," 30 The Public Interest 132 (1973).

Wilson, Alan B., "Social Class and Equal Educational Opportunity," in HER/ EEO/HUP, p. 80 (1969).

Education Law (Books)

Academic Freedom in the Secondary Schools (New York: American Civil Liberties Union, 1971).

Alexander, Kern, Ray Corns, and Walter McCann, *Public School Law: Cases and Materials* (St. Paul, Minn.: West Publishing Company, 1969).

Alexander, Kern, and K. Forbis Jordan, *Legal Aspects of Educational Choice: Compulsory Attendance and Student Assignment* (Topeka, Kan.: National Organization on Legal Problems of Education, 1973).

Appenzeller, Herb, *From the Gym to the Jury*, (Charlottesville, Va.: The Michie Company, 1970).

Bender, John F., *The Functions of Courts in Enforcing School Attendance Laws* (New York: Teachers College, Columbia University, 1927; reprinted by AMS Press, 1972).

Benedetti, Eugene, *School Law in California* (Dubuque, Iowa: Willima C. Brown Company, 1968).

Blackwell, Thomas E., *College Law: A Guide for Administrators* (Washington, D.C.: American Council on Education, 1961).

Bolmeier, Edward C., *Landmark Supreme Court Decisions on Public School Issues* (Charlottesville, Va.: The Michie Company, 1973).

_____*Legal Issues in Education.* Abridged, Duke Doctoral Dissertations (Charlottesville, Va.: The Michie Company, 1970).

_____*The School in the Legal Structure* (Cincinnati, Ohio: W.H. Anderson Company, 1973).

_____*Teachers' Legal Rights, Restraints, and Liabilities* (Cincinnati, Ohio: W.H. Anderson Company, 1971).

Buss, William G., *Legal Aspects of Crime Investigation in the Public Schools* (Topeka, Kan.: National Organization on Legal Problems of Education, 1971).

Calhoun, John W., *The Aftermath of the Amish Case* (Topeka, Kan.: National Organization on Legal Problems of Education, 1973).

Drury, Robert L., and Kenneth C. Ray, *Essentials of School Law* (New York: Appleton-Century-Crofts, 1967).

_____*Principles of School Law With Cases* (New York: Appleton-Century-Crofts, 1965).

Edwards, Newton, *The Courts and the Public Schools: The Legal Basis of School Organization and Administration* (Chicago: University of Chicago Press, 1971).

Edwards, Newton, and H.G. Richey, *The School in American Social Order* (Boston: Houghton Mifflin Company, 1963).

Ely, Dale F., et al., *California Laws Relating to Minors* (Los Angeles: College Book Company, 1973).

Fourteen Leading Cases on Education, Religion, and Financing Schools: Complete and Unabridged Text of the Court Opinions (Wheaton, Ill.: Lincoln Bureau of Research, 1972).

Garber, Lee O., *Education as a Function of the State* (Minneapolis, Minn.: Educational Test Bureau, Inc., 1934).

Garber, Lee O., and Newton Edwards, *The Law Relating to the Creation, Alteration, and Dissolution of School Districts* (Danville, Ill.: Interstate Printers and Publishers, 1962).

Garber, Lee O., *The Public School in Our Governmental Structure* (Danville, Ill.: Interstate Printers and Publishers, 1962).

Garber, Lee O., and E. Edmund Reutter, Jr., *The Yearbook of School Law, 1970* (Danville, Ill.: Interstate Printers and Publishers, 1970).

Gauerke, Warren E., *School Law* (New York: The Center for Applied Research in Education, Inc., 1965).

Gittell, Marilyn, et al., *School Boards and School Policy: An Evaluation of Decentralization in New York City* (New York: Praeger, Inc., 1973).

Hamilton, Otto T., *The Courts and the Curriculum* (New York: Teachers College, Columbia University, 1927; reprinted by AMS Press, 1972).

Hamilton, Robert R., and Paul R. Mort, *The Law and Public Education: With Cases* (Chicago: The Foundation Press, 1959).

Hazard, William R., *Education and the Law: Cases and Materials on Public Schools* (New York: The Free Press, 1971).

Henning, Joel F., and Norman Gross, *Law Related Education in the Public Schools* (Topeka Kan.: National Organization on Legal Problems of Education, 1973).

Howlett, Erwin, *Teachers' Guide to School Law: State Mandated and Permissive Responsibilities and Rights of Certificated Personnel* (Burlingame, Calif.: California Teachers Association, 1971, and 1972 Supplement).

Kallen, Laurence, *Teachers' Rights and Liabilities Under the Law* (New York: ARCO Publishing Company, 1971).

Lippman, Leopold, and Ignacy Goldberg, *Right to Education: Anatomy of the Pennsylvania Case and Its Implications for Exceptional Children* (New York: Teachers College Press, 1973).

Matthews, Howard A., *The Courts and Married Students* (Washington, D.C.: U.S. Office of Education, 1961).

Milstein, Mike M., *Educational Policy-Making and the State Legislature: The New York Experience* (New York: Praeger Publishers, 1973).

Morehart, Grover C., *The Legal Status of City School Boards* (New York: Teachers College, Columbia University, 1927; reprinted by AMS Press, 1972).

National Education Association, *The Pupil's Day in Court: Review of 1969* (Washington, D.C.: National Educational Association, 1970). See also issues for 1970-1973.

_____ *The Teacher's Day in Court: Review of 1969* (Washington, D.C.: National Education Association, 1970). See also issues for 1970-1973.

Nedurian, Vram, *Guidelines: Police—School Cooperation: Search in School Buildings or on School Property* (Topeka, Kan.: National Organization on Legal Problems of Education, 1973).

NOLPE. The National Organization on Legal Problems of Education (NOLPE) was organized in 1954 to provide an avenue for the study of school law problems. NOLPE publications include the *NOLPE School Law Reporter, NOLPE Notes,* and the *NOLPE School Law Journal.* In addition, NOLPE publishes books and monographs on school law subjects.

Nolte, M. Chester, *School Law in Action: 101 Key Decisions With Guidelines for School Administrators*, (West Nyack, N.Y.: Parker Publishing Company, 1971).

Peterson, LeRoy J., Richard A. Rossmiller, and Marlin M. Volz, *The Law and Public School Operation* (New York: Harper and Row, Publishers, 1968).

Poe, Arthur C., *School Liability for Injuries to Pupils: A Study of the Legal Liability for the Injury of Children in Public Schools* (New York: Teachers College, Columbia University, 1941; reprinted by AMS Press, 1972).

Practicing Law Institute, *Legal Problems in Public Education* (New York: Practicing Law Institute, 1972).

Remmlein, Madaline K., *School Law* (New York: McGraw-Hill Book Company, 1950).

Reutter, E. Edmund, and Robert R. Hamilton, *The Law of Public Education* (Mineola, N.Y.: The Foundation Press, Inc., 1970).

State of California, *California Administrative Code: Title 5. Education* (Sacramento, Calif.: Office of Administrative Procedures, Department of General Services, through 1973).

Strayer, George D., *Centralizing Tendencies in the Administration of Public Education: A Study of Legislation for Schools Since 1900* (New York: Teachers College, Columbia University, 1900; reprinted by AMS Press, 1972).

Vacca, Richard S., *Analysis of Court Decisions* (Topeka, Kan.: National Organization on Legal Problems of Education, 1973).

Zimet, Melvin, *Decentralization and School Effectiveness: A Case Study of the 1969 Decentralization Law in New York City* (New York: Teachers College Press, 1973).

Education Law (Articles)

"Constitutional Law—Application of the Fourteenth Amendment to Private Schools," 23 Southern California Law Review 805 (1971).

Cox, Archibald, "Constitutional Adjudication and the Promotion of Human Rights: Foreword to the Supreme Court 1965 Term," 80 Harvard Law Review 91 (1966).

232

"Discrimination Against the Poor and the Fourteenth Amendment," 81 Harvard Law Review 435 (1968).

Foster, Jr., H.H. Freed, and D.J. Freed, "Bill of Rights For Children," 6 Family Law Quarterly 343 (1972).

Giles, Michael W., "Lawyers and the Supreme Court: A Comparative Look at Some Attitudinal Linkages," 35 Journal of Politics 480 (1973).

Gilliom, M. Eugene, "The Case Method: Adapted for Social Studies," 42 The Clearing House 217 (1967).

Hoffman, Earl, "The Classroom Teacher and School Law," *Educational Horizons*, Winter 1970-71, p. 33.

Hogan, John C., "The Roles of the Courts in Certain Educational Policy Formation," 1 Policy Sciences 289 (1970).

Hutchins, Robert M., "The Constitution of Public Education," *The Center Magazine*, July 1969, p. 8.

Keesecker, Ward W., "Supreme Court Decisions Affecting Education," 31 School Life 4 (1949).

Marshall, Robert B., and Richard M. Ritchie, "One Man, One Vote Doesn't Apply in Education," Phi Delta Kappan, December 1971, p. 248.

Michelman, M., "The Supreme Court, 1968 Term. Foreword: On Protecting the Poor Through the Fourteenth Amendment," 83 Harvard Law Review 7 (1969).

Minimum Schooling, Legislation, Externalities, and a "Child Tax." 15 Journal of Law and Economics 353 (1972).

O'Neil, Robert M., "The Limits of Pluralism: Division Without Diversity," 23 American Council of Learned Societies Newsletter 14 (1972).

Problemas Constitucionales del Regiamento de Estudiantes del Sistema de Instruction Publica. 41 Revista Judicada de Universidad de Puerto Rico 319 (1972).

Rousselot, Peter F., "Achieving Educational Opportunity for Negroes in the Public Schools of the North and West: The Emerging Role For Private Constitutional Litigation," 35 George Washington Law Review 698 (1967).

Schoen, R.B., "Nationalization of Public Education: The Constitutional Question," 4 Texas Tech Law Review 63 (1972).

"School Law '71: What Happened and Why," 89 Nation's Schools 43 (1972).

"Symposium: One Hundred Years of the Fourteenth Amendment—Its Implications for the Future," Washington Law Quarterly 381 (1972).

"Symposium on the Legal Rights of Women," 17 New York Law Forum 335 (1971).

Taylor, W.L., "Law As a Catalyst for Change: The Mississippi Experience," 50 North Carolina Law Review 1038 (1972).

Wasby, Stephen L., "The Supreme Court's Impact: Some Problems of Conceptualization and Measurement," 5 Law and Society Review 41 (1970).

Wechsler, Herbert, "Toward Neutral Principles of Constitutional Law," 73 Harvard Law Review 1 (1959).

General Works on Education, Schooling, and Law (Books)

Bruno, James E. (Ed.), *Emerging Issues in Education: Policy Implications for the Schools* (Lexington, Mass.: D.C. Heath and Company, 1972).

Callahan, Raymond E., *Education and the Cult of Efficiency* (Chicago: University of Chicago Press, 1962).

Campbell, Roald F., Luvern L. Cunningham, Roderick F. McPhee, and Raphael O. Nystrand, *The Organization and Control of American Schools* (Columbus, Ohio: Charles E. Merrill Publishing Company, 1970).

Campbell, Roald F., and Donald H. Layton, *Policy Making for American Education* (Chicago: University of Chicago Press, 1969).

Coleman, James S., and Nancy L. Karweit, *Information Systems and Performance Measures in Schools* (Englewood Cliffs, N.J.: Educational Technological Publications, 1972).

Conant, James B., *General Education in a Free Society: Report of the Harvard Committee* (Cambridge, Mass.: Harvard University Press, 1955).

Council of Europe, European Committee on Crime Problems, *The Role of the School in the Prevention of Juvenile Delinquency: A Study Presented by the Co-ordinated Criminological Research Fellowship Team of 1969*. New York: Manhattan Publishing Company, 1972).

Dalkey, Norman C., *Studies in the Quality of Life: Delphi and Decision-Making* (Lexington, Mass.: D.C. Heath and Company, 1972).

Educational Policies Commission, *Education for All American Youth: A Further Look* (Washington, D.C.: National Education Association, 1952).

Kay, F. George, *The Family in Transition: Its Past, Present, and Future Patterns* (New York: Halsted Press, 1973).

Fawcett, Claude W., *School Personnel Administration* (New York: The Macmillan Company, 1964).

Gallager, Arlene, *Law-Focused Education in the Elementary School* (Chicago: Law in American Society Foundation, 1972).

Golden Gate Law Review, A Legal Research and Service Group, *High School Legal Education* (San Francisco: Golden Gate College, School of Law, 1972).

Groton, Richard A., *Conflict, Controversy, and Crisis in School Administration and Supervision: Issues, Cases, and Concepts for the '70's* (Dubuque, Iowa: William C. Brown Company, 1972).

History of Education Society, *Studies in the Government and Control of Education Since 1860* (London: Methuen and Company, Ltd., 1970).

Jenks, Henry F., *Catalogue of the Boston Public Latin School* (Boston, Mass.: The Boston Latin School Association, 1886).

Kneller, George F., *The Philosophy of Education* (New York: John Wiley and Sons, 1967).

Lazerson, Marvin, *Origins of the Urban School: Public Education in Massachusetts, 1870-1915* (Cambridge, Mass.: Harvard University Press, 1971).

Lieberman, Myron, *The Future of Public Education* (Chicago: The University of Chicago Press, 1968).

Nunnery, Michael T., and Ralph B. Kimbrough, *Politics, Power, Polls, and School Elections* (Berkeley, Calif.: McCutchan Publishing Company, 1973).

Pfeiffer, John, *New Look at Education: Systems Analysis in Our Schools and Colleges* (New York: The Odyssey Press, 1968).

Professor X, *This Beats Working for a Living: The Dark Secrets of a College Professor* (New Rochelle, N.Y.: Arlington House Publishers, 1973).

Schultz, Theodore W., *The Economic Value of Education* (New York: Columbia University Press, 1967).

Skinner, B.F., *Beyond Freedom and Dignity* (New York: Alfred A. Knopf, 1972).

Thomas, J. Alan, *The Productive School: A Systems Analysis Approach to Educational Administration* (New York: John Wiley and Sons, 1971).

Vredevoe, Lawrence E., *Discipline* (Dubuque, Iowa: Kendall/Hunt Publishing Company, 1971).

_____*An Introduction and Outline of Secondary Education* (Ann Arbor, Mich.: J.W. Edwards, Publisher, 1957).

Whitehead, Alfred N., *The Aims of Education and Other Essays* (New York: The Free Press, 1957).

General Works on Education, Schooling, and Law (Articles)

"All in the 'Family': Legal Problems of Communes," 7 Harvard Civil Rights—Civil Liberties Law Review 393 (1972).

Bowles, Samuel, "The Determinants of Scholastic Achievement—An Appraisal of Some Recent Evidence," 3 Journal of Human Resources 2 (1968).

_____"Education Production Function, U.S. Department of Health, Education, and Welfare, Office of Education," Final Report, OEC-1-7-000451-2651, Harvard University, February 1969.

_____"Education Production Function," in W.L. Hansen (Ed.), *Education, Income, and Human Capital* (New York: National Bureau of Economic Research, 1970).

Brazziel, William F., "Quality Education for Minorities," Phi Delta Kappan, May 1972, p. 547.

Burgest, David R., "Racism in Everyday Speech and Social Work Jargon," *Social Work*, July 1973, p. 20.

Burd, Gene, "Urban Magazine Journalism Thrives During City Crisis," *Journalism Quarterly*, Spring 1973, p. 77.

Campbell, Robert E., "Accountability and Stone Soup," Phi Delta Kappan, November 1971, p. 176.

235

Cronbach, Lee J., and Lita Furby, "How We Should Measure 'Change'—Or Should We?" 74 Psychological Bulletin 68 (1970).

Curran, W.J., "Cross-Professional Education in Law and Medicine: The Promise and the Conflict," 24 Journal of Legal Education 42 (1971).

El Derecho a la Educacion y la Distribucion de los Recursos para la Ensenanza Escolar, 40 Revista Judicada de la Universidad de Puerto Rico 295 (1971).

"Freedom of Religion and Compulsory Education," 26 Arkansas Law Review 555 (1973).

Gallup, George H., "The Third Annual Survey of the Public's Attitudes Towards the Public Schools, 1971," Phi Delta Kappan, September 1971, p. 33.

_____ "Fourth Annual Gallup Poll of Public Attitudes Toward Education," Phi Delta Kappan, September 1972, p. 33.

_____ "Fifth Annual Gallup Poll of Public Attitudes Toward Education," Phi Delta Kappan, September 1973, p. 38.

_____ "The Gallup Polls of Attitudes Toward Education (1969-1973)," Phi Delta Kappan, 1973, forthcoming.

Hall, Morrill, and Warren G. Findley, "Ability Grouping: Helpful or Harmful?" Phi Delta Kappan, May 1971, p. 566.

Hanusheck, E., "Teacher Characteristics and Gains in Student Achievement," 61 American Economic Review (Papers and Proceedings) 280 (1971).

_____ "The Value of Teachers in Teaching," RM-6362-CC/RC, The Rand Corporation, December 1970.

"Gauging Public Opinion," *Channels*, October 1, 1972, p. 2.

Hogan, John C., " 'Obtaining an Education' As A Right of the People," 3 NOLPE School Law Journal 15 (1973). Reprinted in 68 The Brief, Phi Delta Phi Quarterly 249 (1973).

Howard, Alvin W., "Teacher Liability and the Law," *The Clearing House*, March 1968, p. 411.

Jacobson, Barbara, and John M. Kendrick, "Education and Mobility: From Achievement to Ascription," 38 American Sociological Review 439 (1973).

Jensen, Arthur R., "Personality and Scholastic Achievement in Three Ethnic Groups," *British Journal of Educational Psychology*, June 1973, p. 115.

Kiesling, H.J., "Input and Output in California Education Projects," R-781-CC/RC, The Rand Corporation, October 1971.

_____ "Multivariate Analysis of Schools and Educational Policy," P-4595, The Rand Corporation, 1971.

Klitgaard, Robert E., and George R. Hall, "A Statistical Search for Unusually Effective Schools," R-1210-CC/RC, The Rand Corporation, 1973.

"Legality of Homosexual Marriage," 82 Yale Law Journal 573 (1973).

Levin, H.M., "A Cost-Effective Analysis of Teacher Selection," 5 Journal of Human Resources 24 (1970).

McClung, Merle, "School Classification: Some Legal Approaches to Labels," 14 Inequality in Education 17 (1973).

McDonald, Donald, "A Six Million Dollar Misunderstanding," *Center Magazine*, September/October 1973, p. 32.

McFarland, Anne S., "Suability of School Boards and School Board Members," 21 Cleveland State Law Review 181 (1972).

Millman, Jason, "Reporting Student Progress: A Case for a Criterion-Referenced Making System," Phi Delta Kappan, December 1970, p. 226.

Mollenkopf, William C., and S. Donald Melville,"A Study of Secondary School Characteristics as Related to Test Scores," Princeton: Educational Testing Service, 1956.

Mousley, Woodrow, "Report Cards Across the Nation," Phi Delta Kappan, March 1972, p. 436.

Mueller, Ernst F., and John R.P. French, Jr., "Relationship Between Uric Acid Level and Achievement Motivation," Ann Arbor, Mich.: Institute for Social Research, Michigan University, December 1970.

Raywid, Mary Anne, "The Politicalization of Education," *Education Theory*, Spring 1973, p. 119.

Ritterband, Paul, and Richard Silberstein, "Group Disorders in the Public Schools," 38 American Sociological Review 461 (1973).

Saretsky, Gary, "The O.E.O. P.C. Experiment and the John Henry Effect," Phi Delta Kappan, May 1972, p. 579.

Stake, Robert E., "Testing Hazards in Performance Constracting," Phi Delta Kappan, June 1971, p. 583.

"Testimonial Privileges and the Student Counselor Relationship in Secondary Schools," 56 Indiana Law Review 1232 (1971).

Van Hover, James B., "Reporting Pupil Progress: A Broad Rationale for New Practices," Phi Delta Kappan, February 1972, p. 365.

Vredevoe, Lawrence E., "Secondary Education," in George F. Kneller (Ed.), *Foundations of Education* (New York: John Wiley and Sons, 1971).

Doctoral Dissertations[**]

1973

Campbell, Bruce A., "Law and Experience in the Early Republic: The Evolution of the Dartmouth College Doctrine, 1780-1819," Michigan State University, 1973.

[**]*Doctoral Dissertations*

DATRIX (Direct Access to Reference Information: A Xerox Service) is a computerized information retrieval service provided to scholars by University Microfilms of Ann Arbor, Michigan. The data base includes the majority of all dissertations published since 1938 to the current month. A "Key Word List" is provided to facilitate the search in two general areas: "Humanities/Social Sciences" and "Sciences." The basic fee is $10.00 and includes the first sixty (or less) references. Additional references are 10 cents each. *Dissertation Abstracts*, also published by University Microfilms, can be consulted preliminarily before ordering xerox prints of the complete dissertation. The following dissertation titles were retrieved by means of DATRIX and by the author's own hand-search of *Dissertation Abstracts*.

Gaddis, Roger G., "An Examination of the Legal Control of the Conduct of Students in the Secondary Schools of South Carolina," University of South Carolina, 1973.

LeConte, Michael J., "The Legal Status of Paraprofessionals In Education," Miami University, 1973.

Murphy, Larry G., "Equality Before the Law: The Struggle of Nineteenth-Century Black Californians for Social and Political Justice," Graduate Theological Union, 1973.

Sullins, Ernest W., "The Legal Status of Principals of Public Schools in the Commonwealth of Virginia," University of Virginia, 1973.

Torres, Antonio I., "Tort Liability of Public School Districts, in Selected States, as Affected by Either a Common Law or a Statutory Immunity," Loyola University of Chicago, 1973.

Warner, Laird P., "*Serrano v. Priest:* School Finance Inequalities and Potential Remedies," University of Massachusetts, 1973.

1972

Brackbill, Jr., Albert L., "The Concept of Child-Benefit Analysis," Temple University, 1972.

Canada, Brian L., "Significance of Proprietary School Law," Colorado State University, 1972.

Childs, Robert D., "The Pregnant Public School Student: Legal Implications for School Administrators," University of Denver, 1972.

Hansma, Earl A., "American Indian Education: Law and Policy," University of Miami, 1972.

Hogan, John C., "An Analysis of Selected Court Decisions Which Have Applied the Fourteenth Amendment to the Organization, Administration, and Programs of the Public Schools, 1950-1972," University of California, Los Angeles, 1972.

James, Edmund G., "The Law and Student Rights," The Ohio State University, 1972.

Koch, Jr., Carl, "A Historical Review of Compulsory School Attendance and Child Labor Laws," University of Wyoming, 1972.

Larson, Bernard A., "Equal Protection of the Law and Equality of Educational Opportunity," University of Minnesota, 1972.

Moore, Hollis H., "California Law and the Non-Retention of Probationary Teachers," Stanford University, 1972.

Smith, William R., "The Influence of the Civil Rights Act of 1871 on the Legal Status of American Public School Students," University of Denver, 1972.

Stephens, III, John H., "An Instructional Program in Selected Concepts of the Law for Secondary Schools," University of Pittsburg, 1972.

Theisen, William M., "Implementing a Child Abuse Law: An Inquiry into the Formulation and Execution of Social Policy," Washington University, 1972.

Washburn, David A., "The Development of Law Concerning Pupil Conduct

238

and Discipline: Constitutional Rights and Procedural Guarantees in Public
School Systems," University of Illinois, Urbana-Champaign, 1972.
Van Schuyer, Billye M., "An Analysis of Legal Enactments and Judicial
Decisions Pertaining to Certain Human-Civil Rights of Pupils in Public
Schools," University of Oklahoma, 1972.

1971

Davis, Jr., Clifford Linden, "Black Student Movements and Their Influence in
the High Schools in the Los Angeles City Unified School District," University
of California, Los Angeles, 1971.
Haigh, Roger W., "Mr. Justice Hugo L. Black, Due Process of Law and the
Judicial Role," Fordham University, 1971.
Murdock, Bernard J., "Programmed School Law Materials for Pre-Service
Teachers in Ohio," University of Akron, 1971.
Severino, Michael, "School Vandalism: Legal Implications," University of
Denver, 1971.
Zotos, Michael Harry, "An Examination of Relationships Between Certain
School Financial and Staffing Variables and a Measure of the Educational
Process," Columbia University, 1971.

1970

Ball, Howard, "The Warren Court's Conceptions of Democracy: An Evaluation
of the Supreme Court's Apportionment Opinions," Rutgers University, 1970.
Blackman, Paul Herbert, "Judicial Biography and Public Law: An Analysis, with
Emphasis on the New Deal Court," University of Virginia, 1970.
Collins, Clinton, "The Concept of Equality in the Context of Educational
Policies of Desegregation and Ability Grouping," Indiana University, 1970.
Daniels, William James, "Public Perceptions of the United States Supreme
Court," The University of Iowa, 1970.
Davis, Samuel Calvin, "Education, Law, and the Negro," University of Illinois at
Urbana-Champaign, 1970.
Dicker, Saul S., "The Theory and Practice of Corporal Punishment in the Public
and Private Secondary Schools of Boston: 1821-1890," The Catholic Univer-
sity of America, 1970.
Falkenstein, Edward John, "A Case Law Approach to the Classification and
Analysis of Public School Finance in Ohio from January 1, 1945 through
December 31, 1969," Miami University, 1970.
Graves, Donald Wayne, "An Investigation of Attitudes and Practices Regarding
Bible Reading and Prayer in the Public Schools of Oklahoma," The University
of Oklahoma, 1970.
Haddad, John, "Supreme Court Decisions: 'Wall of Separation between Church
and State?' " University of Pittsburgh, 1970.

Hampton, Claudia Hudley, "The Effects of Desegregation on the Scholastic Achievement of Relatively Advanced Negro Children," University of Southern California, 1970.

Harwood, Charles Edward, "Legal Trends in Relation to the Dismissal of High School Students," University of Minnesota, 1970.

Hood, Max Harry, "An Analysis of Court Decisions Determining the Duties and the Liabilities of the Teacher," West Virginia University, 1970.

Hood, Milton Herbert, "An Examination of State Control in California of Private Education Beyond the High School Level," University of California, Los Angeles, 1970.

Jandura, Ronald Matthew, "An Interpretation of United States Supreme Court Cases Since 1954 as They Affect School Segregation," University of Alabama, 1970.

Leavitt, Donald Carl, "Attitudes and Ideology on the White Supreme Court, 1910-1920," Michigan State University, 1970.

Love, Frederick Perry, "An Analysis of the Litigation Concerning Courses of Study Within the Public School Curriculum with Recommendations for Handling Subjects That Are Controversial," University of Pennsylvania, 1970.

McDonough, Robert Eugene, "American Orthodoxy and the First Amendment Freedoms: The Law and Public Dialogue of Early Virginia," University of Notre Dame, 1970.

McLendon, Dorothy Fullenwider, "Some Effects of Integrated Schooling on Bussed Urban Black Children," Boston University School of Education, 1970.

McMillan, Richard Cupp, "Religious Content in Selected Social Studies Textbooks," Duke University, 1970.

Mallios, Harry Carl, "A Study of Legal Opinion Pertaining to Control of Pupil Dress and Appearance in Public Schools, 1960-1969," University of Miami, 1970.

Moore, Duane Ora, "The Fiscal Impact of Local Nonproperty Tax Revenues on School Districts," The University of Florida, 1970.

Panawek, Gregory, "Relationship Between Knowledge of Criminal Law and Attitudes and Deterrents," United States International University, 1970.

Vance, Donald Frazier, "The Supreme Court and the Definition of Religion," Indiana University, 1970.

Voelz, Stephen John, "The Legal Status of Pupil Suspension and Expulsion and Due Process," The University of Iowa, 1970.

Wagner, Kenneth Arthur, "Lawyers and the Public: Shaping Attitudes Toward the Judicial System," The University of Iowa, 1970.

Weaver, Jr., Robert Roy, "An Analysis of Selected Court Cases which Define the Law in Regard to the Control of Student Behavior," Arizona State University, 1970.

Wheat, Thomas Earl, "A Study of the Reading Achievement of Pupils Bussed to Predominately White Schools as Compared with the Reading Achievement of Pupils Remaining in Predominately Negro Central City Schools," Ball State University, 1970.

240

Zetler, Alan George, "Riding Time and School Size as Factors in the Achievement of Bus Transported Pupils," Montana State University, 1970.

1969

Fulford, Jr., William Edward, "The Legal Aspects of Property Rights and Public Education," Duke University, 1969.

Hayes, Edward Majella, "The Relationship of Race and Sex to Academic Achievement in Selected Rural Elementary and High Schools Before and After Desegregation," University of Virginia, 1969.

Hinton, Milton Waverly, "Enforced Integration Where Whites are the Minority Group," Columbia University, 1969.

LaMorte, Michael Wolfgang, "The Courts and Student Conduct," University of California, Berkeley, 1969.

O'Connor, Francis Patrick, "Student Conduct and Discipline: The Schools and the Courts, 1960-1969," The University of Wisconsin, 1969.

Reiter, Michael Alan, "Legal Reasoning as Applied to the Interpretation of Statutes," The University of Wisconsin, 1969.

Sherain, Howard, "The United States Supreme Court: Studies in Judicial Self-Restraint," University of California, Berkeley, 1969.

Six, Gene David, "Dress and Grooming Standards in California Secondary Schools," University of Southern California, 1969.

Tucker, Eugene, "The Effects of an In-Service Education Program in Modifying Teacher Behavior as Measured by Pupil Growth," University of California, Los Angeles, 1969.

Van Every, Donald Francis, "Effect of Desegregation on Public School Groups of Sixth Graders in Terms of Achievement Levels and Attitudes Towards School," Wayne State University, 1969.

Wood, Bruce Hartley, "The Effects of Bussing Versus Non-Bussing on the Intellectual Functioning of Inner City, Disadvantaged Elementary School Children," University of Massachusetts, 1969.

1968

Dresser, William Lawrence, "An Historical Study of the Role of the Federal Government in Education, 1776-1966," Brigham Young University, 1968.

Hanushek, Eric, "The Education of Negroes and Whites," Massachusetts Institute of Technology, 1968.

Iezzi, Anthony Joseph, "Public School Prayers and the Religion Clauses of the Constitution," Case Western Reserve University, 1968.

Orloff, Leonard Mark, "Legal Analysis of Selected Rights of Pupils in the Public Schools," The George Washington University, 1968.

Poindexter, Robert Craig, "An Analysis of Recent Federal Court Decisions

Concerning Public School District Desegregation in the United States," Indiana University, 1968.

Porter, Hugh Calvert, "A Determination of the Physical Components, Spatial Sizes and Spatial Relationships of a Secondary School Instructional Materials Center and Their Application to Selected Secondary Schools in the State of Indiana," Indiana University, 1968.

Russell, Daryl Daw, "A Compilation and Analysis of Federal Legislation Concerned with Education: 1949-1966," Washington State University, 1968.

Schalm, Philip, "School Administrators' Perceptions of Problems Arising from the Integration of Indian and Non-Indian Children in Publicly Supported Schools in Saskatchewan," Unpublished Master's thesis, University of Saskatchewan, Saskatoon, Saskatchewan, 1968.

Serra, Joseph Robert, "In Loco Parentis: A Survey of the Attitudes of Parents of Undergraduate Students," Indiana University, 1968.

Young, William Harry, "Teaching About Religion in Secondary School Social Studies," Columbia University, 1968.

1966

MacDonald, Roberta Clare, "What the Appellate Courts Have Said—Decisions-Dicta-Dissent—in Matters Relating to College Admissions, Dismissals, Credits, and Degrees," The University of Florida, 1966.

1964

Werkema, Gordon R., "Law and the Non-Public School," University of Denver, 1964.

Table of Cases

Table of Cases

245

247

Index

Index

Core area schools, 43, 53-54
Corns, Ray, cited, 200n
Corporal punishment, use of, 79, 108, 115-119, 146, 155, 193n
Cost of Living Council and Emergency Appeals Court, 140
Courts. *See* specific type of court
Cox, Archibald, cited, 156, 203n
Crisis in the Classroom: The Remaking of American Education (Silberman), 166n
Cubberly, Ellwood P., cited 181
Cultural bias, 132
Curricula, opportunities in, 14, 52, 120, 157

Dallas Independent School District, 97, 118-119, 174n
Dane, Dr. Robert, Cited, 118
Davis, Frederick D., cited, 196n
Davis, Cal., 136
Decision-making powers, 6, 155
Degrees, awarding of, 140-132
DeJure/DeFacto, distinction between, 44-45
Del Olmo, Frank, cited, 194n
Delinquency, 118
Delon, Floyd G., cited, 183n
Democracy, 3, 68-69
Demonstrations, group, 84, 94-95, 113-114
Denver, Colo., 33, 37-41, 44, 51-54
Deschooling Society (Illich), 166n
Desegregation, problems of, 10-13, 19, 121, 150-151, 154
Detroit, Mich., 30-33, 171n
Diplomas, illegal, 130-132
Disadvantaged children, 120
Disciplinary actions, 97, 101, 108-111, 115-116, 132, 141
Discipline, problems of, 12-13, 79, 83, 86, 92-93, 105, 109, 114-115, 118, 133-135, 143, 184-185n
Discipline (Vredevoe), 184, 191-193
Discrimination, 20-21, 24-25, 67-68; racial, 3, 16, 36, 45, 56, 73, 98, 125, 129, 155; by sex, 135
Distel, Dave, cited, 199n
District courts, 42, 67, 95, 122, 133, 135, 137, 139, 143
District of Columbia, 176n, 195n
Doe, Peter N., 132-133

Douglas, William O., Justice, 17, 27, 39, 43-44, 103-104, 106, 168-169n, 172-173n, 176n, 188n, 196n, 203-204n
Dowling, Noel T., cited, 156, 180n, 184n, 187n, 203n
Dress, code of, 101-102. *See also* Grooming
Dropouts, potential, 133
Drugs, use of, 14, 83
Dual school system, 11, 26, 28, 38, 40, 53, 55, 136
Due Process Clause, 4, 9, 15, 84, 104-105, 108-110, 151

East, The, educational problems in, 46, 55
Education: opportunities for, 1-3; private, 1; public, 1, 7-8; and society, 1, 4-5, 11-12; and state power, 6-8, 59-60
Education Code. See California Education Code
Education Digest, 184n
Education Daily, 170n, 180n
"Education to the educators" policy, 2, 8, 81, 149
Education and the Practice Digest (Spurlock), 7
Eighth Amendment, 103, 117
Elementary grade school level, 1, 20, 33, 44, 50-51, 90
Employment practices, pupil, 119-121, 127, 153; teacher, 79, 125-126; tests for, 126, 130
Emporia High School, 134-135
Environment, school, 84, 132
Equal educational opportunity, 1, 10, 15, 21, 56, 149-152
Equal Educational Opportunity (Coleman), 161n
Equal protection clause, 2-4, 16, 26, 43, 51, 53, 55, 60, 67, 71, 73, 105, 128-129, 138, 141, 149. *See also* Fourteenth Amendment
Equal Protection Standard, new, 61-62, 64, 150, 156, 168n
Equality, concept of, 2-4, 21-23, 135-136
Ertl, John, cited, 123-124
Estes, Dr. Nolan, 118
Ethnic compositions, 39, 132

Taylor, William M., Judge, 119, 174n
Taxes: exise, 139; exemption from, 20, 139; and free schools, 2, 71; levying of, 8, 10, 136, 150; property, 73, 76; state, 27
Teacher aides, 154
Teachers, 2, 18, 141; black, 44; certification, 132; dismissal of, 10; disrespect toward, 94; employment of, 79, 125-126; evaluation performances of, 10, 127, 153-154; and pupil ratio, 10, 36; rights, 9, 79-83, 86; salaries, 10-11, 153-154; white, 127
Teenage marriages, 141
Tennessee, 94, 140
Temple Law Quarterly, 178n
Tenth Amendment, 7, 30, 33, 58-59, 150, 154
Territorial uniformity, question of, 69
Tests: for black students, 122; for employment, 126; programs of, 123, 125, 130, 146, 153; scores and measurements of, 79, 120, 144. *See also* specific type testing program
Texas, 70, 72, 155, 174n; law schools, 24-25; school districts, 141; statutory law in, 118-119
Texas Law Review, 167n
Third Amendment, 103
Thirteenth Amendment, 167n
Time Magazine, 197n, 202n
Torts (Prosser), 193n
Track system and the use of tests, 120-121
Transportation: compulsory, 50-51; student, 28, 43, 48-49, 52. *See also* Busing
Treatise on Labor Law (Forkosch), 161n
Trial courts, 70, 107, 131, 138, 155-156
Tulane Law Review, 178n
Two-Court rule, 54
Tyler, Harold L., cited, 163n

Uintah-Ouray Indian Tribe, 188n
Underprivileged pupils, 10
Uniform General Laws, 179n
Unitary school system, 10, 42, 55, 121
United States Government Organizational Manual, 1971/72, 165n

United States Law Week, The, 170n
United States Supreme Court Digest, 7
University of California, 129-130, 181n
University of Chicago Law Review, 178n
University High School in West Los Angeles, 87
University of Mississippi, 129
University of Pennsylvania Law Review, 166n, 188
University of Southern California, 140
University of Texas Law School, 24-25
University of Washington Law School, 131
Up Against the Law: The Legal Rights of People Under Twenty-one (Strouse), 183n
Urban school systems, 46
Utah, 191n

Van Alstyne, William W., cited, 167n
Vandalism, juvenile, 110
VanHoven, James B., cited, 196n
Vanderbilt Law Review, 170-171n
Vietnam policy, protests against, 84-85, 94
Vinson, Frederick M., Chief Justice, 24, 112
Virginia, 19-20, 29
Vredovoe, Lawrence E., cited, 184n, 191n, 193n

Wage price freeze, 139-140
Walkouts, 114
Wallace, George, cited, 13
Wanke, Robert, cited, 186n
Warren, Earl, Chief Justice, 17
Washington, state Supreme Court of, 131
Washington, D.C., 31, 120
Washington Law Review, 178n
Washington Post, 170n, 198n
Weaver, Warren, Jr., cited, 31
Wechsler Intelligence Scale for Children (WISC), 124
Welfare functions, 1
Wells, William W., cited, 179n
West, the, educational problems in, 13, 37, 46, 55
Westlake School: Student Handbook, 1972-1973, 202n
West's California Legislative Service, 169n

White, Byron R., Justice, 172n, 185n
Williams, Jerre, cited, 20, 167
Wisdom, Judge, 43
Wise, Arthur E., cited, 70, 181n
Women and the Law (Kanowitz), 200n
Women's Liberation Movement, 115

Wooten, James T., cited, 164
Wright, J. Skelly, Judge, 5, 72, 77, 120, 156, 163
Wyoming, 35

Zadeh, Stella, cited, 198n

About the Author

John C. Hogan, an administrator for The Rand Corporation, is Adjunct Professor of Education and Administration of Justice at California Lutheran College. He received the Ph.D. from the University of California, Los Angeles, in 1972. A contributor to the *Encyclopaedia Britannica*, he is the author of numerous articles on legal and educational subjects, and co-author of *An Author's Guide to Scholarly Publishing and the Law, Programmed Statistics: With Chapters on Probability, Computer Theory, and Programmed Instruction*, and *Joseph Story: A Collection of Writings By and About an Eminent American Jurist.*